W9-BMH-494

WINNING IN EMERGING MARKETS

Tarun Khanna
Krishna G. Palepu
With Richard J. Bullock

WINNING
IN EMERGING
MARKETS

A Road Map for Strategy and Execution

Harvard Business Press
Boston, Massachusetts

Copyright 2010 Tarun Khanna and Krishna G. Palepu
All rights reserved
Printed in the United States of America
14 13 12 11 10   5 4 3 2 1

No part of this publication may be reproduced, stored in or introduced into a retrieval
system, or transmitted, in any form, or by any means (electronic, mechanical, photo-
copying, recording, or otherwise), without the prior permission of the publisher.
Requests for permission should be directed to permissions@hbsp.harvard.edu, or
mailed to Permissions, Harvard Business Schooi Publishing, 60 Harvard Way, Boston,
Massachusetts 02163.

Library of Congress Cataloging-in-Publication Data

Palepu, Krishna G., 1954–
    Winning in emerging markets : a road map for strategy and execution /
Krishna G. Palepu, Tarun Khanna.
        p. cm.
    ISBN 978-1-4221-6695-6 (hardcover : alk. paper)
    1. Commerce.   2. International business enterprises.   3. Globalization—
Economic aspects.   4. Marketing—Management.   I. Khanna, Tarun.   II. Title.
    HF1008.P35 2010
    658.4'012091724—dc22

                                                    2009036019

The paper used in this publication meets the requirements of the American National
Standard for Permanence of Paper for Publications and Documents in Libraries and
Archives Z39.48-1992.

To Ruhi, Simran, and Rishi

To Laurie, Kalyan, and Anjali

Contents

Preface

The research journey for this book began fifteen years ago when we were teaching in a Harvard Business School Executive Program, Managing Global Opportunities in China and India. The program targeted Western multinationals and investors interested in business opportunities in the then rapidly growing Chinese market and the newly liberalizing Indian market. In Mumbai, as part of that executive program, we invited Ratan Tata, chairman of Tata Sons Limited, to share with the group Tata's strategy for the new Indian market. We were surprised to see Western executives' reaction to Tata's ambitious plans for exploiting the new ambient opportunities. Their experience in Western markets had convinced these executives that emerging market business groups like the Tata's, consisting of several dozen companies in disparate, seemingly unrelated businesses, were anachronisms, doomed to go the way of the dinosaurs unless they radically restructured and focused on one or two core businesses. The disconnect between how emerging market senior leaders like Ratan Tata and leaders of Western multinationals in our executive program thought about the strategic implication of emerging market opportunities was truly fascinating to us.

Diverging perceptions about the right way to do business in emerging markets varied not only in our program. As we examined the subject more widely, we observed that many multinational executives, academics, and consultants had developed their ideas about strategy and execution based primarily on data from mature Western markets, and assumed that what worked in the West would work in emerging markets as well. Why, they reasoned, should emerging markets not take a page out of the painful evolutionary lessons from the mature markets and embrace their best practices *in toto*? But business leaders and entrepreneurs in emerging markets, drawing from their ground-level experience, intuitively felt that emerging markets were different. Who was right? Why were the perceptions of doing business in emerging markets so different between the two sides? What was the most reliable advice one could give to top executives of Western multinationals and investors—and emerging market business leaders and entrepreneurs—on how to win in emerging markets? These are the questions that led us on our fifteen-year research and teaching journey.

During this journey, we studied many companies and wrote dozens of cases on doing business in emerging markets—emerging market entrepreneurs trying to build world-class companies, multinational companies trying to seize new opportunities in large emerging markets, and investors financing both sides. The multinational companies we studied include: General Motors in China, L'Oréal in India, Monsanto in Brazil, McDonald's in Russia, Home Depot in Chile, Tetrapak in Argentina, Microsoft and GE Healthcare in China and India, and Metro Cash & Carry in Russia, China, and India. Emerging market companies we studied include: Haier from China, the Tata Group from India, Doğuş Group from Turkey, Cemex from Mexico, Agora from Poland, Jollibee Foods from the Philippines, South African Breweries from South Africa, Li & Fung from Hong Kong, and Blue River Capital from India. We published more than a dozen articles in academic journals in strategy, economics, and finance journals using data from a dozen emerging markets and hundreds of companies doing business there. And we wrote several *Harvard Business Review* articles outlining our findings and recommendations: "Why Focused Strategies Might Be Wrong for Emerging Markets," "The Right Way to Restructure Conglomerates in Emerging Markets," "Strategies That Fit Emerging Markets," and "Emerging Giants: Building World-Class Companies." We also taught these ideas to hundreds of executives and MBA students both at Harvard Business School and at many companies around the world.

The crux of this book is to advance a structural framework for thinking about the nature and extent of differences between emerging markets and mature markets on the one hand, and among emerging markets on the other. That is, the so-called BRIC economies—Brazil, Russia, India, and China—differ from the United States, the United Kingdom, and Japan on the one hand, but they also differ from each other quite extensively. We specify how. In particular, we articulate a framework to calibrate the differences in soft and hard institutional infrastructure—we refer to the absence in emerging markets of things we take for granted in our backyard in Boston as institutional voids—that permeate emerging markets, and then offer solutions for dealing with these.

This book is thus an important marker in our exciting ongoing intellectual odyssey. In a way, we are fortunate that we started our journey when emerging markets were not as fashionable as they are today. That way, we could take our time, dig deeper, and learn what we consider to be robust lessons. Fortunately, emerging markets are of great continued interest to many executives, scholars, and business students. The recent financial crisis, originating in the West but sweeping the whole globe, has made emerging markets even more relevant than ever for two reasons. First, many in business and government are convinced that a significant part of growth in the next several decades is likely to come from emerging markets. Second, lessons and innovations from emerging markets may be relevant for Western mature markets, as consumers become more cost and value conscious, as their economies work their way through the debris of the financial crisis. We feel fortunate that we are able to offer ideas, based on unhurried research, on a timely topic.

We are the beneficiaries of immense help from many different sources. First and foremost, we are grateful to Harvard Business School for providing the intellectual environment to focus on our research, providing the financial and institutional resources to pursue it over a period of fifteen years, and creating the educational opportunities to test the ideas with hundreds of MBA students and participants in our senior executive programs. We owe these students, and many of our faculty colleagues, deep gratitude for helping us hone these ideas. Second, we are grateful to the many business leaders who agreed to share their insights with us as we developed many of the cases discussed in this book. Without their willingness to help us learn, we would not be in a position to create the ideas in this book. Third, we are grateful to Richard Bullock, our research associate for three years, for helping us synthesize our work and for helping create this manuscript. He has been an invaluable partner. Finally, we are grateful to Harvard Business Publishing for publishing all our cases and articles in *Harvard Business Review*, and thus helping us disseminate many of the ideas in this book as they were being developed. Thanks are particularly due to two *Harvard Business Review* editors, David Champion and Anand Raman, who worked tirelessly to help sharpen our ideas. The book benefited immensely from the encouragement and support of our editors: Kirsten Sandberg, who guided us through the initiation of this project, and Jaqueline Murphy, who helped us through its completion. We also wish to thank the other members of the Harvard Business team who worked with us on this project—David Goehring, Ania Wieckowski, Stephanie Finks, and Allison Peter. It was indeed a pleasure to work with these world-class publishing professionals.

Since we are Boston based, working in the field in emerging markets meant logging many, many airline miles. This would not have been possible without the unbelievable support of our families. We owe an immense and heartfelt debt of gratitude to our understanding young children and to our incredibly supportive spouses.

Tarun Khanna and Krishna G. Palepu

Boston, MA

November 2009

Introduction

THE WORLD IS FOCUSED on emerging markets.[1] The liberalization, growth, and globalization of these still-nascent
economies have made them tremendous sources of interest, opportunity,
and anxiety over the past twenty years. For households, emerging markets are a source of cheap consumer goods. For frustrated computer
users, they are often the location of outsourced technical support. For
executives of multinationals, emerging markets are growth drivers amid
stagnation and financial crisis in developed economies—and the home
turfs of powerful new corporate competitors.

In the first six months of 2009, the FTSE International Emerging Markets Index was up 41.1 percent, whereas the FTSE All World Developed
Markets Index was up 7.2 percent. China, India, and Brazil have reported
robust and significant growth during this period as the developed world
struggled to recover from financial crisis.[2] For companies drowning in
the crisis, these markets have offered life preservers of capital and growth.
For upstart entrepreneurs and well-established companies alike, emerging markets are becoming testing grounds and incubators for innovation.
For entrepreneurs, business leaders, and citizens in emerging markets,
this newfound global standing is a great source of pride.

For some workers in the developed world, however, these markets are
a source of job security angst. This anxiety has only increased in the wake

1

2 | Winning in Emerging Markets

of the financial crisis and recession in developed markets. For others—such as Wall Street investment bankers displaced by the U.S. financial crisis—emerging markets can be havens of new job opportunities. For new university graduates and young professionals in emerging markets, this growth has created tremendous opportunities and recalibrated career aspirations.

For politicians and pundits in the developed world, emerging economies are both derided as the destinations of offshored jobs and pitched as prospective customers for vaunted innovative products and green technologies of the future. For national treasuries in the developed world, the savings held in emerging markets have helped finance government deficits. For politicians from all over the world, emerging markets figure prominently in global trade and multilateral agendas. For environmental and labor rights activists, the rapid industrialization and undeveloped safeguards in these economies are cause for serious concern.

In a small but telling sign of a growing perception that emerging markets were both important and distinctive, the *Economist* in 1994 began including a page of emerging market economic and financial indicators at the back of each weekly issue. The rationale for the feature, the editors noted, rested on a simple premise: "Rich industrial countries dominate the world economy rather less than they used to."[3] In 2007, the *Economist* discontinued the feature, lumping the world's major economies together in a single table of indicators.[4] Whether the change was made for substantive reasons or simply to save space, the place of emerging markets in the global economy changed dramatically in that thirteen-year period.

Consider a few items that appeared in that 1994 issue of the *Economist* in which the emerging market indicators debuted. The magazine's summary of the week's news included a capsule noting the enactment of the North American Free Trade Agreement (NAFTA), linking emerging market Mexico more closely with its more developed northern neighbors—the United States and Canada.[5] One article forecast that India would be "a power in its own neighbourhood but its frail economy and its physical isolation between the Himalayas and the sea will almost certainly keep it out

of the global competition" to be among the world's preeminent powers.[6]
A two-page advertisement touted companies from Taiwan, noting, "Many
of the computers crunching numbers and making their reputations on
Wall Street are made in Taiwan. That's right, Taiwan."[7]

Since then, agreements similar to NAFTA have dismantled trade barriers in many emerging markets. India's economy has boomed, in part by
leveraging global communications technology that renders moot many
of the challenges of its "physical isolation." The promotional advertisement rebutting the incredulity that Taiwan could produce sophisticated
computers is now almost laughable: four of every five personal computers now produced by contracted manufacturers are made by Taiwan-
based firms.[8]

What Is an Emerging Market?

As economic globalization has brought down trade and investment barriers and has connected far-flung countries in integrated global supply
chains—and emerging markets seem to be converging with the world's
"rich industrial countries"—distinguishing these economies from developed markets may seem to matter less than before. We disagree. One fundamental premise of this book is that businesses still need to distinguish
emerging markets—collectively from developed markets and individu-
ally from each other.

But what, really, is an emerging market? The term *emerging markets*
was coined by economists at the International Finance Corporation
(IFC) in 1981, when the group was promoting the first mutual fund
investments in developing countries.[9] Since then, references to emerging
markets have become ubiquitous in the media, foreign policy and trade
debates, investment fund prospectuses, and multinationals' annual
reports, but definitions of the term vary widely (see table I-1).

The term is often reduced to the unhelpful tautology that emerging
markets are "emerging" because they have not "emerged." To understand
emerging markets, we need to consider carefully the ways in which they
are emerging and the extent to which they are genuine markets.

TABLE I-1

Frequently used criteria for defining emerging markets

Category	Criteria
Poverty	Low- or middle-income country
	Low average living standards
	Not industrialized
Capital markets	Low market capitalization relative to GDP
	Low stock market turnover and few listed stocks
	Low sovereign debt ratings
Growth potential	Economic liberalization
	Open to foreign investment
	Recent economic growth

Source: Standard & Poor's; International Finance Corporation; Trade Association for the Emerging Markets; J. Mark Mobius, *Mobius on Emerging Markets* (London: Pitman Publishing, 1996), 6–23.

If you ask a conference room full of business executives how they would distinguish emerging markets from developed economies, variants of three stories will likely arise. Emerging markets such as Brazil, China, India, and Russia, some will certainly say, are emerging by virtue of their recent fast economic growth. The opening of these large economies to global capital, technology, and talent over the past two decades has fundamentally changed their economic and business environments. As a result, the GDP growth rates of these countries have dramatically outpaced those of more developed economies, lifting millions out of poverty and creating new middle classes—and vast new markets for consumer products and services. Large, low-cost, and increasingly educated labor pools, meanwhile, give these markets tremendous competitive advantage in production, and information technology is enabling companies to exploit labor in these markets in unique ways.[10]

Other executives will focus on emerging markets as emerging competitors. On the macro level, a landmark Goldman Sachs report published in 2003 forecast that the economies of Brazil, China, India, and Russia could grow to be collectively larger than the G-6 economies

(United States, Japan, United Kingdom, Germany, France, and Italy) in U.S. dollar terms before the middle of the twenty-first century.[11] Commentator Fareed Zakaria sees this "rise of the rest" as a transformative, tectonic shift in the distribution of global power.[12] Companies based in these economies, meanwhile, are already challenging multinationals based in the developed world—and not only in their home emerging markets. China-based Lenovo's purchase of IBM's personal computer business in 2004 and the acquisition of Jaguar and Land Rover by India's Tata Motors in 2008 are only two examples of the increasing global mergers and acquisitions activity by emerging market-based firms. Some observers see the financial crisis of 2008–2009 as an inflection point, accelerating the emergence of these markets as dominant players in the global economy.

A deeper discussion might elicit a list of the persistent headaches of doing business in emerging markets. These markets, the executives might say, are prone to financial crises. Intellectual property rights are insecure. Navigating government bureaucracies can be thorny. Product quality is unreliable. Local talent is insufficient to staff operations. Reliably assessing customer credit is difficult. Overcoming impediments to distribution can be frustrating. Sorting through investment opportunities or performing due diligence on potential partners is often a guessing game. Others might throw up their hands and say that corruption is so endemic in emerging markets that the risks simply outweigh the potential rewards.

Based on many of these signs of emergence, some might say, emerging markets are not distinctly different from other markets; rather, they are simply starting from a lower base and rapidly catching up. Indicators such as the growing numbers of emerging market-based companies listed on the New York Stock Exchange or the growing ranks of billionaires from emerging markets listed annually by *Forbes* illustrate this trend.[13] Behind those indicators, however, is a more complicated story of why firms based in these economies have sought out overseas listings and how those moguls have amassed fortunes in developing countries that are, by many standards, still quite poor.

All these criteria—the indicators of opportunity and the causes for complaint—are important features of many emerging markets, but they do not delineate the underlying characteristics that predispose an economy to be emerging, nor are they particularly helpful for businesses that seek to address the consequences of emerging market conditions. We see these features of emerging markets as symptoms of underlying market structures that share common, important, and persistent differences from those in developed economies.

A fundamental premise of our work is that emerging markets reflect those transactional arenas where buyers and sellers are not easily or efficiently able to come together.[14] Ideally, every economy would provide a range of institutions to facilitate the functioning of markets, but developing countries fall short in a number of ways.[15] These *institutional voids* make a market "emerging" and are a prime source of the higher transaction costs and operating challenges in these markets. By relying on outcome criteria to assess markets, managers often overlook the ways in which emerging markets operate differently than do developed economies. Ranking the world's economies by per capita gross domestic product would suggest that the United Arab Emirates, for example, is among the world's most developed economies, but it is an emerging market nonetheless because of its market structure.

Intuitively, managers know that operating a business in an emerging market is different from doing so in a developed economy. It is tempting to chalk up these differences simply to country context. Indeed, market structures are the products of idiosyncratic historical, political, legal, economic, and cultural forces within any country. All emerging markets feature institutional voids, however, although the particular combination and severity of these voids varies from market to market.

An Actionable Framework

The chapters in this book identify ways in which the uniqueness of emerging markets is shaping the business opportunities and challenges in these economies. We offer a simple actionable framework to help managers map the institutional context of any emerging market. By developing a granular understanding of the underlying market structure of emerging economies—and not only cataloging symptoms to be incorporated in an overall risk assessment—companies can tailor their strategies and execution in emerging markets to avoid mistakes and outcompete rivals. Familiarity with the framework and toolkits in this book can help organizations address key questions:

- In this particular market, which market institutions are working, and which institutions are missing?

- Which parts of our business model can be adversely affected by these institutional voids?

- How can we build competitive advantage based on our ability to navigate institutional voids?

- How can we profit from the structural reality of emerging markets by identifying opportunities to fill voids, serving as market intermediaries?

In part I of this book, we unpack our structural definition of emerging markets by examining the institutional anatomy of these economies. In part II, we apply this framework to the challenges facing various actors as they manage in these contexts: companies filling voids as intermediaries; multinationals based in developed markets; and domestic companies based in emerging markets, which we call *emerging giants*.

Companies of various stripes face similar strategic choices as they respond to institutional voids in emerging markets.

Replicate or adapt? Institutional voids invariably challenge the execution of business models in emerging markets. Businesses need to determine the extent to which business models can be replicated in emerging markets or adapted to fill institutional voids. Multinationals need to weigh the extent to which they can transfer business models cultivated in developed markets to emerging economies rife with institutional voids or determine how they should adapt. Local companies with global aspirations can learn from the business models of developed market-based multinationals but also can exploit their local knowledge by developing models based on their intimate understanding of institutional voids in their home markets.

Compete alone or collaborate? Developed market-based multinationals and emerging market-based companies each bring inherent advantages to bear in emerging markets, but each might also gain from collaboration with other parties. Multinationals bring brands, capital, talent, and other resources to emerging markets, and yet their track records in these economies have been mixed. Local knowledge is a particularly valuable asset for firms to exploit in navigating institutional voids, and multinationals need to decide whether some form of collaboration with a local player makes sense for their business. Sharing is a two-way street in such collaborations, however, and multinationals need to weigh the benefits of local knowledge against the risk of empowering a partner that could turn into a well-trained and well-informed competitor. Local companies can exploit their inherent advantage in navigating institutional voids as a source of competitive advantage vis-à-vis incoming multinationals, but these firms can gain capabilities and credibility through global partnerships.

Accept or attempt to change market context? Businesses operating in emerging markets can take the institutional contexts of these markets as a given or can work actively to change them by filling institutional voids. Multinationals based in developed markets can either sidestep voids as best they can or strive to fill them in service of their businesses. Given regulatory constraints and other sensitivities, however, it can be difficult for multinationals to fill some voids in emerging markets. Local companies are in some ways better equipped than multinationals to operate amid institutional voids, but they also can exploit their local knowledge to fill voids and create a barrier to entry and expansion by foreign competitors. As we discuss in chapter 3, changing market context can be an entrepreneurial opportunity in its own right for intermediary-based businesses that fill institutional voids.

Enter, wait, or exit? Based on an assessment of institutional voids, companies need to decide whether to enter and operate in an emerging market, to wait and emphasize opportunities elsewhere, or to exit if they are already in the market. Multinationals can bring their global capabilities to bear in an emerging market or say, "Not now" if the challenges posed by institutional voids are too daunting. Exercising the option to wait is relatively easy for multinationals, because they can choose where to compete and have the resources to move to different markets. Although not entering is not an option for local companies based in emerging markets, these firms do have an exit option. Local companies with capabilities unrewarded in their home market contexts can say, "Not here" and exit their markets early in their corporate histories. Exercising this option is difficult for emerging market-based firms, because often they lack the resources needed to go global soon after their founding. Emerging market-based companies operating in different industries might emphasize opportunities elsewhere by waiting to enter a particular industry where institutional voids are more serious obstacles.

Overview of This Book

Part I (chapters 1 and 2) describes the importance of market intermediaries to businesses in all markets and offers a toolkit for companies operating in emerging markets to spot and respond to institutional voids (see figure I-1). Part II begins, in chapter 3, by looking at how companies can see voids as entrepreneurial opportunities and examines the challenges of building intermediary-based businesses in emerging markets. Chapters 4 and 5 then discuss how developed market-based multinationals and emerging giants from a wide range of industries, operating in a wide range of contexts, have wrestled with the strategic choices above to compete in emerging markets. Chapter 6 looks at how the institutional contexts of emerging markets shape the globalization journeys of emerging giants. We conclude the book in chapter 7 by summarizing an agenda for companies to use in developing and deploying strategies that fit emerging markets.

FIGURE I-1

Book structure and organization

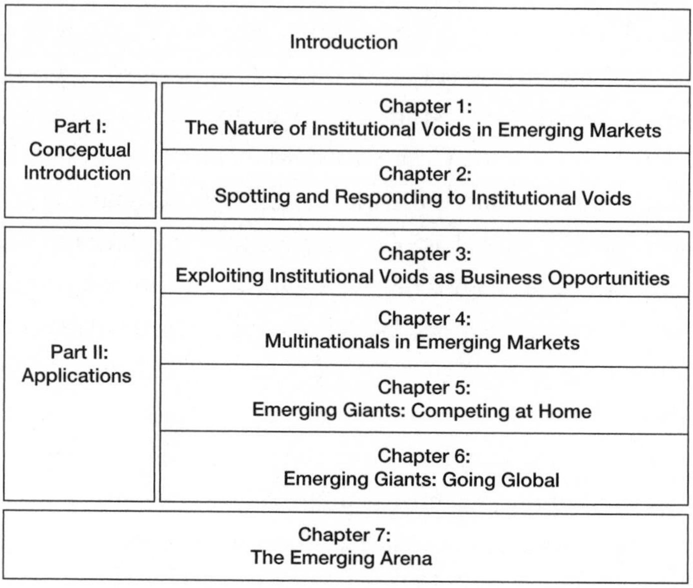

Introduction	
Part I: Conceptual Introduction	**Chapter 1:** The Nature of Institutional Voids in Emerging Markets
	Chapter 2: Spotting and Responding to Institutional Voids
Part II: Applications	**Chapter 3:** Exploiting Institutional Voids as Business Opportunities
	Chapter 4: Multinationals in Emerging Markets
	Chapter 5: Emerging Giants: Competing at Home
	Chapter 6: Emerging Giants: Going Global
Chapter 7: The Emerging Arena	

Part I

Conceptual Introduction

One

The Nature of Institutional Voids in Emerging Markets

CONVENTIONAL WISDOM holds that the diffusion of skills, processes, and technologies throughout global markets is resulting in convergence; the gap between emerging economies and their more developed counterparts is quickly closing.[1] This optimism has been bolstered by the development of high-tech global supply chains and the offshoring of professional services, but market transition and emergence often take more time than most decision makers anticipate. What is emerging in emerging markets is not only their forecast potential or liberalizing investment environments but also the institutional infrastructure needed to support their nascent market-oriented economies.

Institutional development is a complex and lengthy process shaped by a country's history, political and social systems, and culture. Dismantling government intervention and reducing barriers to international trade and investment can spark market development, but they do not immediately produce well-functioning markets. The world may be becoming flatter, as columnist Thomas Friedman has argued, but the landscape of emerging markets, in particular, remains deeply striated by institutional legacies.[2]

Many observers of emerging markets are quick to recognize that, for them to be fully developed, it is important to create physical infrastructure—roads, bridges, telecommunication networks, water and sanitation facilities, and power plants. Without adequate physical infrastructure, it is hard for participants in product, labor, and capital markets to function effectively. However, less recognized is the importance of institutional development that underpins the functioning of mature markets.

The most important feature of any market is the ease with which buyers and sellers can come together to do business. In developed markets, a range of specialized intermediaries provides the requisite information and contract enforcement needed to consummate transactions. Most developing markets fall short on this count. Investors and companies quickly realize that these regions do not have the infrastructure, both physical and institutional, needed for the smooth functioning of markets. It is difficult for buyers and sellers to access information to find each other and to evaluate the quality of products and services. When disputes arise, there are limited contractual or other means, such as arbitration mechanisms, to resolve these issues. Because of a tremendous backlog of cases, resolving disputes in Indian courts, for example, can take five to fifteen years.[3] Some joke that "if you litigate here, your sons and daughters will inherit your dispute."[4] Anticipation of these transactional difficulties also hinders contracting. We use the term *institutional voids* to refer to the lacunae created by the absence of such market intermediaries.[5]

definition

To understand institutional voids in more concrete terms, consider the plight of an independent traveler from the United States visiting an emerging market on vacation. Beyond the challenges of operating in an environment having a different language, culture, and currency, the traveler also must navigate a different way of doing business, even as a tourist. Accustomed to booking flights through Expedia, Orbitz, or Travelocity, choosing hotels based on easily accessible and reliable reviews, obtaining travel-planning assistance from the AAA, paying for goods and services with a credit card in virtually any location, purchasing goods that meet enforced regulatory standards and possess enforceable warranties, paying taxi drivers according to standardized rates, receiving flight status updates by mobile phone text message, and finding restaurant phone numbers by simply dialing 4-1-1, the traveler must adapt to a different environment in the emerging market.

Although they might come in different forms, most other developed markets, such as European countries or Japan, have a comparable tourism market infrastructure to that of the United States. The institutional arrangement of an emerging market's travel and hospitality marketplace, however, differs in fundamental ways. Internet-based airline ticket vendors, published travel reviewers, telephone directory assistance providers, credit card payment systems, and other such intermediaries are businesses, but they are also part of the U.S. market infrastructure. They help bring together buyers and sellers of travel services. (Nonprofit organizations, such as AAA, can also serve as market intermediaries, and governments provide many intermediary functions through regulatory bodies and civic services.)

In developed economies, companies can rely on a variety of similar outside institutions to minimize sources of market failure. Emerging markets have developed some of these institutions, but missing intermediaries are a frequent source of market failures. Informal institutions have developed in many emerging markets to serve intermediary roles. To reach rural consumers in India, for example, many brands rely on traveling salespeople to promote products in villages that have limited television, radio, and newspaper penetration. Salespeople stage live, infomercial-like performances out of the backs of trucks, explaining products while entertaining crowds with skits and banter. One such salesman, profiled in the *Wall Street Journal*, traveled more than five thousand miles per month, moving from village to village pitching products as wide ranging as tooth powder and mobile phones.[6]

Although some informal institutions may look like functional substitutes for the intermediaries found in developed markets, they often exist on an uneven playing field—accessible only to certain local players. A local loan provider might seem like a substitute for a venture capital industry, but only if the loan provider evaluates applicants on their merits or business plan. Seldom are informal market intermediaries truly open to all market participants.

Institutional voids come in many forms and play a defining role in shaping the capital, product, and labor markets in emerging economies. Absent or unreliable sources of market information, an uncertain regulatory environment, and inefficient judicial systems are three main sources of market failure, and they make foreign and domestic consumers, employers, and investors reluctant to do business in emerging markets. When businesses do operate in emerging markets, they often must perform these basic functions themselves.

[margin note: types of instituthal voids]

Institutional voids, however, are not only roadblocks. They are also palpable opportunities for entrepreneurial foreign or domestic companies to build businesses based on filling these voids. To return to the example of the travel industry, Ctrip.com has emerged as China's leading travel booking Web site, offering services similar to those of Expedia, Orbitz, and Travelocity. Established in 1999, Ctrip.com fills voids by aggregating hotel reservation and airline ticket information, providing rates and schedules, and offering a platform for customers to complete transactions—a powerful proposition in a market without a well-developed network of alternative intermediaries, such as travel agents.[7] Ctrip.com registered $210.9 million in revenue in the year ending September 30, 2008, with a profit margin of 31.8 percent.[8] Listed on NASDAQ, the company had a market capitalization of $1.3 billion as of January 13, 2009.[9] The significant value that can be created by intermediary-based businesses illustrates the importance of such market institutions—and the cost of their absence. Transaction costs in markets, the role of market institutions in mitigating them, and the challenges of designing market institutions have been analyzed by several Nobel Prize–winning economists: Ronald Coase, Douglass North, George Akerlof, and Oliver Williamson. We draw on this vast literature in institutional economics in the following discussion.

Why Markets Fail and How to Make Them Work

Transactions vary in difficulty. It is generally easier to transact in developed than in developing markets. For example, renting a car in Boston is far easier than it is in Mumbai, São Paulo, or Ankara. Purchasing a home in London, although increasingly cost prohibitive, is a much easier feat than buying real estate in Moscow, with its infant mortgage market. Even in developed economies, however, there are degrees of transactional difficulty. For instance, U.S. consumers find it far more complex to buy health-care services than to buy groceries or consumer electronics.

Transaction costs, which offer one measure of how well a market works, include all the costs associated with conducting a purchase, sale, or other enterprise-related transaction. Well-functioning markets tend to have relatively low transaction costs and high liquidity, as well as greater degrees of transparency and shorter time periods to complete transactions.

The World Bank Group's World Development Indicators highlight the variance in market performance between countries. Brazil, China, and India required more than twice the number of start-up procedures to register a business in 2007 than the six procedures required in the United States; Australia required only two. Another transaction cost measure is the time required to build a warehouse. A warehouse could be completed in leading developed countries in fewer than 200 days in 2007—in some cases far fewer—whereas in major developing markets such as Brazil, China, India, and Russia, it took 411, 336, 224, and 704 days, respectively. Other indicators, such as time to enforce a contract, time to register property, and time to start a business, also suggest higher transaction costs in many developing regions (see table 1-1).

All markets, irrespective of development phase, are less than perfectly efficient. Compared with emerging markets, however, developed markets are more likely to approach consistent standards for efficient transactions. Conducting even simple transactions in developing economies can be a time- and resource-intensive process, posing hazards for those expecting the fluidity of developed markets.

The challenge of transacting in the absence of well-developed market infrastructure is best illustrated through the Nobel Prize–winning economist George Akerlof's example of a used car market. Akerlof's work showed the difficulty of creating a well-functioning market when the quality of goods and services being bought and sold is uncertain.[10] After

TABLE 1-1

Comparing transaction costs in emerging and developed markets (2007)

Country	Start-up procedures to register a business (number)	Time required to build a warehouse (days)	Time required to enforce a contract (days)	Time required to register property (days)	Time required to start a business (days)
Emerging markets					
Argentina	14	338	590	65	31
Brazil	18	411	616	45	152
China	13	336	406	29	35
Czech Republic	10	180	820	123	17
India	13	224	1420	62	33
Indonesia	12	196	570	42	105
Israel	5	235	890	144	34
Republic of Korea	10	34	230	11	17
Nigeria	9	350	457	82	34
Pakistan	11	223	880	50	24
Russia	8	704	281	52	29
Turkey	6	188	420	6	6
Developed markets					
Australia	2	221	262	5	2
Canada	2	75	570	17	3
Germany	9	100	394	40	18
Japan	8	177	316	14	23
Norway	6	252	310	3	10
United Kingdom	6	144	404	21	13
United States	6	40	300	12	6

Source: World Bank Group, World Development Indicators, WDI Online.

owning and maintaining a car for five years and driving it for sixty-five thousand miles, the seller knows the condition of the car far better than the buyer. Unfamiliar with the car and its seller, the buyer will therefore approach the transaction with a degree of apprehension and mistrust. Is the seller selling a used car in decent working condition, or is he peddling a car with inferior quality relative to its price—a lemon? Is the car worth the price being asked?

The difference in knowledge about the car between buyer and seller—what economists call *information asymmetry*—and lack of trust make the buyer wary of taking the seller's claims of quality at face value. As a result, a prudent buyer generally is reluctant to pay the price asked by the seller. Given these conditions, how can the buyer and seller consummate the transaction to their mutual satisfaction?

One obvious solution, practiced in ancient bazaars for centuries, is price bargaining. Suppose the seller is asking $10,000 for the car. The buyer can respond by offering a lower price—say, $6,000—to compensate for the variety of unknowns. If the seller finds the price acceptable, the transaction will take place; otherwise, the seller will walk away.

But simple bargaining leaves most market participants unsatisfied. Why? The seller has a pretty good idea of the true value of the car, so he will be happy with the $6,000 offer from the buyer only when it exceeds the car's true intrinsic value. This, of course, means that the buyer would have overpaid for the car even though the bid price is substantially lower than the asking price. In contrast, if the seller were honestly representing the facts of the car's quality and asking a reasonable price given its true value, he would find the $6,000 bid from the buyer unattractive, prompting him to walk away from the deal. Thus, with a strategy of bargaining for a price lower than the asking price, the buyer will consummate only deals that are systematically adverse to his interests.[11]

This type of used car market leaves buyers unhappy, because they systematically overpay for any given level of quality. Sellers of genuinely high-quality cars will find no takers, because the market-clearing prices are always lower than sellers' assessment of fair prices. The only participants who will be happy are sellers who sell lemons at an inflated price. Clearly, this type of market will not last very long because sellers of genuinely high-quality cars will learn not to use it, and buyers will regret their purchase decisions and will learn to avoid it for future transactions.

There is, fortunately, a simple way to fix the problem in the used car market. The buyer and seller can agree to take the car to an independent expert mechanic who tests the car for its quality and provides an assessment of its intrinsic value. Based on this independent expert opinion, the buyer and seller can agree on a price.

How does the independent expert alter the situation? The expert opinion reduces information asymmetry between the buyer and seller and creates a basis for agreeing to a price based on common information. As a result, genuinely good-quality cars are likely to receive a fair price, so sellers and buyers of those cars will be happy with the transactions. Moreover, lemons will be exposed for what they are and accordingly will be priced lower. So buyers will either avoid them or, if they choose to buy them, will not overpay. The only players who will be unhappy with the introduction of the independent expert mechanic will be potential sellers of lemons. Because the used car market with the independent expert functions far more reliably than the one without such an expert, both the buyers and the sellers of good cars will be happy to pay for the services of such an expert.

All purchase and sale transactions in product markets for goods, in labor markets for talent, and in financial markets for capital and securities involve information problems and incentive conflicts. As a result, there are plenty of ways in which these markets in any economy may fail to work efficiently and effectively.

We can draw three important lessons from the used car market example. First, information asymmetries and incentive conflicts between buyers and sellers create significant problems in markets. If these issues are not addressed properly, they will lead to a loss of confidence among market participants and potentially to the breakdown of the market. Second, it is possible to devise institutional arrangements—such as the independent mechanic's expert evaluation in a used car market, or passive intermediaries such as Kelley Blue Book and Autobytel—to mitigate these problems and make the markets work significantly better than they would otherwise. Developed economies have devised many such institutions to make their markets work well.

Third, even though such institutional arrangements make many market participants better off, their emergence will adversely affect those benefiting from institutional voids, such as those who sell faulty cars. The creation of market institutions will be resisted by such groups. Building market infrastructure is thus a matter of both economics and politics.

How Developed Markets Work

Developed markets for products, talent, and capital are full of institutions that are the equivalents of the independent car mechanic in the used car market. To reduce the transaction costs that arise from the differential information between buyers and sellers and to limit potential conflicts of interest, markets need institutions to intermediate between buyers and sellers of goods, services, and capital. High transaction costs make an economy inefficient, leading to higher cost of capital, less labor mobility, and increased cost of trading. Beyond transaction costs, absent market institutions are critical sources of operating challenges.

From protecting intellectual property to reaching customers, businesses need market institutions. Developed economies, in their quest to mitigate transaction costs and facilitate commerce, have developed several complementary solutions that together make information disclosure credible, enforce constraints reliably, and regulate markets fairly. Disclosure of high-quality, credible information reduces information asymmetries. Enforceable contracts ensure that buyers can be confident that sellers will not behave opportunistically. By providing aggregation, certification, analysis, and advice, market intermediaries help buyers and sellers come together to conduct transactions efficiently. Finally, market regulation ensures fair play by all parties by defining and enforcing a clear set of rules.[12] Consider the important roles played by market intermediaries in product, capital, and labor markets.

Product Markets

In developed product markets, consumers are able to search for their desired products based on information provided by companies through advertising in newspapers and magazines, direct mail marketing, telemarketing, Web sites, and other forms of communication. Further, consumers have access to third-party information providers, such as the

Consumer Reports magazine and CNET, which produce extensive independent rating information on the quality and efficacy of a variety of products and services.

Retail chains also perform several valuable intermediary functions. They analyze consumer preferences; screen producers that seek to meet these preferences based on attributes such as quality, price, and delivery; stock and display goods so that consumers can see and evaluate them; advise consumers who visit the stores about product attributes; and allow consumers to return goods if they are dissatisfied.

Contracts between manufacturers and retailers, retailers and credit card issuers, card issuers and consumers, and manufacturers and consumers all play a critical role in ensuring that each performs its part of the obligation. Credit card issuers facilitate transactions by providing credit verification, financing, and collection of cash. Courts and consumer groups ensure that these contracts are enforced and that defaulters are penalized. If a manufacturer produces a low-quality product that fails to work as promised, for example, consumers have the right to return the product and recover their outlay. Similarly, if the consumer fails to pay the credit card company, the card company has recourse to collect the payment. Logistics suppliers such as delivery services meet the needs of transporting purchased goods from seller to buyer. Packaging contractors, shipping companies, and insurance agencies provide valuable services between seller and buyer to facilitate safe, timely, and guaranteed movement of products.

All the parties in the consumer product market are subject to a set of clearly laid-out regulations. For example, companies are prohibited from misleading potential customers through false advertising or promotion. Similarly, credit card companies are prohibited from sharing consumer information that violates customers' privacy. Retailers are required to offer well-defined return policies. Logistics providers must be accredited and are held accountable by both transacting parties to deliver products on time and intact. All sales are accompanied by a certain implied warranty by the manufacturer that the consumer is entitled to expect. Manufacturers are prohibited from taking certain actions, such as resale price maintenance, which can reduce retail competition. Consumers can sue companies for selling goods that cause damage or injury.

All these mechanisms in a developed consumer products market rely on a comprehensive network of soft and hard infrastructure. *Soft infrastructure* includes advertising agencies and media outlets that facilitate corporate communication, market research companies and logistics consultants that assist retailers, and credit rating agencies that collect consumer credit information to assist credit card companies. *Hard infrastructure*, such as roads and bridges, is also essential for low-cost movement of goods from producers to retailers. Public institutions such as national, state, and local governments that promulgate rules, consumer unions that lobby for such rules, and courts that enforce these rules, all play an important role.

Capital Markets

Similarly complicated sets of mechanisms underpin the functioning of capital markets in well-developed economies. Financial reporting facilitates investor communication. Accounting standards and independent auditors enhance the credibility of financial reports. Information intermediaries such as analysts, rating agencies, and the financial press provide analysis. Financial intermediaries such as venture capitalists, commercial banks, insurance companies, and mutual funds help investors channel their funds to attractive investment opportunities and facilitate access to capital for entrepreneurs and established companies. Stock exchanges create liquidity by enabling investors to trade with each other at a low cost.

These markets are strictly regulated. The central bank, securities regulators, and stock exchanges enforce these rules. Courts act as arbiters of disputes between various parties. In developed markets, investors can hold corporate managers and directors accountable through the threat of securities litigation, proxy fights, and hostile takeovers. By reducing risks to investors, these institutions make it possible for new enterprises to raise capital on approximately equal terms as big, established companies.

Labor Markets

In the labor market, educational institutions not only help develop human capital but also certify its quality through graduation requirements. Placement agencies and headhunters help employers find talent. Employment contracts and numerous regulations allow both the employers and the employees to protect their interests. Unions act as intermediaries between rank-and-file labor and big corporations that have substantially more power and resources. Unemployment insurance gives companies the flexibility to hire and fire based on their needs and yet provides employees with a safety net.

In developed economies such as the United States, Canada, Western Europe, Japan, and Australia, dozens of market institutions facilitate the smooth functioning of capital, product, and labor markets. In emerging markets, by contrast, many of these intermediary institutions are either underdeveloped or absent. Chapter 2 describes a framework to help spot these institutional voids in emerging markets. Chapter 3 examines the institutional anatomy of markets in more detail as we consider opportunities for businesses to serve as intermediaries in emerging markets.

Structural Definition of Emerging Markets

This chapter highlights the myriad institutions required in product, labor, and capital markets to support simple or complex transactions between buyers and sellers of goods and services. We define emerging markets as those where these specialized intermediaries are absent or poorly functioning. That is, these markets are emerging as market participants work to find ways to bring buyers and sellers of all sorts together for productive exchange. This structural definition arrays markets along a continuum, from entirely dysfunctional—with a plethora of institutional voids—to highly developed (see figure 1-1).

This definition implies that every market, including those of the United States and other developed economies, has some degree of "emergingness" built in. For example, the subprime mortgage market in

FIGURE 1-1

Continuum of institutional voids and market definitions

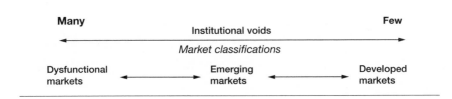

the United States, a key contributor to the financial crisis of 2008–2009, was an emerging market. Although the subprime lending market was serviced by a range of intermediaries—mortgage brokers, credit scorers, rating agencies, investment bankers, credit insurers, and regulators—these intermediaries did not effectively mitigate the information and contracting problems of a market in which the origination and financing of loans were so separated and incentives—such as credit-rating agencies being compensated by the entities whose securities they rated—were misaligned. The fast growth and increasing sophistication of transactions—the bundling and selling of mortgages in complex derivatives—outpaced the capacity of market intermediaries to handle them. More than the absolute growth or potential of a market, it is this gap in market infrastructure that defines an emerging market. The resulting financial crisis—the worst since the Great Depression—shows that institutional weaknesses can lead a market completely astray.

Working with this structural definition, chapter 2 focuses on how to evaluate emerging markets to spot these voids and introduces a general approach for companies to use in responding to institutional voids. Markets do not emerge overnight. Product, labor, and capital markets that are missing critical intermediaries tend to be imperfect for long periods. Even when governments of developing countries establish new intermediaries to fill these voids, they do not immediately function along the same lines as those in developed economies. The existence of intermediaries does not guarantee that they will execute their roles effectively, efficiently, or even-handedly, as the U.S. subprime mortgage market example illustrates.

Institutional voids cannot be mandated away through deregulation and liberalization; it takes both significant time and substantial expertise to eliminate these voids. Indeed, the most predictable feature of an emerging market is the persistence of institutional gaps over the short and medium term. Thus, scanning emerging markets for institutional voids provides an anchor for business analysis, opportunity assessment, and strategic decision making in these markets.

Two

Spotting and Responding
to Institutional Voids

THIS CHAPTER BUILDS ON OUR structural definition of
emerging markets to equip managers with toolkits to spot
and respond to institutional voids.[1] Emerging markets are hardly uniform in the nature and extent of their institutional voids. The development of business strategy in any economy is driven by three primary
markets—product, labor, and capital—and institutional voids can be
found in any, or all, of these markets in developing countries.

The advantage of an institutional approach to considering emerging
markets is that it specifies the particular combination of features that
prevents efficient exchange in each market. Some countries might lack
specialized intermediaries in the labor market but have them in abundance in the capital markets. Others may have effective labor markets
but distorted capital markets. Product and factor markets within developing countries often develop at different rates.

Chile is lauded for its capital market efficiency, whereas Korea's financial markets remain constrained by the entanglement between banks and
its *chaebol* business groups (see figure 2-1). At the same time, Korea has
undergone spectacular development in its product markets, as evidenced
by its world-leading broadband penetration, while Chile's communications

FIGURE 2-1

Comparing financial markets in Korea and Chile

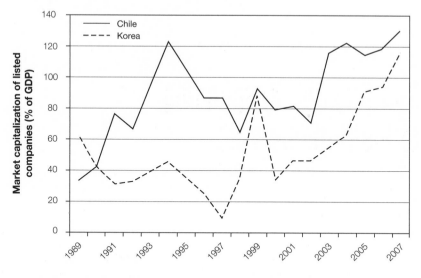

Source: The World Bank Group, World Development Indicators, WDI Online.

infrastructure is not nearly as developed (see figure 2-2). Moreover, different industries are not uniform in the ways in which they rely on market institutions. Some industries are more institution intensive than others, so different industries within the same market are affected differently by institutional voids.

This structural definition has actionable implications for managers. Institutional voids have real and first-order effects on business strategy.[2] Companies rely on intermediaries both to raise the willingness to pay (WTP) of consumers and to lower companies' own costs. Companies need the expertise of market research firms, for example, to understand customer preferences and then adapt their offerings to raise WTP. Identifying and segmenting the market are immeasurably more difficult without market research specialists acting as intermediary.

In terms of company operations, a firm's options for supply chain management, for example, depend entirely on available logistics intermediaries. Operating in a market that lacks logistics providers has predictable and measurable effects on inventory carrying costs. Moreover, financing

FIGURE 2-2

Comparing product markets in Korea and Chile

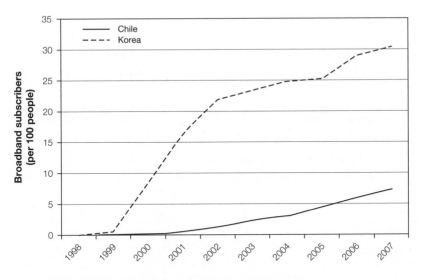

Source: The World Bank Group, World Development Indicators, WDI Online.

options depend on capital market intermediaries, such as commercial and investment banks. Raising external capital requires credibly convincing external capital providers that the money being sought will be used in the way that is intended. This would be highly difficult if there were no independent auditors and if there were no recourse mechanisms available to investors in the face of after-the-fact disputes. Human resource capabilities depend on intermediaries such as business schools and executive search firms. Identifying and screening candidates for managerial positions entirely in-house carry significant costs.

Therefore, for anyone interested in managing or investing in emerging markets, spotting institutional voids is a key first step. To facilitate this task, we have developed a series of questions shown in this chapter's toolkits.[3] Systematically answering these questions can give an organization important insights into the way a particular emerging market is likely to work or not work.

Consider how a few examples of these questions illustrate the variance in market infrastructure between developed and emerging markets, as well as among different emerging markets (see toolkit 2-1).

Toolkit 2-1
Applying the Spotting Institutional Voids Toolkit (Markets)

Product Markets

1. Do large retail chains exist in the country? If so, do they cover the entire country or only the major cities? Do they reach all consumers or only wealthy ones?

   Business Implications: Can we reach the customers we hope to reach in an efficient manner? As an entrepreneur with little market reputation, can we piggyback on the credibility of the chain stores to convince customers to trust the quality of our products?

United States	Brazil	Russia	India	China
Well-developed, highly competitive retail sector with strong and varied retail chains and wide range of Internet-based vendors.	Supermarkets, hypermarkets, department stores, including foreign retailers such as Carrefour and Walmart, have growing presence, though focused in urban centers. Shopping center sales account for almost one-fifth of retail sales. High taxes restrain formal retail growth. 30% of retailing is through informal operators.	Supermarkets, hypermarkets, shopping malls widely present in and around Moscow and St. Petersburg, and now expanding elsewhere. Government has encouraged modern retail, closed down outdoor markets, but retail outlets per capita still lower than more developed countries. Only 5% of retail outlets in chains. Limited foreign retail presence.	Modern retail is growing but represents only 3.5% of retail revenue. Sector remains highly fragmented; independent grocers constitute two-thirds of all retail outlets. Foreign retailers are present; large domestic companies growing retail presence rapidly.	Modernizing but still fragmented retail sector. 100 largest retailers account for 10% of country's retail sales. Shopping mall building is booming.

Sources: Euromonitor International, *Country Market Insight,* "Retailing–US" (May 2007), "Brazilian Retailing" (February 2007), "Russian Retailing" (October 2006), "Indian Retailing: Market Overview" (June 2007), "Chinese Retailing: Market Overview" (March 2007); Nandini Lakshman, "Protesters Tell Wal-Mart to Quit India: Foreign Retail Giants Such as Wal-Mart and Germany's Metro, Along with Local Chain Reliance Retail, Face Pressure from Small-Trade Workers," *BusinessWeek Online,* October 15, 2007.

2. Do consumers use credit cards, or does cash dominate transactions? Can consumers get credit to make purchases? Is data on customer credit worthiness available?

Business Implications: How can we evaluate the creditworthiness of our customers?

United States	Brazil	Russia	India	China
2.34 credit cards per person in 2006; 7.5 financial cards per person. Credit cards constituted almost 55% of financial card transaction value. Financial card and electronic payments more prevalent than paper checks. In 2006, private credit bureau coverage equaled 100% of adults.	One credit card for every 2.26 people in 2006; 2.36 financial cards per person. Credit cards constituted 19.5% of financial card transaction value. Payments with financial cards equaled 21% of private consumption in 2006. In 2006, private credit bureau coverage equaled 43% of adults. Public credit registry coverage equaled 9.2% of adults.	One credit card for every 110 people in 2004; one financial card for every four people. Credit cards constituted less than 4% of financial card transaction value. 90% of population did not use financial organizations or credit. Smart cards—microchip-embedded cards widely used to prevent fraud—constituted 41% of financial cards. In 2006, there was 0% private credit bureau or public credit registry coverage of adults.	One credit card for every 42 people in 2006; one financial card for every 12.5 people. Credit cards constituted 36% of financial card transaction value. Only 6.8 transactions per financial card in 2006 (40% of financial cards not used at all). In 2006, private credit bureau coverage equaled 6.1% of adults. Public credit registry coverage equaled 0% of adults.	One credit card for every 56 people in 2006; 0.93 financial cards per person. Credit cards constituted almost 13% of financial card transaction value. Only 3% of retail shops accepted financial cards at the end of 2005. In 2006, private credit bureau coverage equaled 0% of adults. Public credit registry coverage equaled 10.2% of adults. (A credit information database established by China's central bank in 2006 reportedly covered more than 25% of the Chinese population and some 98% of all Chinese bank consumer loans.)

Sources: Financial card data and analysis from Euromonitor International, *Country Market Insight,* "Financial Cards–US" (March 2007), "Financial Cards–Brazil" (February 2007), "Financial Cards–Russia" (March 2006), "Financial Cards–India" (March 2007), "Financial Cards–China" (May 2007), and data derived from population figures from The World Bank Group, World Development Indicators, WDI Online. Credit coverage data from The World Bank Group, World Development Indicators, WDI Online.

3. Is there a deep network of suppliers? How strong are the logistics and transportation infrastructures?

Business Implications: Can we manage inventory using modern vendor management techniques and collaborate with supply chain partners efficiently to minimize cost and maximize flexibility?

United States	Brazil	Russia	India	China
Companies use national and international suppliers. Firms outsource and move manufacturing and services offshore instead of integrating vertically. A highly developed infrastructure is in place, but urban areas are saturated.	Suppliers are available in the Mercosur region (Argentina, Brazil, Paraguay, Uruguay). A good network of highways, airports, and ports exists.	Companies can rely on local suppliers for simple components. The European region has decent logistics networks, but trans-Ural Russia is not well developed.	Suppliers are available, but their quality and dependability vary greatly. Roads are in poor condition. Ports and airports are underdeveloped.	Several suppliers have strong manufacturing capabilities, but few vendors have advanced technical abilities. The road network is well developed. Port facilities are excellent.

Labor Markets

1. How are the rights of workers protected? How strong are the country's trade unions? Do they defend workers' interests or only advance a political agenda?

Business Implications: What constraints do we face in the hiring, firing, and management of our employees?

United States and European Union	Brazil	Russia	India	China
The level of unionization varies among countries. Industrial actions take place in Europe, especially in the manufacturing and public sectors, but not in the United States.	Trade unions are strong and pragmatic, and this means that companies can sign agreements with them.	Trade unions are present, but their influence is declining except in certain sectors, such as mining and railways.	The trade union movement is active and volatile, although it is becoming less important. Trade unions have strong political connections.	Workers can join the government-controlled All-China Federation of Trade Unions. Historically, there were no industrial actions.

2. Does a deep pool of local management talent exist? Does the local culture accept foreign managers? Can employees move easily from one company to another? Does the local culture support that movement? Do recruitment agencies facilitate executive mobility?

   Business Implications: Can we staff our operations adequately? Can we count on lateral hiring, or do we need to rely exclusively on entry-level hiring and internal talent development?

United States and European Union	Brazil	Russia	India	China
A large and varied pool of well-trained management talent exists.	The large pool of management talent has varying degrees of proficiency in English. Local and expatriate managers hold senior management jobs.	The large pool of management talent has varying degrees of proficiency in English, and it is supplemented by expatriate managers. Employment agencies are booming.	The country has a highly liquid pool of English-speaking management talent fueled by business and technical schools. Local hires are preferred over expatriates.	There is a relatively small and static market for managers, especially away from the eastern seaboard. Many senior and middle managers are not fluent in English. A large number of managers are expatriates. Some members of the Chinese diaspora have returned home to work.

Capital Markets

1. How effective are the country's banks in collecting savings and channeling them into investments? Can companies raise large amounts of equity capital in the stock market? Is there a market for corporate debt?

   Business Implications: Can we raise adequate funding with appropriate capital structures at a reasonable cost?

United States and European Union	Brazil	Russia	India	China
Companies can easily get bank loans. The corporate bond market is well developed. The integration of stock exchanges gives companies access to a deep pool of investors.	A good banking system exists, and there is a healthy market for initial public offerings. Wealthy individuals can invest in offshore accounts.	The banking system is strong but dominated by state-owned banks. The consumer credit market is booming, and the IPO market is growing.	The local banking system in well developed. Multinationals can rely on local banks for local needs. Equity is available to local and foreign entities.	The local banking system and equity markets are underdeveloped. Foreign companies have to raise both debt and equity in home markets.

2. How reliable are sources of information on company performance? Do the accounting standards and disclosure regulations permit investors and creditors to monitor company management?

Business Implications: How can we evaluate potential partners and investment opportunities?

United States and European Union	Brazil	Russia	India	China
Apart from off-balance sheet items, a high level of transparency exists.	The financial-reporting system is based on a common-law system and functions well.	The modified Soviet system of financial reporting works well. Banks are shifting to international accounting standards.	Financial reporting, which is based on a common-law system, functions well.	There is little corporate transparency. China's accounting standards are not strict, although the China Securities Regulatory Commission wants to tighten disclosure rules.

Adapted and reprinted by permission of *Harvard Business Review.* From "Strategies That Fit Emerging Markets," by Tarun Khanna, Krishna G. Palepu, and Jayant Sinha, June 2005. Copyright © 2005 by the Harvard Business School Publishing Corporation; all rights reserved.

The Macro Context

Institutional voids in factor and output markets are shaped by the broader macro context of emerging economies. Politics, history, and culture affect the development, form, and function of institutions and the existence and persistence of institutional voids. In capital markets, for example, the development of financial reporting and independent auditing depends on transparency and trustworthiness. It also depends on the willingness of the state to open its capital markets to analysis and public scrutiny.

The ability to create value in product markets may also be hampered by a closed economic context wherein consumers are uncomfortable or unwilling to share information about their tastes and needs. It may prove troublesome to build market research institutions in this environment. Additionally, the rule of law and the regulatory institutions that govern efficient transacting in developed markets may be conspicuously absent in economies that have significant asymmetries of power resulting from a transitional country's sociopolitical heritage.

It may appear that we are singling out closed economies, but open economies can also impair institutional change. The democratic process, as in India, sometimes hinders the development of a predictable regulatory climate or the rapid development of infrastructure. The political back-and-forth inherent in a democracy slows the rate of change and concurrently makes it hard to ignore the prevailing vested interests that might be affected by the birth of new market institutions. For example, the entry of mass retailers has been subject to severe restrictions in India because of the aggressive lobbying and political clout of the small retailers. In this respect, aggressive state mandates can sometimes be more effective than the democratic process in implementing institutional change.

In light of the importance of the political and social systems in emerging markets and their openness to investment and the flow of information, we have included questions in the "Spotting institutional voids" toolkit relating to macro context (see toolkit 2-2).

Developing the capability to spot institutional voids can help companies from developed markets in two ways. It not only can help them pursue business opportunities in emerging markets but also may open their eyes to opportunities and challenges in their own markets. If top executives, boards, analysts, and regulators of financial firms in the United States had appreciated the institutional voids in the mortgage industry, for example, many of the problems exposed in the financial

Toolkit 2-2
Applying the Spotting Institutional Voids Toolkit (Macro Context)

1. How vibrant and independent are the media? Are nongovernmental organizations, civil rights groups, and environmental groups active in the country?

   Business Implications: What other stakeholders does my business need to consider?

United States	Brazil	Russia	India	China
A dynamic media acts as a check on abuses by companies and governments. Powerful nongovernmental organizations (NGOs) influence corporate policies on social and environmental issues.	Influential local media serves as a watchdog. The influence of local NGOs is marginal.	The media is controlled by the government. NGOs are underdeveloped and disorganized.	A dynamic press and vigilant NGOs act as checks on politicians and companies.	The media is muzzled by the government, and there are few independent NGOs. Companies do not have to worry about criticism, but they cannot count on civil society to check abuses of power.

2. What restrictions does the government place on foreign investment? Can a company make greenfield investments and acquire local companies, or can it break into the market only by entering into joint ventures?

   Business Implications: Is competing alone an option for my business, or do we need to seek out a partner?

United States	Brazil	Russia	India	China
Open to all forms of foreign investment except when government has concerns about potential	Greenfield investments and acquisitions are possible entry strategies. Companies team up with local	Greenfield investments and acquisitions are possible but difficult. Companies form alliances to gain	Restrictions on greenfield investments and acquisitions in some sectors make joint ventures	The government permits greenfield investments as well as acquisitions. Acquired companies are

| monopolies or national security issues. | partners to gain local expertise. | access to government and local inputs. | necessary. Red tape hinders companies in sectors where the government does allow foreign investment. | likely to have been state owned and may have hidden liabilities. Alliances let companies align interests with all levels of government. |

3. How long does it take to start a new venture in the country?

    Business Implications: What bureaucratic impediments to establishing operations can my business expect? What does this signal for government's attitude toward future growth and development of my business in this country?

United States	Brazil	Russia	India	China
6 days	152 days	26 days	33 days	35 days

Source: The World Bank Group, World Development Indicators 2007, WDI Online.

Adapted and reprinted by permission of *Harvard Business Review.* From "Strategies That Fit Emerging Markets," by Tarun Khanna, Krishna G. Palepu, and Jayant Sinha, June 2005. Copyright © 2005 by the Harvard Business School Publishing Corporation; all rights reserved.

crisis might have been avoided. As policy makers in the United States and elsewhere consider reforms to prevent future financial crises, they need to keep institutional voids in mind.

Market Segments in Emerging Markets

Before responding to institutional voids, companies need to audit the local context to identify voids. Companies also need to appreciate the importance of market segments in emerging markets. Different strategies in response to institutional voids position multinationals and domestic firms to reach different segments. Market segments in emerging markets are distinguished not only by income and prices but also by needs, tastes, and psychographic characteristics. Targeting particular segments requires particular capabilities and knowledge, and not simply different price points.

The product markets in emerging economies can be divided into global, emerging middle class, local, and bottom segments, which are distinguished by combinations of three variables: price, quality, and features (see table 2-1).

The *global* segment consists of consumers who want offerings having the same attributes and quality as products in developed countries and who are willing to pay global prices for them. The *emerging middle class* segment consists of consumers who demand products or services having a combination of global and local price, quality, and features. A customer might be willing to pay global prices and expects global quality, but desires local features. For example, Chinese and Indian executives may prefer to stay in a Shangri-La or Taj hotel rather than at a Four Seasons.

Some customers in emerging markets might look for products with global (or near-global) quality but with local features and prices. An example of this *local* segment would be a family in a developing market looking for a washing machine with world-class reliability but tailored to their local living conditions—such as space constraints, power consumption, and water consumption—and local prices. Some combinations of local and global price, quality, and features can be ruled out as not logically viable (such as products with local quality and features but global prices). Lower-middle-class consumers in the local segment are happy with products of local quality and features and at local prices.

TABLE 2-1

Market segments in emerging economies

Segment	Global	Emerging middle class		Local	Bottom
Price	Global	Global	Local	Local	Lowest
Quality	Global	Global	Global	Local	Lowest
Features	Global	Local	Local	Local	Fewest
Advantage	Multinationals	Battleground	Battleground	Domestic	Domestic[a]

Note: Some theoretical combinations can be ruled out by logic.

a. Some foreign players have targeted this segment with products that require foreign-developed technology—though pared-down features—through subsidized initiatives such as One Laptop Per Child.

The *bottom* of the market consists of people who can afford only the least-expensive products. C. K. Prahalad of the University of Michigan has called this market segment the "bottom of the pyramid."[4]

Understanding these segments can help multinationals as well as domestic companies in emerging markets tailor their business models and growth strategies. Before the opening of emerging markets, local companies dominate all segments. Market leaders typically straddle all segments, because these firms are the only game in town.

But when markets open up, multinationals based in developed markets quickly displace local companies in the global segment, because that is their natural niche of global quality at global price. Because of the institutional voids in developing countries, some multinational companies find it difficult to serve anything except this segment. The lack of market research makes it tough for multinational companies to understand customers' tastes, and limited distribution networks often prevent them from delivering products to customers outside large urban centers and thereby reach the local segment.

Local companies, because of their legacy, can dominate the local segment. Local knowledge is a powerful source of competitive advantage in the local segment, both to tailor products and to navigate voids. This large segment is not going away. Even as some customers in this segment move into the emerging middle class, economic growth refills the local segment as poorer consumers move into it.

Neither developed market-based multinationals nor aspiring emerging giants are satisfied with the status quo. The quest for growth leads both types of organizations to vie for the attention of the emerging middle class segment. Neither type, however, can lay claim to this segment with its existing offerings. Multinationals need to localize their products to reach local price points. These companies need local knowledge as they redesign products to successfully pare down features, retaining only those that are truly valued by local customers—without sacrificing quality. Local companies need to deliver higher-quality items and to design products that satisfy unique local needs. (Some local companies can even grab a part of the global segment, provided they can reach global quality levels and offer products and services that truly cater to the local sensibilities and even national or cultural pride of local elites.) Both multinationals and local companies need to stretch to compete in the emerging middle class segment.

Companies operating in emerging markets also need to think about segmentation as it relates to factor markets. In talent markets, multinationals often do not have enough knowledge about the local talent pool to design policies that will attract and motivate employees outside the global segment of employees trained by global institutions and compensated with global salaries. Local companies, by contrast, can take advantage of their local knowledge and familiarity with voids in labor markets to identify and sort talent outside this global segment.

Responding to Institutional Voids

Companies cannot operate in emerging markets without encountering institutional voids, but once they identify the voids that will shape the environment for their businesses, they can find ways to overcome them.[5] Recognizing the costs of institutional voids, companies might decide to build a business to fill institutional voids. In chapter 3 we look at the opportunities and challenges facing companies seeking to exploit voids as entrepreneurial opportunities. Multinationals and emerging market-based companies that do not build full businesses to fill institutional voids face a set of strategic choices and menu of options to respond to them (see table 2-2).

Replicate or Adapt?

Developed market-based multinationals have built their businesses on the foundation of well-developed institutional contexts. Executing these models in emerging markets, which lack such a foundation, is a challenge. Multinationals enter emerging markets without local knowledge or reputation, but often they can exploit their global capabilities by tapping in to global factor markets for capital, talent, or know-how or by leveraging the credibility that comes with being a global brand.

TABLE 2-2

Responding to institutional voids

Strategic choice	Options for multinationals from developed markets	Options for emerging market-based companies
Replicate or adapt?	• Replicate business model, exploiting relative advantage of global brand, credibility, know-how, talent, finance, and other factor inputs. • Adapt business models, products, or organizations to institutional voids.	• Copy business model from developed markets. • Exploit local knowledge, capabilities, and ability to navigate institutional voids to build tailored business models.
Compete alone or collaborate?	• Compete alone. • Acquire capabilities to navigate institutional voids through local partnerships or JVs.	• Compete alone. • Acquire capabilities from developed markets through partnerships or JVs with multinational companies to bypass institutional voids.
Accept or attempt to change market context?	• Take market context as given. • Fill institutional voids in service of own business.	• Take market context as given. • Fill institutional voids in service of own business.
Enter, wait, or exit?	• Enter or stay in market in spite of institutional voids. • Emphasize opportunities elsewhere.	• Build business in home market in spite of institutional voids. • Exit home market early in corporate history if capabilities unrewarded at home.

Simply exploiting these advantages—replicating the model of their home market—can enable multinationals to enter emerging markets without significant disruption and without facing significant institutional voids, but often these strategies position multinationals only to tackle the global market segment. To compete in the emerging middle class and local segments, multinationals need to adapt their products, services, business processes, or organizations. Adaptation is difficult because of institutional voids. When tailoring and marketing a product for a developed market overseas, a multinational can hire an advertising agency or other branding consultant in that country. Emerging markets often lack these intermediaries. Other forms of adaptation can help multinationals circumvent institutional voids.

Replicating business models developed outside their borders—particularly in developed markets—is not a viable option for emerging market-based companies that seek to build competitive advantage. Prospective emerging giants can exploit their local knowledge of product markets or factor markets, their established reputation, or other local resources to gain advantage in the market. By exploiting local knowledge and capabilities, emerging market companies can adapt their offerings, processes, and organizations to institutional voids.

Compete or Collaborate?

Institutional voids often stifle the entry of multinationals into emerging markets because they lack local knowledge or capabilities to get around these voids. Multinationals can counter this disadvantage by launching joint ventures (JVs) or other partnerships with local companies or by quickly localizing their staffs. Many local companies in these markets have internalized some roles served by market intermediaries in developed markets and, as a result, can be resourceful partners for multinationals entering emerging markets. Local companies, meanwhile, can exploit partnerships or other forms of collaboration with multinationals to help develop global capabilities or other resources—as well as credibility.

Accept or Attempt to Change Market Context?

Companies operating in emerging markets can take institutional voids as a given, or they can more actively engage with the institutional context by filling voids in service of their businesses. This strategy can be implemented in a number of ways. Consider the challenges facing a retailer operating in India. Hoping to sell fresh produce in a country that lacks a well-developed cold chain distribution system, the retailer could either build a cold chain itself or could induce another party to build it through cooperation, shared investment, or contracting for a guaranteed minimum amount of business.

If the company chooses to fill the void itself, it could do so simply as a catalyst and later exit its intermediary role, or it could build these operations into a business to serve other companies as well (exploiting the void as an entrepreneurial opportunity). Practical difficulties or regulations might prevent a foreign third-party logistics provider from building comprehensive infrastructure in an emerging market on its own. The company could still fill the void by providing port-to-port logistics and partnering with a local company to connect its operations deeper into the market or by inducing government or another entity to invest in infrastructure development through contracted business guarantees.

Enter, Wait, or Exit?

Some institutional voids are beyond the capabilities of either local or multinational firms to circumvent or otherwise alter. When faced with such situations, companies can emphasize business opportunities in other markets that do not present such voids. This exit option can come in various forms. An emerging market company might maintain a presence in its home market while investing more seriously in markets that are more conducive to growth or learning beyond its borders. Similarly, a multinational might delay significant investment in a particular emerging market until regulations pertaining to foreign firms are changed.

In chapters 4 and 5, we look at how companies operating in emerging markets have faced these strategic choices. In chapter 6, we turn to the globalization journeys of emerging giants. The strategic choices to respond to institutional voids do not apply as clearly to emerging market-based companies as they go global, but the institutional contexts of their home markets do shape their journeys. Emerging giants can replicate their home market-developed capabilities by entering other emerging markets having similar market segments and institutional contexts. To enter developed markets, these companies—like multinationals entering emerging markets—need to adapt their products, capabilities, or organizations to new market contexts, although with better-developed market infrastructure and more-demanding customers than in their home markets.

Emerging giants can go global not only by entering new markets but also by building global capabilities. These companies are increasingly able to "borrow" market institutions from developed markets to augment their capabilities. For example, a company from a country lacking well-developed financial markets could list itself on a foreign stock exchange through a global depository receipt (GDR) or American depository receipt (ADR). Not only can this approach help the company raise capital, but also it serves as a signal that the company meets international standards of corporate governance and sees itself as globally oriented. Foreign acquisitions are another avenue for emerging market companies to use in accessing global brands, talent, or know-how. These companies can also take advantage of connections to networks of their country's diaspora living overseas to tap in to foreign resources.

Persistent Voids, Anchored Strategies

The responses to institutional voids described in this chapter are not mutually exclusive or irrevocable choices. They can be successfully employed simultaneously or in different sequences. As institutional contexts in emerging markets evolve, corporate strategies will often need to change accordingly. Strategic positioning based on institutional voids is likely to be sustainable to some extent, however, because of the likely persistence of institutional voids. Much as markets cannot be mandated into existence, institutional voids cannot be mandated out of existence. Generally, government and private enterprise can fill voids only with the passage of time and experimentation, and not by fiat. As a result, challenges from market gaps—and opportunities to bridge them—persist. The presence or absence of intermediaries matters for strategy and the sustainability of competitive positioning.

There is no simple, straightforward formula for navigating the unique challenges of emerging markets, but companies operating in these markets will inevitably encounter institutional voids and they need not be paralyzed by them. Looking at institutional voids through common-sense approaches—assessing strengths and adapting accordingly, building capabilities, reshaping the environment, or biding time until the context changes—gives companies a palette of ways to assess and seize opportunities in these markets. Developing a more granular appreciation of an emerging market's institutional context up front can help managers avoid easy-to-anticipate mistakes and even identify unexpected sources of competitive advantage.

Toolkit 2-3
Spotting Institutional Voids in an Emerging Market

Product Markets

1. Can companies easily obtain reliable data on customer tastes and purchase behaviors? Are there cultural barriers to market research? Do world-class market research firms operate in the country?

2. Can consumers easily obtain unbiased information on the quality of the goods and services they want to buy? Are there independent consumer organizations and publications that provide such information?

3. Can companies access raw materials and components of good quality? Is there a deep network of suppliers? Are there firms that assess suppliers' quality and reliability? Can companies enforce contracts with suppliers?

4. How strong are the logistics and transportation infrastructures? Have global logistics companies set up local operations?

5. Do large retail chains exist in the country? If so, do they cover the entire country or only the major cities? Do they reach all consumers or only wealthy ones?

6. Are there other types of distribution channels, such as direct-to-consumer channels and discount retail channels, that deliver products to customers?

7. Is it difficult for multinationals to collect receivables from local retailers?

8. Do consumers use credit cards, or does cash dominate transactions? Can consumers get credit to make purchases? Is data on customer creditworthiness available?

9. What recourse do consumers have against false claims by companies or defective products and services?

10. How do companies deliver after-sales service to consumers? Is it possible to set up a nationwide service network? Are third-party service providers reliable?

11. Are consumers willing to try new products and services? Do they trust goods from local companies? How about foreign companies?

12. What kind of product-related environment and safety regulations are in place? How do the authorities enforce regulations?

Labor Markets

1. How strong is the country's education infrastructure, especially for technical and management training? Does it have a good elementary and secondary education system as well?

2. Do people study and do business in English or in another international language, or do they mainly speak a local language?

3. Is data available to help sort out the quality of the country's educational institutions?

4. Can employees move easily from one company to another? Does the local culture support that movement? Do recruitment agencies facilitate executive mobility?

5. What are the major post-recruitment training needs of the people whom multinationals hire locally?

6. Is pay for performance a standard practice? How much weight do executives give seniority, as opposed to merit, in making promotion decisions?

7. Would a company be able to enforce employment contracts with senior executives? Could it protect itself against executives who leave the firm and then compete against it? Could it stop employees from stealing trade secrets and intellectual property?

8. Does the local culture accept foreign managers? Do the laws allow a firm to transfer locally hired people to another country? Do managers want to stay or leave the nation?

9. How are the rights of workers protected? How strong are the country's trade unions? Do they defend workers' interests or only advance a political agenda?

10. Can companies use stock options and stock-based compensation schemes to motivate employees?

11. Do the laws and regulations limit a firm's ability to restructure, downsize, or shut down?

12. If a company were to adopt its local rivals' or suppliers' business practices, such as the use of child labor, would that tarnish its image overseas?

Capital Markets

1. How effective are the country's banks, insurance companies, and mutual funds in collecting savings and channeling them into investments?

2. Are financial institutions managed well? Is their decision making transparent? Do noneconomic considerations, such as family ties, influence their investment decisions?

3. Can companies raise large amounts of equity capital in the stock market? Is there a market for corporate debt?

4. Does a venture capital industry exist? If so, does it allow individuals with good ideas to raise funds?

5. How reliable are sources of information on company performance? Do the accounting standards and disclosure regulations permit investors and creditors to monitor company management?

6. Do independent financial analysts, rating agencies, and the media offer unbiased information on companies?

7. How effective are corporate governance norms and standards in protecting shareholder interests?

8. Are corporate boards independent and empowered, and do they have independent directors?

9. Are regulators effective in monitoring the banking industry and stock markets?

10. How well do the courts deal with fraud?

11. Do the laws permit companies to engage in hostile takeovers? Can shareholders organize themselves to remove entrenched managers through proxy fights?

12. Is there an orderly bankruptcy process that balances the interests of owners, creditors, and other stakeholders?

Macro Context

1. To whom are the country's politicians accountable? Are there strong political groups that oppose the ruling party? Do elections take place regularly?

2. Are the roles of the legislative, executive, and judiciary clearly defined? What is the distribution of power between the central, state, and city governments?

3. Does the government go beyond regulating business to interfering with it or running companies?

4. Do the laws articulate and protect private property rights?

5. What is the quality of the country's bureaucrats? What are bureaucrats' incentives and career trajectories?

6. Is the judiciary independent? Do the courts adjudicate disputes and enforce contracts in a timely and impartial manner? How effective are the quasi-judicial regulatory institutions that set and enforce rules for business activities?

7. Do religious, linguistic, regional, and ethnic groups coexist peacefully, or are there tensions between them?

8. How vibrant and independent is the media? Are newspapers and magazines neutral, or do they represent sectarian interests?

9. Are nongovernmental organizations, civil rights groups, and environmental groups active in the country?

10. Do people tolerate corruption in business and government?

11. What role do family ties play in business?

12. Can strangers be trusted to honor a contract in the country?

13. Are the country's government, media, and people receptive to foreign investment? Do citizens trust companies and individuals from some parts of the world more than others?

14. What restrictions does the government place on foreign investment? Are those restrictions in place to facilitate the growth of domestic companies, to protect state monopolies, or because people are suspicious of multinationals?

15. Can a company make greenfield investments and acquire local companies, or can it break into the market only by entering into joint ventures? Will that company be free to choose partners based purely on economic considerations?

16. Does the country allow the presence of foreign intermediaries such as market research and advertising firms, retailers, media companies, banks, insurance companies, venture capital firms, auditing firms, management consulting firms, and educational institutions?

17. How long does it take to start a new venture in the country? How cumbersome are the government's procedures for permitting the launch of a wholly foreign-owned business?

18. Are there restrictions on portfolio investments by overseas companies or on dividend repatriation by multinationals?

19. Does the market drive exchange rates, or does the government control them? If it's the latter, does the government try to maintain a stable exchange rate, or does it try to favor domestic products over imports by propping up the local currency?

20. What would be the impact of tariffs on a company's capital goods and raw materials imports? How would import duties affect that company's ability to manufacture its products locally versus exporting them from home?

21. Can a company set up its business anywhere in the country? If the government restricts the company's location choices, are its motives political, or is it inspired by a logical regional development strategy?

22. Has the country signed free-trade agreements with other nations? If so, do those agreements favor investments by companies from some parts of the world over others?

23. Does the government allow foreign executives to enter and leave the country freely? How difficult is it to get work permits for managers and engineers?

24. Does the country allow its citizens to travel abroad freely? Can ideas flow into the country unrestricted? Are people permitted to debate and accept those ideas?

Adapted and reprinted by permission of *Harvard Business Review.* From "Strategies That Fit Emerging Markets," by Tarun Khanna, Krishna G. Palepu, and Jayant Sinha, June 2005. Copyright © 2005 by the Harvard Business School Publishing Corporation; all rights reserved.

Part II

Applications

Three

Exploiting Institutional Voids
as Business Opportunities

INSTITUTIONAL VOIDS have a material impact on the operations of firms doing business in emerging markets.[1] They are often a source of frustration. Foreign firms, for example, have trouble replicating models from their home markets in contexts that lack the intermediaries that underpin them. Institutional voids can even derail businesses, as illustrated by the challenges faced by software, film, publishing, and other companies operating in emerging markets, such as China, that have undeveloped intellectual property rights regimes. For domestic firms, institutional voids can frustrate attempts to get off the ground, raise capital, hire employees, and, later, match the resources and capabilities of foreign-based multinationals entering their home markets.

We have discussed institutional voids primarily as obstacles for companies doing business in emerging markets. But they can also be a source of advantage for those companies—foreign or domestic—that have local knowledge, privileged access to resources, or other capabilities that can help substitute for missing market institutions. Because institutional voids impose costs on market participants, entrepreneurial ventures that seek to fill these voids can create significant value. Although some market intermediaries are under the purview of governments, many can be owned and operated by private sector players—developed market-based multinationals, domestic companies, or upstart entrepreneurs. In this chapter, we look at how companies can identify and exploit opportunities to build full businesses by alleviating institutional voids.

Identifying Opportunities to Fill Voids

To build a business that fills institutional voids, companies and entrepreneurs first need to recognize the absence of an intermediary that would add value in an emerging market. As we have discussed, institutional voids occur when specialized intermediaries are absent. Intermediaries are the economic entities that insert themselves between a potential buyer and seller to bring these actors together and reduce transaction costs. In developed market economies, dozens of institutions facilitate the smooth functioning of markets.

Opportunities to fill institutional voids are often born of necessity. Multinationals entering emerging markets, for example, would prefer to focus on their core business but often need to invest in expensive efforts to build market infrastructure to execute their core businesses. Some void-filling businesses have been spin-offs of such initiatives. But how can other companies and entrepreneurs identify opportunities to build businesses dedicated to filling voids?

Taxonomy of Market Intermediaries

Given the bewildering array of such institutions in various markets, it is useful to think about these institutions from a functional perspective—that is, by the nature of the activity they perform in market economies. There are essentially six types of market institutions: credibility enhancers, information analyzers and advisers, aggregators and distributors, transaction facilitators, regulators, and adjudicators.

Each of these types of institutions performs a distinct task that is critical to the functioning of the market. These institutions help resolve the problems arising from information asymmetries and incentive conflicts between buyers (customers) and sellers (producers). Together, they constitute the network of institutions that makes markets work.[2] This intermediation taxonomy is based on the institutional framework discussed in chapters 1 and 2 and provides a comprehensive picture of the market intermediaries that facilitate business transactions across product, labor, and capital markets.

Credibility enhancers provide independent assessments to support or validate business claims. To raise capital, for example, companies must convince providers of finance that the money being sought will be used in the way it is intended. This would be difficult if there were no third-party auditors to certify the credibility of the company and confirm a track record of creditworthiness. ISO (International Organization for Standardization) and other quality certification agencies serve a similar function in the product markets. The Association to Advance Collegiate Schools of Business (AACSB) and Graduate Management Admission Council (GMAC) do the same in the talent market.

Information analyzers and advisers find and generate information that facilitates business decisions, typically by providing data mining, number crunching, and consulting services. To develop and tailor products and processes that meet customer needs, companies rely on intermediaries such as market research firms to solicit information regarding the preferences of consumers or manufacturers. In the absence of a vibrant market research sector, identifying the kinds of goods to provide and performing detailed segmentation exercises would be significantly more difficult. Stock analysts and rating agencies play a similar role in financial markets, as do publications that rank universities and professional schools in the talent market.

Aggregators and distributors are the matchmakers in market intermediation, providing low-cost matching and other value-added services for suppliers and customers through expertise and economies of scale. Mass retailers add value as this type of market institution by compiling retail products into a one-stop shopping experience for consumers. Dedicated logistics companies aggregate the supply chain management operations of many companies by procuring inputs and disseminating outputs. Venture capital firms also provide this service by connecting businesses with sources of capital.

Transaction facilitators provide a transaction platform and facilitate buying and selling in markets. In searching for managerial talent, companies often rely on search firms to identify and screen potential employees, reducing many in-house human resource expenses. Online payment companies add to the cost savings of e-commerce by enabling consumers to complete transactions without waiting for checks or cash to get through the mail. Stock exchanges, eBay, and online job announcement sites are other examples of transaction forums in financial, product, and labor markets, respectively.

Adjudicators help market participants resolve disputes. Courts and arbitrators facilitate communication and resolution, and they issue rulings in a neutral setting.

Regulators and policy makers create and enforce the underlying rules that determine business engagement and industry direction. These intermediaries typically shape policy and make decisions to serve public and regional or national interests.

Table 3-1 applies this taxonomy of market intermediaries to U.S. markets, illustrating the range and depth of institutions underpinning developed capital, product, and talent markets.

The Value of Market Intermediaries

Many of the institutions of the marketplace are themselves privately owned and hence are driven by market forces. The fact that private sector intermediaries exist in a free market setting suggests that their services are valuable to buyers and sellers. John Joseph Wallis and Douglass C. North found that the transaction sector amounted to about one-half of U.S. GNP in 1970.[3] Viewed another way, the fact that so much economic activity is devoted to market intermediation suggests the magnitude of the challenge faced by buyers and sellers in conducting transactions in the absence of intermediaries.

Second, the fact that so many different types of intermediaries exist, and that within each type still many more individual institutions exist, suggests that intermediation is based on deeply specialized knowledge and skills. Nurturing and deploying these skills are challenges; markets,

TABLE 3-1

Institutional infrastructure in a developed market (the United States)

Type of market institution	Function it performs	Examples in capital markets	Examples in product markets	Examples in talent markets
Credibility enhancers	Third-party certification of claims by suppliers or customers	• Audit committees • Auditors	• ISO certification • CMM level certification	• AACSB certification • ETS admission tests
Information analyzers and advisers	Collect and analyze information on producers and consumers in a given market	• Financial analysts • Credit rating agencies for companies and individuals • Financial press • Financial planners • Investment bankers	• *Consumer Reports* magazine • J.D. Power ratings • Press • Industry analysts (Gartner Group) • Market research firms • TripAdvisor • Management consultants • Audit Bureau of Circulation	• Publications that rank universities and professional schools • Career counselors • HR consultants
Aggregators and distributors	Provide low-cost matching and other value-added services for suppliers and customers through expertise and economies of scale	• Banks • Insurance companies • Mutual funds • Venture capital and private equity funds	• Trading companies • Mass retailers	• Universities • Professional training institutions • Labor unions
Transaction facilitators	Provide a platform for exchange of information, goods, and services, support consummating transactions	• Stock, bond, and futures exchanges • Brokerage houses	• eBay • Commodities exchanges • Credit card issuers • PayPal	• Executive recruiters • Online job announcement Web sites

TABLE 3-1 (*continued*)

Type of market institution	Function it performs	Examples in capital markets	Examples in product markets	Examples in talent markets
Adjudicators	Resolve disputes regarding law and private contracts	• Courts and arbitrators • Bankruptcy specialists	• Courts and arbitrators	• Courts and arbitrators • Union arbitration specialists
Regulators and other public institutions	Create and enforce appropriate regulatory and policy frameworks	• SEC • FASB • NASD	• FDA • EPA • Consumer Product Safety Commission • FCC • FTC • FAA	• OSHA • Equal Employment Opportunity Commission • Unemployment insurance agencies

Source: Tarun Khanna and Krishna G. Palepu, "Spotting Institutional Voids in Emerging Markets," Note 9-106-014 (Boston: Harvard Business School Publishing, 2005). Copyright © 2005 by the President and Fellows of Harvard College; reprinted by permission of Harvard Business School Publishing.

can fail if any of the institutions in the network fails to fulfill its function. That is why it is a daunting task to build modern markets.

Third, as discussed earlier, the development of these institutions is a matter not only of economics but also politics. Market failures are beneficial to some economic actors, but they hurt others, so institutions that reduce market failures are not uniformly welcomed by everyone in an economy. Domestic and multinational companies can apply the taxonomy to identify the missing institutions—by function—and the opportunities that might exist in the intermediation space.

Exploiting Opportunities to Fill Institutional Voids

With their expertise, credibility, and experience in developed market contexts, multinational companies may seem to have a natural advantage as market intermediaries. However, emerging market-based businesses bring their own advantages to these ventures. Domestic players often understand the institutional landscape of their home markets more intimately and can identify opportunities—and potential pitfalls—more readily.

Just as multinationals cannot fill some emerging market voids because of government regulation or other political considerations, void-filling domestic firms are limited in their ability to apply their business models outside their home markets. Even without international expansion, however, the sheer size of large emerging markets such as Brazil, China, India, and Russia presents big opportunities for intermediaries to grow into large domestic businesses. Businesses that fill voids in smaller emerging markets can grow into adjacent opportunities. A print media company, for instance, can expand into electronic media; a bank can diversify into asset management and investment banking; and a privately owned business school can set up a medical, law, or technology school. Such diversification often paves the way for these businesses to go global at a later stage.

Executing some types of intermediation, however, is difficult for existing companies. For instance, the success of information intermediaries such as financial analysts depends on their credibility. If a business group with many listed subsidiaries begins a fund, bank, or publication that would conduct such analyses, its credibility could be questioned.

Companies looking to build businesses based on the alleviation of institutional voids face many of the same challenges experienced by other companies operating in emerging markets. When developed market-based companies seek to transfer their intermediary role to an emerging market, they need to determine whether the market is ready for the intermediary and, if so, to what extent the home market model can be replicated in the emerging market and what adaptation is required.

For example, big box retailers—product market aggregators and distributors—rely on a sophisticated supply chain in developed markets. Replicating such a supply chain in an emerging market is complicated, and it is challenged by difficulties in the market's hard as well as soft infrastructure. Distribution for a retail chain requires both hard infrastructure, like roads, to physically move goods efficiently, and soft infrastructure to, for example, reliably identify and assess suppliers and check the creditworthiness of customers. Both hard and soft infrastructures are underdeveloped outside large urban centers in many emerging markets.

Intermediaries that help retailers build and connect their supply chains as well as those that provide market information and facilitate contracting are also missing or underdeveloped in emerging markets.

Similarly, credit card companies—product market transaction facilitators—are intermediaries that themselves depend on other intermediaries. The absence of consumer finance in emerging markets—the institutional void that credit card companies hope to fill—is the source of opportunity but also the source of challenges. The business model of credit card companies is particularly dependent on market infrastructure that has not developed or lacks the scope and sophistication of comparable intermediaries in developed markets. Credit information, which is credible and easily accessible in a developed market such as the United States, is not nearly as pervasive in emerging markets. Marketing through direct mail—a common practice for credit card companies—is difficult in emerging markets. Collection agencies, which credit card companies turn to in the event of delinquencies, are not as well developed. After working to overcome customers' unfamiliarity with credit cards and gain acceptance in the local market, credit card companies face the challenge of managing in the absence of intermediaries on which their business models in developed markets depend.

Consider the ways in which global executive search firms—labor market transaction facilitators—have related their operations to the institutional voids in emerging markets. Some have focused almost exclusively on the global market segment, exploiting their relative advantages, whereas others have adapted their models and acquired new capabilities. Russell Reynolds Associates, for example, exploited its inherent advantages to gain a foothold in emerging markets (as it did in other foreign markets) by following existing multinational clients and maintaining its "one firm" approach to organizational culture and compensation structure.[4] In Brazil, the company initially focused on the country's privatizing telecommunications industry, where it exploited its industry knowledge. "It plays off our strength in telecom in London, in Atlanta," said one company executive. "Those people are as much a part of the telecom practice as they are the Brazilian geography."[5]

Similarly, in China, Heidrick & Struggles followed clients as it developed its operations, even opening an office in Chongqing, a giant municipality in central China—the first such firm to do so.[6] The company also adapted its approach by joining with its JV partner, Beijing Leading Human Resources Consulting, in the development of an online jobs portal, Jobkoo, which catered to the top, or global, market segment.[7] One Heidrick & Struggles executive described the value of flexible business models in emerging markets: "The last thing I want to do is go downstream. But if this works, I will apply the same technologies in India, in Central and Eastern Europe, and in Russia. This will be a completely separate brand, a completely separate company, and the way to create a revenue stream in the emerging markets while simultaneously building a future database for us. Could some of these ventures eventually cannibalize our business? Sure, but given the option of doing nothing, that's a risk I'm willing to take."[8]

Like other multinationals in emerging markets (as we discuss in chapter 4), the foreign intermediary adapted operations and acquired new capabilities to reach a different market segment in an emerging market—and hoped to transfer those capabilities to other emerging markets. Similarly, domestic companies with intermediary-based business models need to identify their sources of relative advantage in filling voids (such as local knowledge), acquire capabilities as needed, and determine which segment (or segments) they can serve.

As with any company operating in emerging markets, the firms that have been most successful in building businesses to fill institutional voids have been those that understand that business models cannot travel seamlessly to emerging markets; these companies adapt effectively and remain open to experimentation. Mapping the institutional context is a good first step. Intermediaries can use the taxonomy described here to identify the missing pieces of market infrastructure that might serve as entrepreneurial opportunities. By then auditing their capabilities, inherent advantages, capacity to adapt, and ability to acquire new capabilities, intermediary businesses can see how they match up to the opportunities identified.

TABLE 3-2

Case examples

Strategic challenge	Examples
Segmentation for intermediaries	Blue River Capital in India
Adapting intermediary models	Deremate.com in Argentina
Moving up the intermediation value chain	Li & Fung in Asia
Displacing substitute intermediaries	Metro Cash & Carry in India

In the rest of this chapter, we look at four companies that identified opportunities to fill various voids in different markets (see table 3-2). These examples illustrate the importance of identifying opportunities as well as the often wrenching challenges companies face when executing these opportunities.

Blue River Capital faced tough competition and execution challenges as it sought to fill voids in India's capital markets. The investment firm differentiated itself by targeting a market segment eschewed by many rivals—middle-market, largely family-owned businesses—and exploiting institutional voids as barriers to entry. Deremate.com sought to replicate the success of auction site eBay in Argentina and found the need to adapt this model to the emerging market. Low barriers to entry in Argentina ensured that fly-by-night operators made competition tough. Further, the country lacked many of the other contextual features that made eBay successful in the United States. Hong Kong–based Li & Fung has identified and successfully filled a range of voids in the global manufacturing supply chain, relentlessly evolving its model and adding more value to customers by adding intermediation roles to its offerings. In many cases, institutional voids in emerging markets remain unfilled because of opposition from governments or other vested interests. Successful execution of these businesses requires a great deal of sensitivity to the impact of filling the void on various stakeholders. German wholesaler Metro Cash & Carry learned this lesson in India when it faced entrenched opposition having a stake in preserving the status quo.

Segmentation for Intermediaries: Blue River Capital

The growth and potential of the Indian economy, and the companies emerging within it, attracted investment firms of all stripes to set up shop in the country in the early 2000s—from Silicon Valley–based venture capitalists to global private equity behemoths to local entrepreneurial start-ups.[9] While chasing the next Infosys or Bharti Airtel, these firms were also filling voids in India's capital markets. India-dedicated private equity firm Blue River Capital was established in 2005 as this flood of foreign investors and financial services firms clamored to enter or step up their presence in the booming market.

Blue River differentiated itself from this competition by targeting a segment it identified as an underserved niche: middle-market businesses established and still managed by families or entrepreneurs. Shallow coverage of companies by research analysts narrowed the pool of companies targeted by foreign private equity firms looking for more known quantities—even at a premium—as they raced into a market that was relatively unfamiliar to them.

Blue River avoided this competition by targeting companies not covered by analysts, including private companies and public firms that were not actively traded or widely covered. Blue River also pursued investments in businesses outside the sectors typically pursued by global venture capital and private equity firms. Sectors in which Blue River invested—such as textile, packaging, and auto components—might be considered mundane and not particularly high-growth prospects in the United States, for example, but could become big businesses in an emerging market like India.

Blue River sought out high-potential, low-risk companies within a segment deemed risky by many investors because they were not prescreened and could be difficult to assess. As with other firms operating in emerging markets, intermediaries need different capabilities to target different segments. Blue River exploited institutional voids directly as sources of investment opportunity by targeting a segment containing more institutional voids (see figure 3-1)—but where it could exploit the relative advantage of its local knowledge. "If it were easy, then it wouldn't be an

FIGURE 3-1

Segmentation for Blue River Capital

Segment	Global	Emerging middle market	Local	Bottom
Institutional voids	Fewer	←————————————————→		More
Capital provider	Global VC/private equity	Battleground between Blue River Capital and global firms	Local banks	Microfinance

opportunity," a company executive said. "Because of all the complications, because of all the challenges, that creates the opportunity for the folks who are able to manage through that."[10]

Providers of risk capital such as Blue River are important market intermediaries in any economy. Venture capital and private equity firms provide seed funding for start-ups and growth capital for companies looking to expand. The value proposition of these firms is particularly strong in emerging markets having other institutional voids in their capital markets. Service-oriented businesses, for example, often lack hard assets sufficient to serve as collateral for bank loans in markets without well-developed cash-flow lending facilities. In the taxonomy of market intermediaries, these firms serve primarily as aggregators and distributors of capital. As the first professional investor in portfolio companies, Blue River was an active investor, providing capital but also working closely with portfolio companies on strategy and a range of business issues and thereby serving several other intermediary functions (see figure 3-2).

Identifying and executing investments in Blue River's target segment were difficult, resource-intensive processes. The firm sourced deals through the research of its own staff and leads from local investment banks, accountants, law firms, and deal brokers. In 2006, the firm reviewed 207 potential deals, issued ten term sheets, and conducted formal due diligence for three deals, all of which were completed. "Historically,

FIGURE 3-2

Institutional voids filled by Blue River Capital

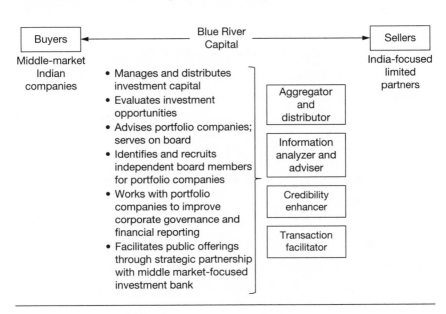

you can say that India has this problem of a lot of tainted entrepreneurs or family businesses, and you do need local expertise to be able to identify who to partner with and who not to partner with," said one Blue River executive.[11] Blue River built its business on the relative advantages of its local knowledge—helped by its strategic partnership with Edelweiss Capital, a middle-market-focused investment bank—and its willingness to invest the time and resources to work with companies that would be outside the comfort zone of most foreign investors in terms of corporate governance.

The absence of information intermediaries and background check services complicated due diligence for Blue River. The firm sought to minimize these risks by investing in firms that had track records long enough to assess meaningfully. Blue River began its due diligence with background checks on the management of prospective investments—a process that often concludes due diligence in the United States and other developed markets—even before evaluating the company in terms of its operations. To do so, Blue River needed to fill an institutional void; background investigation firms and the databases that provide raw data for such firms are undeveloped in India (although KPMG International recently started a background check service in the country). Blue River exploited its network and other sources to make inquiries about the management of potential portfolio companies.

Blue River explicitly sought out companies that needed to revamp financial reporting and corporate governance or needed help with other management issues. By working with portfolio companies on these issues, Blue River served as a credibility enhancer. One of Blue River's portfolio companies, for example, did not differentiate between payables and receivables from one company with which it was both customer and vendor, essentially saying, "Let's net it off," according to one Blue River executive.[12] But he also noted, "Family business does not mean a lack of professionalism."[13] Blue River looked for promising businesses with established track records that needed only to change business practices (and polish their organizations) to unlock and monetize their potential.

Blue River's model required significant "handholding," one company executive said, even before the firm committed capital to portfolio companies.[14] After completing deals, Blue River developed templates for new portfolio companies that were establishing plans for organizational and other changes; the protocols covered the first six months after the investment. With each investment, Blue River insisted on changing statutory auditors, financial controls, and accounting practices; identified related-party transactions; and put the entrepreneurs and any family members working for portfolio companies on employment contracts. "Be more conservative in how you represent yourselves to the outside world," Blue River told portfolio companies.[15]

Blue River has also worked with portfolio companies to develop boards of independent directors—including identifying candidates through its network—a practice that can add value to the firms beyond simply increasing governance credibility. "'You should want something from your board,'" Blue River tells portfolio companies, according to one

Blue River executive. "We say that these are people who will stay with you much longer than we will."[16]

Blue River exploited a provision in Indian law under which contracts can supersede minority shareholder rights to demand rights above those that would be afforded conventionally, including seats on the boards of portfolio companies and approval over some business decisions, such as annual budgets, capital-raising initiatives, changes to senior management, and compensation. The firm knew that it would face resistance from portfolio companies to the organizational changes it sought to implement once they were in its investment portfolio. Blue River dealt with this challenge by investing in only those companies that were amenable to organizational changes. Still, managing the internal dynamics of portfolio company organizations, particularly those run by families, was a challenge. "Sometimes it's like swimming in a sea of glue," said one of Blue River's operating advisers.[17]

To limit resistance, Blue River sought out companies undergoing transitions, particularly family-run firms in which a younger generation of family members was assuming management responsibility. More fundamentally, Blue River's model required its willingness and ability to empathize with portfolio companies. "Arrogance here doesn't work at all," a Blue River executive reflected. "We tell them that we're doing this for your benefit, and they respect us for it. You have to give people that sense of comfort that you're not taking away business flexibility from them."[18]

Intense competition from a range of players compelled Blue River to seek out a market segment where many potential rivals feared to tread, in large part because of institutional voids. The firm exploited its local knowledge and willingness to invest resources in corporate governance and organizational issues. Any investment firm fills a void by providing capital to businesses; Blue River differentiated itself by offering additional intermediary functions to a segment in which institutional voids served as both obstacles and opportunities. Like many successful intermediation businesses, Blue River developed a unique value proposition to an underserved segment.

Adapting Intermediary Models: Deremate.com

Market institutions often migrate from developed to emerging markets after decades of economic development.[19] Many of the myriad new market institutions born of the Internet in developed markets were replicated in emerging market countries much more quickly. Soon after the online auction site eBay took off in the United States, for example, clones were established in many emerging economies. The experience of Deremate.com, one of the first players in Latin America, illustrates the challenges of replicating intermediaries in emerging markets.

eBay was an innovative market intermediary in its own right, but it flourished only because it was built on a foundation of other contextual features (such as high Internet penetration and familiarity with similar transactions through classified ads) and other market intermediaries (such as widely accepted payment systems and reliable delivery services). eBay clones arrived in emerging markets quickly but succeeded only as the institutional ecosystem around them developed.

Internet auction sites are direct market intermediaries, connecting buyers and sellers of goods through a Web site that serves as a transaction facilitator and pricing mechanism. Deremate—literally "at auction" in Spanish—saw the intermediary's value proposition as particularly strong in developing markets by serving, for example, as a pricing guide for customers outside urban centers and without access to other information intermediaries and a useful tool for consumers with low incomes, in particular, to monetize assets (see figure 3-3).[20]

Deremate borrowed global institutions from its inception. Mindful of the power of first-mover advantage in its business and by fast-moving competition—including MercadoLibre.com, a rival founded by a group of graduates of the Stanford Graduate School of Business—Deremate sought assistance from developed markets to get its site up and running. The company partnered with Aucland, a French firm that had developed an online auction platform that operated in multiple European currencies and languages, a useful feature given that Deremate planned to expand beyond its home market, Argentina.

FIGURE 3-3

Institutional voids filled by Deremate.com

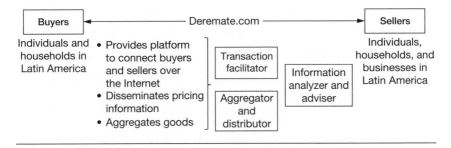

Internet auctions are useful as intermediaries only if the quality and quantity of their product listings are sufficient to attract potential customers. Deremate's management initially listed personal possessions—and cajoled friends and family to do likewise—to help stock the site, but the firm faced challenges acquiring scale in its product listings. eBay had piggybacked on an existing market for collectibles to spur its early growth, but no similar market existed in Latin America. Moreover, even comparable intermediaries such as yard sales and classified ads were not particularly developed in the region. This barrier of unfamiliarity and the low level of Internet penetration in Latin America compelled Deremate to position itself initially primarily as a business-to-consumer (B2C) site, an easier proposition than building a consumer-to-consumer (C2C) base from scratch. Deremate's marketing, meanwhile, focused on increasing awareness of its model, and the company segmented the market, targeting wealthy consumers through advertising on cable television.[21]

Institutional voids, such as underdeveloped payment systems and delivery infrastructure, challenged Deremate across Latin America. Forms of transaction varied widely across the region, from two parties exchanging goods in person and paying by check to the use of debit cards and third-party delivery. The company later established alliances with courier companies in each country to facilitate shipping.[22]

Currency fluctuations, language differences, and trust concerns, meanwhile, limited customer willingness to engage in cross-border transactions.[23] As a Deremate executive noted, even eBay has not been able to compete independently outside the United States (with the exception of the United Kingdom and Canada) and instead has looked to acquire or partner in other foreign markets.[24] Another institutional void—the absence of information intermediaries that might provide data on the marketplace—also challenged Deremate's ability to manage the growth of its organization. "Nobody really understands how big the market is, how big it can be, and very well-reputed organizations disagree by orders of magnitude about the present size of the market, let alone the projections," said one company executive.[25]

By 2000, Deremate had become a leader in the market and faced a "feeding frenzy" of bankers looking to take it public.[26] Deremate had been valued by several Wall Street banks at more than $1 billion, but the IPO was canceled after the burst of the tech bubble.[27] Many of Deremate's competitors continued to spend aggressively, expecting equity prices to recover, but Deremate cut expenditures, focused on organic growth, and remained one of the region's leading players in Internet auctions, along with MercadoLibre.[28] The two firms had discussed merging sixteen times by mid-2002 but never reached agreement.[29] eBay sought to enter Latin America through a partnership and, in October 2001, signed an exclusive strategic partnership agreement with—and took an 18 percent stake in—MercadoLibre.[30] With its noncompete agreement with eBay set to expire in 2006, MercadoLibre sought to acquire Deremate. MercadoLibre bought Deremate's operations in all but Chile and Argentina in 2005 and completed its acquisition with the purchase of those operations in 2008, reportedly giving MercadoLibre a 90–95 percent share of the Internet auction market in Latin America.[31]

It seems relatively easy to transfer the concept of a void-filling business to an emerging market, and this perception of ease, coupled with the palpable opportunity presented by institutional voids, often attracts significant competition. Deremate faced forty-two competitors in 2002, ten of which had received significant funding from institutional investors.[32] The tremendous power of network effects in an intermediary business such as Internet auctions quickly winnowed the competition to essentially one—the firm that had partnered with the global leader in its business.

Replicating developed market-based intermediaries in emerging markets is much more easily conceived than executed. eBay was built on a foundation of market infrastructure that was not present or fully developed in Latin America at the time Deremate and other firms established their businesses. Contextual features challenged not only the ability of these companies to generate business activity but also their ability to manage their growth in a fluid, uncertain environment, and for others to value them. Void-filling businesses can change the context of emerging markets, but they are also dependent on an ecosystem that cannot be transferred overnight. Firms targeting these businesses need to audit the local business context and institutional voids to understand that ecosystem, adapt their models to that context, work to fill those other voids where possible—and otherwise be patient and manage expectations and organizations accordingly.

Moving Up the Intermediation Value Chain: Li & Fung

Li & Fung started by brokering deals between Western companies and Chinese factories in Guangzhou, China, in 1906.[33] The entrepreneurial venture filled a void as a transaction facilitator between buyers and sellers that lacked a common language and shared business connections. The company, based in Hong Kong since the late 1930s, grew into a global giant by providing an ever-widening array of high-value-added intermediary services to global retailers and brands looking to exploit factor markets in emerging economies in Asia and elsewhere. Li & Fung has evolved from a pure transaction facilitator into an aggregator, distributor, credibility enhancer, information analyzer, and adviser in three lines of business—trading, distribution, and retailing—serving different sets of customers (see figure 3-4).

Li & Fung started out in basic trading and then operated as a sourcing agent for raw materials and consumer goods, first in China and Hong Kong and then in other Asian markets. The company was compelled to take on additional intermediary roles to move up the value chain as it tried to outpace declining margins. One company executive noted, "When my grandfather started the company . . . his 'value added' was that he spoke English . . . No one at the Chinese factories spoke English,

FIGURE 3-4

Evolution of Li & Fung's intermediary businesses

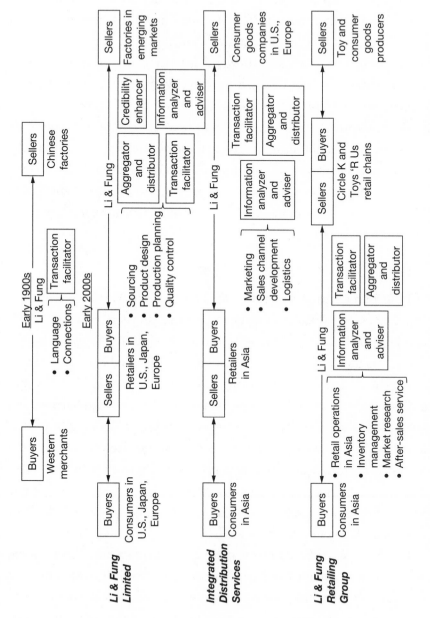

Source: Created by authors based on description of Li & Fung supply chain in Li & Fung Research Center, *Supply Chain Management—The Practical Experience of Li & Fung Group*, 2003, 28, 40, via Feng Bang-yan, *100 Years of Li & Fung: Rise from Family Business to Multinational* (Singapore: Thomson Learning, 2007), 214–217.

and the American merchants spoke no Chinese. As an interpreter, my grandfather's commission was 15%. Continuing through my father's generation, Li & Fung was basically a broker, charging a fee to put buyers and sellers together. But as an intermediary, the company was squeezed between the growing power of the buyers and the factories. Our margins slipped to 10%, then 5%, then 3%."[34]

Li & Fung moved up the value chain of intermediation from serving as a sourcing agent to developing full manufacturing programs for retailers and, later, breaking up supply chains to minimize costs and maximize efficiency and quality in each segment across different suppliers in different countries. "Managing dispersed production was a real breakthrough," said one company executive. "We dissect the manufacturing process and look for the best solution at each step. We're not asking which country can do the best job overall. Instead, we're pulling apart the value chain and optimizing each step—and we're doing it globally. Not only do the benefits outweigh the costs of logistics and transportation, but the higher value added also lets us charge more for our services."[35]

Based on its deep knowledge of several thousand Asian suppliers from which it had sourced over many years, Li & Fung identified and sorted their capabilities, quality, and credibility, matched them to the design and manufacturing needs of Western customers, and met stringent delivery requirements despite the poor quality of local infrastructure. For example, as one company executive noted, the company could help a retailer save costs in putting together a toolkit by sourcing wrenches from a factory in one country and screwdrivers from another. "That has some value in it—not great value, but some."[36]

Through dispersed production, Li & Fung exploited the scale of its reach and the quality of its internal information-sharing systems to respond to customer demands with speed and flexibility, adding more value for customers that needed just-in-time services. By reserving undyed fabric and mill capacity in advance, for example, Li & Fung enabled apparel retailers to respond to changing customer tastes and fashion trends more quickly and to limit excess out-of-style inventory. The company knew that simply squeezing costs by identifying lowest-cost producers and improving operations in hard infrastructure was not a sustainable source of competitive advantage. Instead, Li & Fung sought to improve margins from "the soft money," as one company executive called it, in distribution and value-added services. "It offers a bigger target, and if you take 50 cents out, nobody will even know you are doing it. So it's a much easier place to effect savings for our customers."[37]

Li & Fung earns this soft money by filling voids in soft infrastructure. The company alleviates information and contracting problems for its customers, exploiting its knowledge of suppliers and taking on the risk of contracting with them. Through services as wide ranging as product planning, executing design, managing quality control, managing customs requirements, and handling shipping consolidation and other logistics, Li & Fung fills a range of voids.

In terms of the taxonomy of market intermediaries, Li & Fung serves a number of roles for various constituencies through its three main business lines: trading (Li & Fung Limited), distribution (Integrated Distribution Services), and retailing (Li & Fung Retailing Group). The company is an information analyzer and adviser in assessing suppliers by price, quality, reliability, speed, credibility, regulatory compliance, environmental standards, and labor conditions. The company also evaluates the broader institutional contexts of the markets in which it contracts in light of concerns over protectionism and quotas—a service that is particularly important for its textiles and apparel customers. Li & Fung continually evaluates suppliers and seeks out new production partners based on labor costs, quality, and other features.

The company is also an aggregator and distributor of materials, goods, and information with its wide and deep reach. For suppliers, Li & Fung serves as a credibility enhancer, a role that connects it to global brands and retailers. As one company executive described Li & Fung's business, "In a sense, we are a smokeless factory. We do design. We buy and inspect the raw materials. We have factory managers, people who set up and plan production and balance the lines. We inspect production. But we don't manage the workers, and we don't own factories."[38]

As with any strategy, Li & Fung also needed to determine what it would not do in terms of intermediation. "I could expand the company by another 10% to 20% by giving customers credit," one company executive said. "But while we are very aggressive in merchandising—in finding new sources, for example—when it comes to financial management, we are very conservative."[39]

To deliver its value-added services, Li & Fung adapted its organization and operations both to the institutional contexts of the markets in which it operated and to the high-touch needs of its customers. Partnering with suppliers in Bangladesh, for example, offered cost savings, but Li & Fung needed to manage in light of the market's underdeveloped hard infrastructure, such as communications, that hindered the company's IT-intensive model. Li & Fung also aligned itself with customer needs by organizing its operations in small, autonomous, customer-dedicated units. These units sometimes went so far as to tailor their operations to the business processes and software systems used by their customers. The company sought out entrepreneurial managers in its organization— "little John Waynes," as one company executive dubbed them—to lead these units and incentivized them "to move heaven and earth for the customer."[40]

Li & Fung moved up the value chain and out of its home market through targeted acquisitions. The company sought to fill the mosaic of its place in the intermediation space by buying other intermediaries having specific capabilities or industry expertise it lacked. The company also pursued acquisitions to move up the value chain by buying companies that specialized in private label and proprietary brands. These acquisitions gave Li & Fung an onshore presence in the U.S. market, allowing it to be closer to customers and liaise with them at the beginning of product planning and identify new services the company could provide. "Instead of stopping our role once the ship is loaded, we are moving with the goods into the U.S.," said one company executive. "That way we get more jobs and more value."[41]

Shaken by the U.S. recession—and looking to cut costs wherever possible—some major U.S. retailers saw Li & Fung's services as a particularly valuable proposition in 2008–2009. Liz Claiborne, for example, sold its sourcing operations to Li & Fung in early 2009.[42] "This economic recession is more Darwinian," Liz Claiborne's CEO told *BusinessWeek*.

"Now is the time to reinvent your business model to be more competitive."[43] Through acquisitions of customer sourcing operations and rivals, Li & Fung sought to accelerate its growth through the recession.[44]

Li & Fung's success epitomizes the potential for firms to exploit globalization opportunities, technological capabilities, and deep local knowledge in cross-border intermediation. The intermediary's business evolved incrementally over time and successfully adapted to different contexts.

Our next example illustrates how intermediary-based businesses often displace powerful vested interests profiting from inefficiency and can provoke opposition even to highly compelling—and void-filling—value propositions.

Displacing Substitute Intermediaries: Metro Cash & Carry

Metro Cash & Carry, a division of German company Metro AG, has been an effective wholesaler in many emerging markets.[45] The Düsseldorf-based company sells everything from meats and vegetables to napkins, toothpicks, and hard goods as a B2B supplier to restaurants, hotels, and other businesses. Although Metro has a large and long-established presence in Western and Eastern Europe, the company has recently pushed into emerging markets such as China, India, Russia, Turkey, and Vietnam.

Although food varies widely as a percentage of sales in Metro's outlets, the company's operations often change the context of food supply and distribution in emerging markets where food is a significant line of its business. To supply its stores, the company has built direct links with farmers in rural areas to bring their goods to urban markets. As Metro enters emerging markets, it fills several roles described in the taxonomy of market intermediaries (see figure 3-5). The company serves as a transaction facilitator through its stores, connecting sellers of produce (farmers) with food buyers (restaurants, hotels, and other businesses). Metro is an aggregator and distributor for buyers, offering one-stop shopping for a range of goods, and for sellers, offering farmers and other businesses access to a range of customers. As a reliable seller of goods, Metro helps businesses reduce their inventories. As a reliable buyer of

FIGURE 3-5

Institutional voids filled by Metro Cash & Carry

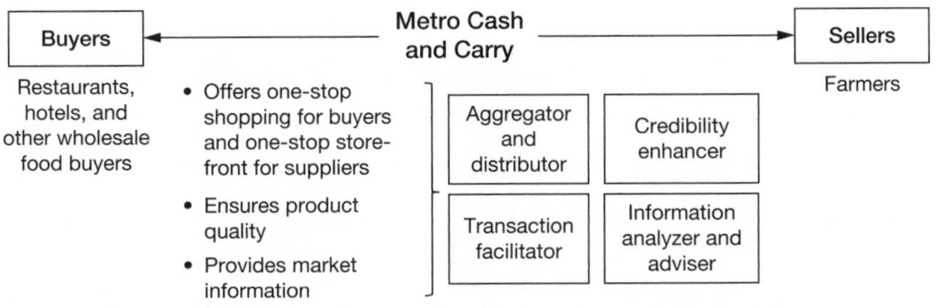

goods, the company helps farmers reduce risk. The company is also a credibility enhancer, helping ensure the quality of goods sold, and an information provider, relating market information to farmers. Moreover, by shifting transactions from roadside markets to state-of-the-art wholesale stores, the company's operations bring primary products into the tax net, a boon to local governments.

Metro expanded quickly in some emerging markets. Within five years, the company had opened twenty-two stores in Russia, an expansion helped in part by support from Moscow mayor Yuri Luzhkov. Metro faced significant competition in China from a wide range of players; within five years, it had eight stores but opened seventeen more in the few years thereafter. The slower pace in China was attributable in part to the extensive local negotiations needed to open each outlet, even with a large local JV partner.

In India, local opposition proved even more problematic. Metro's value proposition was particularly strong in India because of the waste and inefficiency that plagued the country's food distribution system. "Everything that we bring is positive," said one company executive. "It's positive for the farmer; it's positive for the retailer. The cost saving gets passed right down. The immediate mind-set in people is, 'This is too good to be true.' Everybody wins—except us, in the beginning."[46]

In 2000, the company received approval from national authorities to open its cash-and-carry outlets in India. Metro then opened its first two stores in Bangalore in 2003. As a high-tech hub with a significant presence of foreign companies, the city was thought to be a particularly promising entry point for the wholesaler. Metro's first outlets were only half-stocked, however, because the company could not purchase fruits and vegetables directly from farmers, a practice that was central to its business model in other countries. The Agricultural Produce Marketing Committee (APMC) Act required that produce in India be sold only through government-run auction markets called *mandis*.

Designed to prevent the exploitation of farmers by landed gentry in the 1950s, the APMC Act stifled the creation of genuine produce markets, hurting farmers, who were subjected to the *mandis'* inefficiencies. Although central government leaders had decried the APMC Act as an anachronistic impediment, it remained in force in the state of Karnataka—where Bangalore is located—and subject to the will of local authorities, who neglected to make good on continued promises to Metro to lift the measure. Metro's supporters in the central government offered little assistance because political power was decentralized.

Metro soon faced vocal public opposition and even protests from groups opposed to foreign investment and the traders who profited from the inefficiencies in the *mandi* system. "The middle man normally in all of these countries, they only have one investment: it's a cellular phone," said one Metro executive. "They buy cheap and sell high. And they fuel the governments."[47] Metro attracted particular attention in the media and from protesters by virtue of the large size and sophistication of its stores and the fact that Metro was the first major foreign big box operator to enter India.

The company struggled to convince the public that it was a wholesale operation and was not encroaching on the turf of local retailers, all of whom sold directly to the end consumer as retail players. At the same time, it needed to confront the political opposition with sensitivity, as one company executive recalled: "The farmers wanted to go on the street to protest for us. The small traders wanted to go on the street to protest for us. We said no, because you only generate a conflict. Maybe for a short time you are winning, but then you are a political instrument, and you don't have control on that. You have to be very balanced, especially in an environment like India where there are political chameleons that are changing from today to tomorrow."[48]

Market contexts are the product of history, culture, and politics as much as economics. A changing market context thus poses historical, cultural, and political challenges that are difficult to overcome, particularly for multinationals. Even without perishable foods—which typically represented 30 to 40 percent of an outlet's sales—Metro's stores in Bangalore achieved higher sales than foreseen in the budget, an indication that the cash-and-carry model was accepted by customers. As a foreign company displacing established interests in a sensitive political environment, however, Metro was vulnerable to opposition from other stakeholders.

Multinationals bring many business advantages to emerging markets when they seek to fill institutional voids, but they must work to overcome entrenched interests and latent suspicions to be seen as a partner in progress. One company executive explained:

> We know that the concept is right for India. We can communicate this, but you have to then build trust to be given the chance to show you can do it. The trust leads then to the operation, leads to credibility, leads then to the speed of expansion that we will have. Once the concept is really in place and we can show the benefit to the customer, the benefit to the supplier, the benefit to the taxman, the benefits all around, then everybody will support it. And then you have a different mind-set. But in a developing market, if you come in as a foreigner, there's a lack of trust. That is a big challenge for any foreign company going into a developing market, because ultimately we are there to make money. You can make money, and everybody can still benefit, but that's very difficult in a developing market for people to accept.[49]

Metro expanded its operations to other cities in India, but the APMC Act continued to be a barrier in Karnataka as of 2008. As one company executive noted, "There's a very nice saying in India, which is, 'You might have the clocks, but we have the time.'"[50]

Emerging markets develop not through the simple addition of intermediaries serving to connect buyers and sellers but through an incremental, often halting, process of development. Intermediary-based businesses with strong value propositions must contend with the informal institutions and substitute intermediaries that have a stake in the status quo—illustrating the critical importance of carefully mapping the institutional context in emerging markets.

Filling Voids in Emerging Markets

Intermediaries face tough contextual challenges, competition, and incumbent substitutes, as the examples in this chapter show. Any company seeking to build a business based on filling institutional voids in emerging markets should first recognize that an institutional void exists and that filling it could create significant value (see toolkit 3-1).

Prospective intermediaries need to match their capabilities to the broader institutional context of the emerging market. Void-filling multinational businesses need to determine whether the market is ready for their services or whether they should emphasize opportunities elsewhere. Domestic firms need to identify a source of relative advantage in filling the void.

Next, prospective intermediary businesses need to identify which segment of the market they can serve with their current capabilities or which skills or other capabilities they need to acquire to serve it. Intermediaries often depend on other market institutions or contextual features, so these businesses need to map, evaluate, and adapt accordingly. Firms often need to fill other voids as a means of serving their primary intermediary functions. As they establish themselves, firms need to consider how to expand into adjacent intermediary roles and grow their businesses by adding value through their intermediation. Finally, successfully changing the market context requires a great deal of sensitivity to stakeholders that are affected or displaced and the broader ecosystem that often underpins market intermediaries.

Toolkit 3-1
Toolkit for Intermediaries Looking to Fill Institutional Voids

Where can we identify voids to fill as entrepreneurial opportunities?

Taxonomy of institutional infrastructure	Function	Capital market	Product market	Talent market
Credibility enhancers	Third-party certification of the claims by suppliers or customers			
Information analyzers and advisers	Collect and analyze information on producers and consumers in a given market			
Aggregators and distributors	Provide low-cost matching and other value-added services for suppliers and customers through expertise and economies of scale			
Transaction facilitators	Provide a platform for exchange of information, goods, and services and provide support functions for consummating transactions			
Regulators and other public institutions	Create and enforce the appropriate regulatory and policy framework			
Adjudicators	Resolve disputes regarding law and private contracts			

What segment can we reach?

Segment	Global	Emerging middle market	Local	Bottom
Institutional voids	Fewer	←——————————————————→		More

- What other contextual features or market institutions does this intermediary role depend on in developed markets?

- How do we need to adapt this intermediary-based business to the local context?

- How can we expand our business into adjacent intermediary services and move up the intermediation value chain?

- What vested interests are we displacing or might we encounter as we seek to fill this void?

Four

Multinationals in Emerging Markets

THE RISE OF EMERGING MARKETS has not gone unnoticed by multinationals based in developed markets, such as the United States, Europe, and Japan.[1] In many cases, multinationals landed in the larger emerging markets immediately after liberalization and have been operating in those markets for years. Emerging markets are playing pivotal roles in the strategies of multinationals based in developed markets. Developing markets accounted for 30 percent of U.S.-based Procter & Gamble's net sales in 2008, up from 21 percent in 2004.[2] Historically hesitant to move into developing countries, Japan's largest automakers—Honda, Nissan, and Toyota—have moved aggressively into emerging markets in recent years. In May 2008, Nissan broke ground on a $1.1 billion production facility in Chennai, India. The company is also setting up plants in China, Morocco, and Russia. Nissan sold only 500 vehicles at its five dealerships in India in 2007; by 2012, the company hopes to sell 200,000 through fifty-five dealerships. Toyota has built production facilities in Russia and India, and Honda is expanding its production capacity in Brazil, India, and Argentina.[3]

Emerging markets have already become major growth drivers for telecommunications-related multinationals. After registering 15 percent growth in 2008, emerging markets accounted for 57 percent of Sweden-based Ericsson's telecom network sales.[4] Nokia of Finland, meanwhile, has designed a wide range of handsets particularly for emerging markets, offering not only voice communication but also mobile Internet service.[5] In 2008, Nokia's net sales in China, India, Indonesia, and Russia each surpassed its sales in the United States.[6]

Despite the advantages enjoyed by developed market-based multinationals—scale, brand recognition, superior technology, demonstrated success based on existing organization, and access to developed markets for talent, finance, and other inputs—their track record in emerging markets has been mixed. These companies face two overarching challenges in emerging markets: the prevalence of institutional voids and the new class of nimble, ambitious competitors that are developing world-class capabilities.

Multinationals can succeed in emerging markets only by adapting to or shaping the institutional voids in the markets they enter, particularly given that they must compete against local companies having an inherent advantage in navigating the business contexts of their home markets. Chapters 1 and 2 explain the uniqueness of emerging markets in terms of institutional context. This chapter examines what this unique institutional context means for multinationals looking to tap in to the growth of these markets as they confront and respond to institutional voids.

Facing Institutional Voids

The opportunities for developed market-based multinationals in emerging markets are fairly clear, but what does it mean for these companies to operate amid institutional voids? We introduce the concept of institutional voids in chapter 1 with the example of an independent foreign traveler touring an emerging market. The traveler would miss the institutions that facilitate travel in his home market.

Now consider the plight of a foreign entrepreneur or multinational setting up a business in an emerging market. Like travelers, foreign businesses rely on a range of institutions to facilitate transactions and manage operations in their home markets and often are forced to internalize the added costs of their absence in emerging markets. Consider a consumer goods company. Products designed for developed markets often need to be modified to suit local needs, tastes, and price points in emerging markets—a difficult task in the absence of market information intermediaries. Reaching a significant share of the large consumer markets that attract many multinationals to emerging economies, meanwhile, is not as simple as contracting with retail chains or enlisting third-party logistics providers, because often these entities are not as well established or widespread in emerging markets. Any company operating in a foreign market faces challenges not encountered at home, but when a U.S.-based multinational, for example, sells its products in other developed markets—say, Europe or Japan—its market expertise may not be as deep, but it can still draw on deep networks of local market intermediaries for research, marketing, and distribution. These capabilities are not as widely available or as well developed in emerging markets.

Developed market-based multinationals have built businesses on foundations of strong market infrastructure. Often, these institutions are noticed only when they are missing, and they cannot be taken for granted in emerging markets. Soft infrastructure—market institutions, in contrast to hard infrastructure, such as roads and ports—plays a critical role in the ability of developed market-based multinationals to execute their standard business models in emerging markets, and it should not be overlooked.

Emerging markets can be exploited as consumer markets, regional or global production platforms, innovation and product development hubs, sources of talent, raw materials, or other inputs, and untapped opportunities to develop market infrastructure. Multinationals will confront institutional voids while pursuing any of these opportunities, so firms need to be clear about how they want to engage any emerging market in relation to the market's institutional context.

Initially mesmerized by the size of these markets, many early-mover multinationals quickly discover that selling in emerging markets is a complicated exercise, requiring deep knowledge of customer needs, distribution networks, and a broadly supportive institutional framework. Low-cost labor makes emerging markets attractive as sourcing and production venues for multinationals. Through sourcing and local production, multinationals gain market entry and also infuse capital into the economy, improve the quality and processing standards of domestic industry, and share technology, management, and other expertise—an attractive proposition for governments in emerging markets. An incoming global company can build relationships and market know-how through sourcing deals to fuel future business and growth in target markets even while waiting to tackle the local consumer market.

Institutional context is a critical determinant of the ways multinationals choose to exploit factor markets. Using an emerging market as a hub for innovation and product development, for example, depends on the market's intellectual property rights regime and the technical capabilities of its workforce.

Understanding the institutional context can help multinationals determine whether to sell or source in the emerging market; whether to engage the market through greenfield entry, acquisitions, joint ventures, or another form of collaboration with local players; and whether to focus on B2B or B2C initiatives. If the government exhibits a lack of openness, for example, joint ventures may be the most effective way to enter a market. If transportation and logistics networks are poor, a B2B strategy might be a better strategy than a B2C approach to get products into the market. Thus, companies create value by matching their strategies to the contexts in which they operate.[7]

As a first step, firms need a clear understanding of the existing voids. Firms that scan the institutional context and develop a clear and realistic understanding of intermediation gaps or other market voids and the ways they align with their own core competencies and value propositions are more likely to choose the best markets to enter, select optimal strategies, and extract the most value from operating in emerging markets. By being able and willing to experiment, multinationals can navigate emerging market contexts and even exploit some institutional voids for competitive advantage.

Responding to Institutional Voids

Multinationals face a series of strategic choices as they confront institutional voids in emerging markets (see table 4-1). These choices are faced by multinational firms that exploit their global brands and reputation to sell into product markets in emerging markets and those that exploit local factor markets to produce and source in emerging markets. These choices are closely tied to the various market segments within emerging markets. As described in chapter 2, emerging markets—both output markets and input markets—can be segmented into four tiers: global, emerging middle class, local, and bottom of the market. Different strategies in response to institutional voids position multinationals to reach different market segments, as we discuss next.

Replicate or Adapt?

Equipped with business models developed for markets having deep networks of market intermediaries, multinationals need to decide the extent to which they can replicate those models in emerging markets having institutional voids. By virtue of their global brands, credibility, know-how,

TABLE 4-1

Responding to institutional voids in emerging markets

Strategic choice	Options for multinationals from developed markets
Replicate or adapt?	• Replicate business model, exploiting relative advantage of global brand, credibility, know-how, talent, finance, and other factor inputs. • Adapt business models, products, or organizations to institutional voids.
Compete alone or collaborate?	• Compete alone. • Acquire capabilities to navigate institutional voids through local partnerships or JVs.
Accept or attempt to change market context?	• Take market context as given. • Fill institutional voids in service of own business.
Enter, wait, or exit?	• Enter or stay in market in spite of institutional voids. • Emphasize opportunities elsewhere.

talent, and resources, multinationals have unique competitive advantages in emerging markets. These advantages are so valuable in emerging markets—where domestic rivals lack access to the intermediaries that help companies acquire and build these capabilities—that multinationals can build strategies around them. Multinationals can exploit their relative advantage to gain traction, replicating their home-market business models with little modification. This approach enables multinationals to sidestep some institutional voids and does not particularly strain their organizations, but often it limits companies to serving only the global market segment, where those capabilities are most rewarded.

The global segment features infrastructure, tastes, talent, and resources similar to those in developed market-based multinationals' home markets. It thus offers these companies an easy entry point into emerging markets where institutional voids are relatively moot. The absence of market research, product design, brand-building, or distribution intermediaries, for example, does not impede multinationals from reaching the global segment. Many Western fashion houses entering China brought their standard global lines with global pricing to retail outlets in the shopping plazas in five-star hotel properties; in this way, the fashion houses exploited their global brands and existing design expertise at easily accessible retail locations frequented by members of the country's market segment having both wealth and global tastes.

Multinationals' experience in catering to this segment in developed markets gives them a natural advantage vis-à-vis emerging market-based entrepreneurs. By limiting their ambition to serving—or producing from—this segment, multinationals can treat emerging markets like small outposts of their home markets. However, the global segment is small in most emerging markets—much smaller than many multinationals anticipate.

Multinationals can establish footholds and test the waters in emerging markets by simply exploiting their natural endowments without significant modification. To reach customers and access talent and resources in the emerging middle class, local, and bottom-of-the-market segments—the mass markets that attract many firms to invest heavily in emerging markets—multinationals need to adapt their product offerings, business processes, and organizational structures in light of the institutional voids that they may sidestep in the global segment.

Adaptation is difficult for multinationals in emerging markets for a number of reasons. To reach customers in the other market segments, multinationals first need to identify these. These segments are not easily distinguished purely on the basis of income, so local knowledge is critical to targeting segments effectively. Acquiring this local knowledge is difficult in the absence of sophisticated market research intermediaries. Even after identifying segments, multinationals need local knowledge to tailor products to local needs. This could mean deciding which elements to eliminate from products to meet lower price points than in the companies' home markets. Meeting lower price points can also be a source of internal stress for multinationals as they accommodate new cost structures. Beyond product development and marketing, often multinationals also need to adapt their approaches to distribution to reach customers outside urban centers in the absence of retail chains and third-party logistics providers. In the talent market, these companies need to work around the absence of information and certification intermediaries to attract, sort, and motivate employees.

Before adapting standard approaches to target emerging markets, firms must compare the benefits of doing so with the additional coordination costs they will incur. Multinationals can localize too much in emerging markets, thereby undermining their advantages of scale and branding while creating operational complexity. Different forms of localization are often needed in different emerging markets, and these divergent adaptations can strain multinational organizations. Multinationals need to determine which pieces of their business models are sacrosanct and carefully manage any modification of the pieces that are not.

Compete Alone or Collaborate?

Multinationals entering and operating in emerging markets also need to relate their business models and organizations to competitors and other stakeholders, such as the government, in emerging markets. Partnerships or joint ventures (JVs) with local companies can be the price of admission for multinationals in some emerging markets. Partners can also serve as valuable sources of local knowledge, substituting for missing market intermediaries, such as offering insight into customer preferences in the absence of market research firms.

However, institutional voids can also make it more difficult for multinationals to acquire new capabilities through collaboration—for instance, in evaluating potential local partners. Partnerships can bring risks as well as rewards for multinationals. Technology transfer agreements, for example, can create powerful potential competitors out of former partners.

Accept or Attempt to Change the Market Context?

Through adaptation, multinationals can often circumvent voids. Partnerships, for example, can substitute for voids. In the face of particularly challenging market contexts, multinationals need to determine whether they need to work proactively to fill voids. Multinationals can fill voids independently to serve their own business, such as a retailer developing a more comprehensive distribution infrastructure than necessary in a developed market where third-party providers are better established, or an automotive company establishing a financing arm. Alternatively, multinationals can induce other businesses in the emerging market to fill the void by offering a guaranteed stream of business through contracting. Given the challenges of filling voids in emerging markets discussed in chapter 3, however, multinationals need to consider carefully the extent to which they can shape the institutional context in emerging markets.

Enter, Wait, or Exit?

It may be impractical or uneconomical for some firms to adapt their business models to emerging markets and daunting to attempt to change the market context. The first-mover advantage can be powerful in emerging markets, but waiting—emphasizing opportunities elsewhere—can also be a viable, and even wise, strategy for multinationals facing institutional voids.

Delayed entrance strategies can take a number of forms. Waiting might mean avoiding a high-risk consumer-facing environment while getting the company's feet wet through exploring or establishing sourcing relationships or by considering setting up a part of the value chain in-country. Indirect engagement often limits the need for multinationals to adapt existing business models or significantly localize offerings. The ability to enter a market under the radar and to spend time learning about the local market and customer needs can be an excellent entry path into developing regions. Following existing customers into emerging markets and helping fill market gaps can be a wise entrance strategy for multinationals. For multinationals already established in emerging markets, it is sometimes necessary simply to cut their losses and exit in the face of challenging institutional voids.

Multinationals in Emerging Markets: Examples

In the rest of this chapter, we look at examples of multinationals based in developed markets that confronted these strategic choices in the face of institutional voids in emerging markets (see table 4-2). Although each of these companies has confronted each of these strategic choices, we focus on the most salient choice for each example.

When General Motors entered China, the automaker replicated its model and targeted the global segment of the country's nascent car market. Similarly, L'Oréal exploited the advantages of its global brand and

TABLE 4-2

Case examples

Strategic choice	Example
Replicate or adapt?	General Motors in China L'Oréal in India Organizational adaptation in emerging markets
Compete alone or collaborate?	Microsoft in China GE Healthcare in emerging markets
Accept or attempt to change market context?	McDonald's in Russia Monsanto in Brazil
Enter, wait, or exit?	The Home Depot in emerging markets Tetra Pak in Argentina

capabilities in India, but only after retreating from an earlier failure to adapt to the country's local market segment. Adaptation for multinationals can also mean tailoring operations and organizational structures in emerging markets.

Adaptation is not enough for many multinationals to manage institutional voids in emerging markets. Microsoft's initial attempt to adapt on its own in China failed. The company found that it needed to collaborate with local stakeholders and position itself as a partner in progress to make headway in the market. GE Healthcare sought to take advantage of cost savings in emerging markets without sacrificing the quality of its sophisticated imaging and other medical equipment. Replicating global standards in emerging market-made products required the company to collaborate closely with its supply chain.

McDonald's sought to replicate its menu around the world. To deliver this in Russia, the company found that it could not simply take the market context as a given. It needed to work actively to fill voids in its supply chain. In Brazil, Monsanto faced contextual challenges of intellectual property rights infringement that undermined its business. In part by borrowing foreign market institutions, the company pressured stakeholders to change that context.

Institutional voids prevented The Home Depot from executing its standard business model in emerging markets. The company opted to adapt in some markets and wait in others, emphasizing opportunities elsewhere. Tetra Pak's operations in Argentina faced serious contextual challenges during the country's financial crisis in 2001–2002. Instead of exiting, however, the company exploited the relative advantages of its global organization to weather the crisis and recommit to the market.

Replicate or Adapt? GM in China

When U.S.-based automaker General Motors (GM) made its first major push into the China market in 1997—beating out global rivals to sign a $1.6 billion joint venture agreement with Shanghai Automotive Industry Corporation (SAIC)—the company saw a market with extraordinary potential. At the time, China boasted only 5.25 passenger cars per 1,000 people, but that figure was poised to increase dramatically as the country's economic growth created a new middle class.[8] China's hard infrastructure of roads and highways was underdeveloped at the time, limiting GM's potential customer base to some extent, but the company also faced the underdeveloped soft infrastructure needed to produce and sell vehicles there.

Automakers depend on a number of market intermediaries. Car research and development and product design depend on market research firms—product market information analyzers and advisers. Developing products requires employees having technical expertise developed in universities and other training institutions—labor market aggregators, distributors, and credibility enhancers. Producing complex products such as vehicles depends not only on the hard infrastructure of logistics and transportation but also on soft infrastructure to develop a deep supplier network—including, for example, information analyzers and advisers to identify suppliers, credibility enhancers to certify them, and regulators and adjudicators to ensure intellectual property protections.

Because vehicles are a major purchase for consumers, distributing and selling vehicles depend on extensive dealer networks where customers can test-drive cars. Before making a car purchase, customers in developed markets turn to a wide range of information analyzers and advisers such as ratings and awards from organizations like J.D. Power and publications like *Consumer Reports* magazine. Financing a large purchase like an automobile depends on capital market aggregators and distributors to advance loans as well as capital market information analyzers and advisers to provide credit scoring. Automotive standards depend on regulators and other public institutions. Disputes over car warranties are resolved by adjudicators.

In short, successfully bringing together buyers and sellers of cars is a complex enterprise facilitated by a wide range of market intermediaries. Many of these intermediaries were missing or underdeveloped in China when GM entered the market. The company had no choice except to collaborate with SAIC as a price for admission into the China market. The company's main strategic choice was to replicate its U.S. business model in China instead of significantly adapting to the market. GM accepted the market context in China initially and then later sought to change it.

GM exploited its relative advantage as it entered the Chinese market by using its global brand, quality, and capabilities to target a narrow segment. The company built a first-class, global-quality facility in Shanghai to produce luxury Buick-branded cars for a market that was still quite poor.[9] The venture was a big bet on the China market in general and the global segment in particular. Although panned by many observers at the time of its announcement, GM's strategy proved to be a successful avenue because of the market's institutional voids.

The Buick brand had a built-in advantage in China because of its long history in the country. Buicks had been popular among elites in China before the country's 1949 revolution and retained their cachet nearly fifty years later when GM reintroduced the brand to newly prosperous Chinese customers.[10] This ambient familiarity with the brand partially substituted for the missing information analyzers and advisers GM would rely on to build its brand in more developed markets.

GM's focus on delivering global-quality products was a response in part to the changing context of information awareness in the country. The proliferation of Internet services gave a wider pool of potential customers access to information on car models marketed around the world, increasing demand for global-quality products in China, the company said.[11] However, because of voids—such as the lack of personal computers and limited Internet penetration—this information awareness did not extend far beyond the global market segment in 1997.

Market research, product design, and other intermediaries for tailoring products to customers were also underdeveloped in China at the time. Instead of adapting its products to its initial understanding of the Chinese marketplace, GM identified a market segment whose preferences were most aligned with its existing product base: executives of state-owned and foreign-invested enterprises, and government officials who could afford a luxury vehicle or whose vehicles were purchased by their employers. As of 2000, only 10 percent of GM's customers in China were individuals; more than half were state-owned enterprises, joint ventures, or government entities.[12] The company tailored vehicles for the China market, adding features and styling to the rear seats to accommodate the preferences of the chauffeured passengers who were the vehicle's target customers, but these modifications were relatively superficial.[13] "We're trying to strike a balance between global economies of scale and local-market adaptations," said GM's head engineer in China. "We used to let people change things too quickly, too easily. It's human nature. If you can change it, you will."[14]

To save on costs while still modifying models to meet local preferences, GM developed flexible platforms for its vehicles but restricted engineering and design changes to a certain "bandwidth" within those platforms.[15] Within this bandwidth, GM also marketed vehicles in new ways, such as marketing a luxury version of a minivan as an "executive wagon" for chauffeured businesspeople and government officials.[16] Such experimentation has been critical to the success of many multinationals in emerging markets. Deploying an existing product to a new market segment was a low-cost way for GM to exploit its relative advantage.

GM was also limited to the global segment early on because of institutional voids that prevented suppliers in the country from developing world-class capabilities and prevented GM from identifying and assessing potential partners. As part of its JV agreement, GM was required to source a significant percentage of car parts produced at the plant locally. It would take some time for the automaker to develop a highly efficient supply chain in China that could deliver high-quality but low-cost vehicles. The cheapest Buick model initially produced at the plant was listed at $38,000—$10,000 *more* than the comparable model in the United States, in a market with a per capita income that was a fraction of that in the United States.[17]

Perhaps because of these voids, Shanghai GM also established "all-inclusive" operations and replicated again by adopting GM's global manufacturing system to ensure and certify—as a credibility enhancer—standardization, quality, speed, and improvement in its manufacturing process.[18] At the time GM established its joint venture with SAIC in 1997, the company also established a joint venture—Pan Asia Technical Automotive Center—for automotive engineering and design, in one attempt to change the market context in technical training and expertise in China.[19]

The company later launched several other context-changing initiatives (see table 4-3). In 1999, GM started a wholly owned warehousing and trading company (later expanded beyond Shanghai) to serve GM operations in China, as well as other automakers, with parts distribution (and, by extension, certification of quality), warehousing, customs clearance, and other consulting services.[20] After catering to a segment of the market that could afford to pay cash for vehicles early in its engagement in China, GM set up an automotive finance joint venture, the country's first to be approved and operational, in 2004.[21] In 2008, GM established a cooperative R&D and technical training institute with Shanghai Jiao Tong University, filling voids in China's educational infrastructure.[22]

These initiatives were not unlike those undertaken by GM earlier in its history when its home market, the United States, was an emerging automotive market. The company established General Motors Acceptance Corporation (GMAC) in 1919 to fill voids in U.S. capital markets. GM's founder, William C. Durant, wrote of the rationale for GMAC's establishment, "The magnitude of the business has presented new problems in financing which the present banking facilities seem not to be elastic enough to overcome."[23] The initiative served as a substitute for consumer lending by banks at the time. As with GM's efforts to develop education and technical training in China, GM's acquisition and development of what became the General Motors Institute in Flint, Michigan, filled voids in the U.S. education infrastructure.

GM has faced challenges in China, including competition from its JV partner, SAIC, which was helped by transferred technology and training by GM.[24] But delivering global-quality models with limited modification to targeted market segments enabled GM to establish a solid foothold and foundation for its business early in its engagement with China. As it expanded its portfolio of brands in the country to reach other market segments, GM undertook additional initiatives to fill institutional voids. In 2007, GM sold more than 1 million vehicles in China, accounting for 11 percent of its global sales by volume.[25]

TABLE 4-3

GM in China: Responding to institutional voids

Spotting voids question	Specific void	Response
Can consumers easily obtain unbiased information on the quality of the goods and services they want to buy? Are there independent consumer organizations and publications that provide such information?	Absent consumer information providers (product market information analyzers and advisers)	Replicated: Exploited lingering brand awareness of Buick from status in pre-1949 China
Can companies easily obtain reliable data on customer tastes and purchase behaviors?	Absent market research providers (product market information analyzers and advisers)	Replicated: Targeted segment with relatively known tastes and where information for small product modification could easily be acquired
Do consumers use credit cards, or does cash dominate transactions? Can consumers get credit to make purchases? Is data on customer creditworthiness available?	Undeveloped credit system (product market transaction facilitators; information analyzers and advisers)	Early: Replicated: Targeted high-end and corporate segment that would not need to finance purchase Later: Attempted to change market context: Established China's first automotive finance provider
Can companies access raw materials and components of good quality? Is there a deep network of suppliers? Are there firms that assess suppliers' quality and reliability? Can companies enforce contracts with suppliers?	Limited intermediaries to identify and assess suppliers (factor market aggregators and distributors; information analyzers and advisers)	Adapted: Built first-class plant with all-inclusive production Attempted to change market context: Established technical center for design, engineering, and testing
How strong are the logistics and transportation infrastructures? Have global logistics companies set up local operations?	Underdeveloped hard and soft logistics infrastructure (product market aggregators and distributors)	Attempted to change market context: Established warehousing and trading operation
How strong is the country's education infrastructure, especially for technical and management training?	Limited technical training institutions (labor market aggregators and distributors; credibility enhancers)	Attempted to change market context: Established cooperative technology institute with Jiao Tong University

As GM headed toward bankruptcy in 2009—because of its operations and major losses in developed markets—the company's business in emerging markets continued to grow. In 2008, GM's sales in Brazil grew 10 percent, sales in China grew 6 percent, and sales in India grew 9 percent.[26] In China, the company maintained ambitious, "self-financing" growth plans, including the introduction of ten new models in the country over the next two years.[27] Some observers suggested that the "new GM" to emerge from restructuring might adopt a business model more like the company's successful operations in emerging markets, emphasizing product experimentation, such as catering to lower price points and emphasizing fuel economy.[28]

Replicate or Adapt? L'Oréal in India

Producers of discretionary consumer goods, such as French cosmetics company L'Oréal, depend on some of the same intermediaries as automakers like GM: product market information analyzers, advisers, aggregators, and distributors (retail chains instead of dealer networks), and transaction facilitators (credit cards instead of car loans).[29] In India, L'Oréal also faced the challenge of convincing customers to part with cash for truly new and unfamiliar cosmetics products in the absence of information intermediaries.

L'Oréal had successfully reached the mass market in the United States, but it did not initially appreciate the challenges of reaching the comparable segment in India in the face of institutional voids when it entered the market in 1991. L'Oréal introduced a shampoo in India, Garnier Ultra Doux, but localized the product only by eliminating certain ingredients and thus reducing its price. The product failed, because it offered nothing to differentiate itself from foreign and local competition. The company had offered a largely replicated product in a segment that required adaptation. Successful localization in emerging markets depends on adapting products and processes based on acquired local knowledge, and not simply reformulating products at a different price point.

L'Oréal later retooled its approach in India, repositioning itself as a higher-end brand in the mid-1990s. At that time, the company noticed and sought to understand the new and growing demographic of middle-class Indian women, many of whom were entering the country's workforce. As it revamped its strategy for the market, L'Oréal drew on product market information analyzers and advisers, enlisting the help of advertising executives and foreign fashion magazine *Elle*, which entered the India market in 1996.

Market research identified hair dyes as a promising product segment, because henna and ammonia, traditionally used by Indian women, had drawbacks and Western-style products were not prevalent. L'Oréal introduced its Excellence Crème in India at the same price as in Europe but marketed it as a luxury product. To reach the emerging middle-class segment successfully, L'Oréal attempted to change the market context by working with partners in the marketplace (see table 4-4). L'Oréal worked with shopkeepers to spruce up their shops—making them more like

TABLE 4-4

L'Oréal in India: Responding to institutional voids

Spotting void question	Specific void	Response
Can companies easily obtain reliable data on customer tastes and purchase behaviors? Do world-class market research firms operate in the country?	Absent market research providers (product market information analyzers and advisers)	Early: Replicated: Unsuccessfully attempted to replicate in segment where replication unrewarded Later: Replicated: Repositioned to segment where relative advantage could be exploited
Are customers willing to try new products and services? Do they trust goods from local companies? How about foreign companies?	Absent consumer information providers (product market information analyzers and advisers)	Early: Replicated: Didn't compensate for void Later: Replicated: Used incoming foreign product market information analyzers and advisers
Do large retail chains exist in the country? If so, do they cover the entire country or only the major cities? Do they reach all consumers or only wealthy ones?	Low retail chain penetration (product market aggregators and distributors)	Attempted to change market context: Worked with salons to upgrade facilities, trained hairdressers

Western drugstores—and began training hairdressers (twenty thousand per year) to use its products in salons.

Excellence Crème and salon products helped L'Oréal's India operations attain profitability starting in 2004. After establishing a successful foothold in the emerging middle-class consumer segment—a demographic that continues to grow in India—L'Oréal reintroduced products aimed at the local segment with its improved brand image. Still, according to the L'Oréal executive who oversaw the company's strategic shift in India, "We don't do poor products for poor people."[30] When a large share of a market such as India remains poor, however, the company discovered the importance of targeting particular segments. Although different multinationals can find different opportunities in emerging markets—as shown by, for example, Hindustan Unilever's success at the bottom of the market in India—L'Oréal found success only after it replicated its global model with customers who could afford to pay global prices.

Organizational Adaptation

Developed market-based multinationals need to consider not only adapting their offerings to local needs and preferences in emerging markets but also adapting their organizations to the business demands and institutional contexts of the emerging markets in which they operate. Adaptation can be a painful process for multinationals. Modification of products, business processes, and organizations can create organizational tension and stress a multinational's core value proposition. An in-country operation might anticipate big growth opportunities from a modification that headquarters sees as eroding the company's global brand. Alternatively, headquarters, desperate for growth, might expect too much from a product not tailored to the emerging market. The leadership of multinationals that invest and operate in emerging markets needs to think clearly about what in the company's business model is open for modification and what is off the table—while understanding that the first time is very rarely the charm in these markets.

In light of these tensions, multinationals need to align their organizational structures and reporting lines with their strategies and goals for specific emerging markets. The organizational structures of subsidiaries in various emerging markets often evolve independently, with varying degrees of connection to headquarters. Connections between local subsidiaries and headquarters reflect priorities, but they can also impact performance. Emerging markets share common characteristics, and multinationals are well served by facilitating the transfer of knowledge about them across their organizations.

Motorola's organizations in China and India, for example, reflect the variance in subsidiaries within multinationals. Motorola's top management cultivated close ties to China's top political leadership as it invested heavily in the country. As a result, the company's headquarters was closely and directly involved in its China operations. The reporting lines of the company's India operations, by contrast, wind through Singapore, and Motorola's presence in the market has developed more slowly.[31]

The scale of opportunities in China and India pushed Microsoft to adapt its organization. The company's Greater China and India operations were made subsidiaries independent of regional operations, reporting directly to headquarters. In addition, Microsoft established teams (the Emerging Segments Market Development Group and Market Expansion Group) based at its headquarters devoted to emerging markets more generally. These teams were devoted in part to helping the company fulfill the goals of the Beijing Declaration, an initiative announced by Bill Gates in 2007 to help expand global computer access dramatically from 1 billion people in 2007 to 2 billion in 2015. The scale of such an initiative and Microsoft's unprecedented organizational response reflect the company's deep commitment to building its business in emerging markets, because these markets—even in the face of such contextual challenges as piracy (as we discuss later in this chapter)—will be critical to its future.[32]

Similarly, U.S.-based Cisco decided to establish its Globalization Center East in Bangalore, India, in 2007. The center is slated to house one-fifth of Cisco's top executives and ten thousand employees by 2011.[33] The importance of emerging markets should also be reflected in the composition of multinationals' senior management and boards of directors. One large German multinational's CEO noted concern over the lack of diversity in his company's leadership in mid-2008. "The management board are all white males," he said. "Our top 600 managers are predominantly white German males. We are too one-dimensional."[34]

A central organizational question for multinationals in emerging markets is when—and to what extent—they should localize the management of their operations in these markets. Relying on foreign managers to navigate unfamiliar business contexts poses obvious challenges. "Sending expats in is not a sustainable strategy because you make all of the cultural mistakes that it's possible to make," said one Microsoft executive. "In any country if you look at two direct competitors and see who has localized management first, you tend to see success correlations out there."[35]

However, expatriate management can bring certain benefits to multinationals. Reflecting on German wholesaler Metro Cash & Carry's entry into India, one company executive said that with the benefit of hindsight he would choose to open operations with a non-Indian country manager. The interaction between an Indian country manager, for example, and the Indian government or other stakeholders will be bound up in complicated relational norms. "But if you have a leader [who is not constrained by local norms], then you already get out of a lot of problems," the executive said. "It's like Forrest Gump. You don't see these problems. It's a very good approach, but it has to be done with politeness, not with arrogance. With a certain Forrest Gump approach, it goes much easier. But a local person sees more complexity."[36]

There are benefits and costs to either expatriate or local management. Local personnel often have better market information but more complicating entanglements, whereas the contextual unfamiliarity of expatriate management can be an asset or liability. Multinationals need to think carefully about which approach would work best for their business in particular emerging market contexts—and decide how to offset the costs of either approach.

Compete Alone or Collaborate? Microsoft in China

Microsoft faced intellectual property-related institutional voids in emerging markets so pervasive that they threatened to undermine its business in these markets.[37] When Microsoft began its engagement with China in the early 1990s, for example, piracy prevailed at a rate of 98 percent—the highest in the world—and stifled the company's ability to build a viable business by reaching paying customers. Adaptation was necessary but not sufficient for Microsoft to build a business in China. The company was compelled to collaborate with local firms and other stakeholders and work to be seen as a partner in progress.

When Microsoft first entered China, the company attempted to compete alone by developing its own Chinese-language version of Windows at a software development facility in Taiwan. When the company introduced the product in 1993, the Chinese government promptly blacklisted it for failing to meet mainland software standards. Microsoft sold fewer than twenty thousand copies in its first year.

Chastened by this initial failure, Microsoft found that it could not thrive in China without adapting to engage more effectively with relevant Chinese stakeholders and work around the market's profligate piracy. After extensive negotiations with the Ministry of Electronics Industry, Microsoft adopted a more cooperative approach in 1994 and began to codevelop a localized version of Windows with a major Chinese software vendor. Microsoft also established joint ventures with six other local software vendors to work on future software development projects.

Piracy still prevented Microsoft from producing significant revenue despite the huge scale of opportunities in the market. When Microsoft raised the piracy issue with the Chinese government, the government asked how Microsoft could help China develop its domestic software industry. Recognizing the importance of the China market but also the need to confront its contextual barriers and build relations with government and other stakeholders, in 1998 Microsoft launched a new engagement with China that emphasized changing the market context by aiding the development of China's domestic software and IT sectors through alliances and investments in educational and research initiatives. As *Newsweek* noted, "China is more likely to fight pirates if it has its own software industry."[38] Localizing its operations through partnerships with stakeholders and investing in the development of China's software industry helped Microsoft build the institutional support it needed to develop its business in the market.

Microsoft also sought to address piracy through adaptation. The company introduced differentiated versions of products to meet local price constraints and potentially help confront piracy. Windows Starter edition, for example, was introduced as a simple, low-cost product for first-time PC users. By offering the product at a price within reach of lower-income consumers in emerging markets, Microsoft hoped to reduce demand for pirated versions of the software. The company has also experimented with subscription-based offerings and cheap software packages for students to introduce—and hopefully instill—the brand among new segments and generations of customers. These efforts substituted for the absence of consumer credit for low-income customers.

To piggyback on the explosive growth of cellular phones in China and India and to expand access to basic PC applications to customers who did not own conventional PCs, Microsoft developed FonePlus, a "starter edition" of Windows Mobile. The product offers some PC capabilities on a cellular phone, which can then be linked to a television and used as a basic home computer with external keyboard. Microsoft has viewed experimentation as essential to the company's adaptation to the contexts and preferences of emerging markets, as one company executive has noted:

> You've got to view these potentially disruptive innovations
> and models as sources of long-term business advantage for
> you because, sooner or later, these same business models will
> scale to other countries—both developing and developed.
> So I've been arguing for the two and a half years I've been at
> Microsoft that [we should] view India, first and foremost, as a
> lab for disruptive innovation. Even more than a resource base,
> view us as strategically important because we are a laboratory
> for these kinds of crazy innovations, which in the short term
> are disruptive, but tomorrow open up whole new sources of
> competitive advantage.[39]

Lecturing the government about the problems posed by intellectual property rights (IPR) infringement did not work. Instead, Microsoft joined with local partners, positioned itself as a partner in progress, and pursued experimental adaptations such as differentiated pricing (see table 4-5). Microsoft worked to develop research and development capabilities with local talent in China, exploiting the country's factor markets where it could work around institutional voids and also offer jobs and training to the market—a positive proposition for the country's government and a seed of public support for Microsoft.

TABLE 4-5

Microsoft in China: Responding to institutional voids

Spotting void question	Specific void	Response
What restrictions does the government place on foreign investment? Are those restrictions in place to facilitate the growth of domestic companies, to protect state monopolies, or because people are suspicious of multinationals?	Foreign companies not treated even-handedly by regulators (regulators)	Collaborated: Codeveloped localized version of Windows with local software firm
Can companies access raw materials and components of good quality? Is there a deep network of suppliers? Are there firms that assess suppliers' quality and reliability? Can companies enforce contracts with suppliers?	Limited expertise in domestic software industry (aggregators and distributors; credibility enhancers)	Collaborated: Invested in the development of Chinese software industry
Do consumers use credit cards, or does cash dominate transactions? Can consumers get credit to make purchases? Is data on customer creditworthiness available?	Limited access to credit for cash-strapped customers (transaction facilitators)	Adapted: Experimented with subscription model, differentiated versions of products
Do the laws articulate and protect private property rights?	Intellectual property rights not protected (regulators)	Attempted to change context: Offered seminars on IPR law, scholarships for law students focusing on IPR law

Although piracy remains a significant challenge, Microsoft has found some success in confronting it in China by stimulating the local industry. Instead of public rebukes, Microsoft has also drawn attention to IPR issues through seminars and attempts to address the problem by offering scholarships to law students in emerging markets who focus on IPR law.

Although these context-changing initiatives may be long-term propositions, they have been important efforts for Microsoft to be seen as a partner in progress. One company executive reflected on Microsoft's engagement with emerging markets:

> When a company like Microsoft comes in and says, "We're going to use your talent," it's not seen as doing you a favor. It's seen as exploiting the talent pool out there. Somehow we have to each figure out how we are seen as good for the economy, good for the country. That requires first of all humility. Second thing it requires is significant investments, and investments particularly in developing talent, investments in developing this partner ecosystem and helping local software companies, for instance, be more successful as a result of your being in that country. If you can't do that, sooner or later you get some backlash from one group or the other. Usually they're able to successfully mobilize local politicians, local government to create some pain. In most cases they can be very successful in distracting you from running your business. So earning trust, earning goodwill, learning to be seen as good for the country is super important. These are most of the things we have learned from China, and we're trying to avoid making similar mistakes in India.[40]

Microsoft has needed to be patient given the persistence of the voids surrounding IPR violations and has needed to be sensitive to the local context; "Nobody wants to be told that we're a country of pirates," one company executive noted.[41] It has also found the need to be open to adaptation, experimentation, and collaboration to manage institutional voids in emerging markets such as China.

GE Healthcare in Emerging Markets

Starting in 1997, GE Healthcare (then called GE Medical Systems) began moving production and sourcing for its diagnostic imaging and other medical equipment to emerging markets, with the goal of incorporating lower-cost components and products into standard global lines, initially for export.[42] To replicate global-quality products from factories in emerging markets, GE needed to collaborate closely with local supply chains.

GE Healthcare enlisted outside suppliers to produce a large share of the components used in its sophisticated diagnostic imaging and other medical equipment. "Because we buy so many things, the game for us is very much a supply-chain game and not a manufacturing game," said one company executive.[43] GE produced the proprietary "crown jewels," and inputs from other suppliers constituted some $2 billion of the company's $2.3 billion variable manufacturing costs. By shifting this sourcing to lower-cost emerging markets, GE could save a great deal of money.

Finding suppliers in these markets—particularly those capable of meeting GE's exacting quality standards for technically complex parts and subassemblies—was a challenge because of institutional voids, particularly missing information analyzers and advisers and credibility enhancers. "You just can't go to the local chamber of commerce in India or China and find workable suppliers," said one company executive. "It must be a long-term strategy."[44]

To replicate the quality and sophistication of products made in developed markets, GE Healthcare deployed sourcing and quality teams from existing facilities to work closely with new suppliers to ensure seamless transitions. These collaborations were time- and resource-intensive efforts. When working with Bharat Electronics Ltd. of India, for example, GE sent a sourcing team of twenty engineers (spending 25 percent of their time with the company) and a quality team of seven GE employees (allocating half of their time to the company). GE also trained the senior management of Bharat Electronics in six sigma. The company's training and certification of vendors filled the void of credibility-enhancing institutions.

GE's relationship with Bharat Electronics, as with other suppliers, evolved from sourcing simpler to more sophisticated components. Although GE did not finance its suppliers, GE's business signaled credibility in the capital markets of emerging economies, often helping suppliers get financing through other avenues.

GE's collaboration in emerging markets also took the form of investing in educating end users and regulators on the diagnostic health care enabled by its products—a marketing initiative, to be sure, but also an effort to position the company as a partner in progress. One company executive described the initiative this way:

> [General Electric Medical Systems] held a round-table for Eastern European customers in Budapest last year. The Croatian contingent made clear that their radiologists needed to be trained to use advanced equipment. It became apparent to us that a real differentiation opportunity exists here. We plan to hold seminars for users, regardless of whether or not they are using our products currently. We also spend a lot of time marketing to the regulators, explaining to them that it is not cost effective to save on capital investment in, say, [magnetic resonance] machines.[45]

Collaboration in emerging markets was not without challenges for GE Healthcare. In China, for example, GE had established joint ventures and partnerships with manufacturers that were part of the country's health regulatory agencies. "In one joint venture," one company executive explained, "the partner firm would receive orders for equipment, and then service the orders from its separately and wholly owned factory, thus cutting us out. We couldn't stop this practice. So we had to renegotiate."[46] GE later acquired full ownership of two of these ventures and 90 percent of the third. As GE Healthcare built more-sophisticated operations on the ground in emerging markets, it needed to adapt to the institutional void of underdeveloped intellectual property regimes, as one company executive noted:

The only concern I have is we educate these people and teach them how to do sophisticated algorithms that do CT reconstruction to take electronic signals into an image in some way, that I don't lose them. The only concern I have, if they walk across the street and then sign up for a competitor who might be new—or Siemens and Philips—you lose that . . . In these new kinds of facilities we put up, we'll take our best engineers and put a lot of handcuffs on them, in the sense of stock options and earnings and different things so they're not easily stolen.[47]

Close collaboration enabled GE Healthcare to produce global-level quality products in emerging markets. Successfully executing these collaborations required the company to fill and adapt to institutional voids (see table 4-6).

TABLE 4-6

GE Healthcare in emerging markets: Responding to institutional voids

Spotting void question	Specific void	Response
Can companies access raw materials and components of good quality? Is there a deep network of suppliers? Are there firms that assess suppliers' quality and reliability? Can companies enforce contracts with suppliers?	Low standards and undeveloped certification (factor market information analyzers and advisers; credibility enhancers)	Collaborated: Became information analyzers and credibility enhancers by bringing six sigma training to supply chain
Would a company be able to enforce employment contracts with senior executives? Could it protect itself against executives who leave the firm and then compete against it? Could it stop employees from stealing trade secrets and intellectual property?	Underdeveloped intellectual property rights regime (labor market regulators)	Adapted: Used stock options and other devices to reduce risk of IPR loss through employees

Later in its engagement with emerging markets, GE Healthcare shifted its strategy from exploiting emerging market inputs for exported products to serving the domestic markets of these economies. As it moved toward this new "In Country For Country" model, GE Healthcare adapted products to local needs and thus was compelled to acquire local capabilities. GE introduced an "economy" CT scanner in China, for example, costing one-third of the price of a CT scanner sold in the United States. "People in the U.S. can't design a low-end product for China," said one company executive. "They will add needless bells and whistles and they just won't get it right. Similarly, China can't design a product for the Mayo Clinic."[48]

Some of GE Healthcare's adaptations and experiments in emerging markets may even migrate back to developed markets. Under GE's "healthy-magination" initiative—announced in 2009—the company plans to focus on health-care needs in emerging markets and underserved areas in developed countries. GE has allocated $3 billion over six years for R&D of low-cost health-care equipment. Cost-cutting by U.S. hospitals has hurt GE Healthcare's sales of expensive MRI and CT machines but may offer new opportunities for adoption of products like the CT scanner developed for China or the portable electrocardiograph machines developed for India.[49]

Accept or Attempt to Change Market Context? McDonald's in Russia

For any multinational with the ambition to reach beyond the narrow global segment in emerging markets, it is necessary to adapt to the local context or work to augment capabilities through collaboration or context-changing initiatives.[50] One executive of a major Turkish business group described the challenges for multinationals that have entered his home country and encountered institutional voids without any form of adaptation:

Unfortunately, just putting your money to a new market doesn't bring you success. You have to think and know the ways of the local realities. Even, for example, some companies come to Turkey. They are used to operating in certain ways. Sometimes certain things that they outsource do not exist in Turkey. How are they going to do it? . . . It's a McDonald's approach. They just open the bun, put the hamburger, close it, go, take the money, give the hamburger. Maybe it's a different style where I come from.[51]

In fact, the operations of McDonald's itself in emerging markets illustrates this principle. Although the fast food chain has been able to deliver a relatively standard output in markets around the world—while occasionally adapting its menu to local tastes—it has done so only by tailoring its inputs to the institutional voids in the markets in which it has operated.

In the United States, McDonald's outsources most of its supply chain operations. When the fast food franchise tried to move into Russia in 1990, however, it was unable to find adequate local suppliers, in large part because of institutional voids (see table 4-7). The chain asked several of its

TABLE 4-7

McDonald's in Russia: Responding to institutional voids

Spotting void question	Specific void	Response
Can companies access raw materials and components of good quality? Is there a deep network of suppliers? Are there firms that assess suppliers' quality and reliability?	Limited access to capital and limited expertise in supply chain (aggregators and distributors; transaction facilitators)	Attempted to change market context: Built McComplex; financed and worked to improve capabilities of suppliers
What kind of product-related environment and safety regulations are in place? How do the authorities enforce regulations?	Limited standards (credibility enhancers)	Attempted to change market context: Instituted training programs for service and quality standards
How strong is the country's education infrastructure, especially for technical and management training?	Limited agriculture management training (labor market aggregators and distributors)	Attempted to change market context: Imported agriculture specialists to train farmers
How strong are the logistics and transportation infrastructures? Have global logistics companies set up local operations?	Underdeveloped hard and soft infrastructure for logistics (product market aggregators and distributors)	Attempted to change market context: Established own trucking fleet

European vendors for their assistance, but they were not interested in taking on the regulatory and other challenges posed by the Russian market.

Instead of giving up, McDonald's decided to tackle the local supply chain voids on its own, working to change the market context in service of its business to an even greater extent than the other examples in this chapter. With the help of its joint venture partner—the Moscow city administration—the company identified Russian farmers and bakers as additional partners. It imported cattle from Holland and russet potatoes from the United States, brought in agricultural specialists from Canada and Europe to improve the farmers' management practices, and advanced the capital streams to farmers so that they could invest in better seeds and equipment.

Next, the company built a 100,000-square-foot McComplex in Moscow to produce beef, ketchup, mustard, Big Mac sauce, and bakery, potato, and dairy products. It set up a trucking fleet to move supplies to restaurants and financed its suppliers so that they would have enough working capital to buy modern equipment. The company also brought in some fifty expatriate managers to teach Russian employees about its service standards, quality measurements, and operating procedures, and it sent a team of twenty-three Russian managers to Canada for a four-month training program.

In response to institutional voids, McDonald's created a vertically integrated operation in Russia, but the company clung to one principle: it would sell only hamburgers, fries, and soda to Russians in a clean environment—fast. The strategy paid off. Fifteen years after serving its first Big Mac in Moscow's Pushkin Square, McDonald's had invested more than $250 million in the country and controlled 80 percent of the Russian fast food market.

Accept or Attempt to Change Market Context? Monsanto in Brazil

Like Microsoft, U.S.-based Monsanto faced contextual challenges in Brazil so serious that they threatened to undermine the company's business.[52] In response, Monsanto worked actively to change the market context. Monsanto was a pioneer in developing biotechnology for the agricultural sector, creating products such as seeds that could increase crop yields, exhibit particular desired characteristics (in fewer generations than in traditional agronomy), and resist plant pathogens.

In the United States, the company relied on a sophisticated soft infrastructure to develop and protect its technology. Monsanto's research and development operations relied on a robust education and technical training infrastructure to identify, sort, and train employees and identify capital markets that could support the long time horizon of new product development. After selling its sophisticated seed varieties, Monsanto relied on intellectual property rights protections, either through patenting genetically modified plants, obtaining plant variety protection certificates from the U.S. Department of Agriculture (or, in some cases, both), and then licensing use to farmers. In the United States, as in other developed markets, Monsanto could turn to the well-developed court system—adjudicators, in the taxonomy of market intermediaries—to resolve disputes and enforce protections, such as filing suits against growers who replanted seeds without paying new license fees.

Monsanto's developed market-made technology had a compelling value proposition in developing countries, where farmers were competing in global markets without local substitutes for technology such as Monsanto's seeds—in part the result of institutional voids in technical training and high-tech expertise. Demand for this technology in emerging markets presented Monsanto with tremendous business opportunities, but many of these markets lacked the sophisticated soft infrastructure to protect its technology.

As the world's largest soybean exporter, Brazil was a promising market for Monsanto's Roundup Ready soybean seeds, which were genetically engineered to resist—and thus intended to be used in conjunction with—the company's Roundup herbicide. The product was a blockbuster success in the United States—planted in 50 percent of the country's total soybean area in three years—and Monsanto sought to introduce it in Brazil only one year after its U.S. debut.

The company received a patent for Roundup Ready soybeans in Brazil as well as approval for commercial sale from the country's biosafety commission in 1998, but objections from both environmental and peasant groups—and a subsequent injunction from a local judge—put the product in legal limbo. Although the court order made it illegal for Monsanto to sell its Roundup Ready soybeans in Brazil, the product was widely used in southern Brazil, where farmers purchased smuggled seeds from Argentina. Monsanto tried to approach the problem through government relations but succeeded only when it worked to change the context (see table 4-8).

TABLE 4-8

Monsanto in Brazil: Responding to institutional voids

Spotting void question	Specific void	Response
Are the country's government, media, and people receptive to foreign investment? Do citizens trust companies and individuals from some parts of the world more than others?	Objections from peasant groups fearful of multi-national role in agriculture	Attempted to change context: Launched major communication effort to farmers
Do the courts adjudicate disputes and enforce contracts in a timely and impartial manner? How effective are the quasi-judicial regulatory institutions that set and enforce rules for business activities?	Slow resolution of legal matters, including the legal limbo of Monsanto's Roundup Ready soybean seed (adjudicators)	Attempted to change market context: Borrowed global market institutions
Do the laws articulate and protect private property rights?	Underdeveloped intellectual property rights enforcement regime (regulators)	Attempted to change market context: Devised point of delivery (POD) system to collect on technology and "borrowed" intellectual property protections in destination markets in Europe
How effective are the country's banks, insurance companies, and mutual funds at collecting savings and channeling them into investments?	Limited access for farmers to capital and insurance (aggregators and distributors; transaction facilitators)	Attempted to change market context: Became risk-sharing partner and credit provider, in effect, through POD program

Monsanto challenged the injunction, but institutional voids in Brazil's court system delayed adjudication. In the face of legal and regulatory uncertainty—and pressure from U.S. customers complaining about their Brazilian competitors using the smuggled seed—Monsanto looked to devise a way to collect on its technology. Because Monsanto was barred from selling Roundup Ready soybeans and collecting payment up front, the company sought to collect payment after harvest. The company developed a point of delivery (POD) collection system, which charged farmers an indemnification fee, clearing them of future legal challenges to their unlicensed use of the Roundup Ready patented technology.

Executing this system required Monsanto to engage and incentivize relevant stakeholders and borrow market institutions based outside Brazil. The primary customers of the Brazilian farmers using Roundup Ready were large developed market-based multinationals such as Archer Daniels Midland (ADM), Bunge, and Cargill. Monsanto told these companies that it would collect on its technology, even through customs enforcement in destination markets in Europe if necessary. This threat was credible only because Roundup Ready was patented both in Brazil and in Europe.

However, "borrowing" developed market institutions in this way was not sufficient for Monsanto to collect on Roundup Ready. The company succeeded only by convincing the farmers that POD would fill a void for their businesses. As one company executive described it, "The breakthrough came when we sat down with the farmers' groups and the cooperatives. We explained that since we were collecting at harvest, we would actually be sharing in both the production risk and the price risk."[53] Farmers using Roundup Ready paid only for what they produced in the POD system. By offering to share in the risks of farming, Monsanto exploited its relative advantage as a large multinational that could afford to do so. Monsanto also served as a de facto credit provider for farmers by charging farmers who self-declared their use of Roundup Ready a lower price than farmers were charged in the United States. (Farmers who volunteered that they used Roundup Ready seeds were charged a lower indemnification fee than those who did not volunteer but whose produce tested positive for the presence of Roundup Ready seeds.)

Starting in January 2004, Monsanto enlisted the grain companies such as ADM, Bunge, and Cargill to serve as collection agents for POD at their elevators and in turn gave them a share of the proceeds. The POD initiative required a major effort in communication and negotiation with the grain companies and elevators, but it worked: some 95 percent of farmers self-declared in the first year.

In the face of pervasive institutional voids—lack of enforcement of intellectual property rights (IPR) protection and slow adjudication of disputes in the court system—Monsanto devised a creative solution to collect on its Roundup Ready technology. Although the idea of collecting at harvest was not new, Monsanto successfully executed this approach by engaging—and getting buy in from—stakeholders all along the value chain. When the context changed and the Brazilian government approved the sale of the seed, Monsanto set up a dual system, allowing farmers to pay either up front or at the time of harvest, and giving incentives for farmers to pay earlier.

POD was devised as a response to specific contextual features. In Argentina, for example, Monsanto was unable to secure a patent for Roundup Ready, so the company had no legal basis to enforce its claims as it did in Brazil. Nonetheless, Monsanto's response to institutional voids in Brazil illustrates a creative attempt to change the market context by ultimately compelling IPR, which did not exist prior to that time.

Enter, Wait, or Exit?

All the developed market-based multinationals discussed in this chapter chose to enter emerging markets in spite of institutional voids. In several cases, this was a strategic decision based on the benefits of early-mover advantage. Early entry was important to GE Healthcare in China, for example, not only because of the market's fast growth but also because of the importance of building customer brand allegiance and government relations in the country's still-nascent health-care sector. One company executive explained: "You go to China right now because you want to influence future decision making in that health-care market, both at a macroeconomic level of working with the government, which we certainly do, but also at a micro level of teaching physicians how to use your equipment, working with nurses on how they can use patient monitoring to save lives . . . It's at that level that you're trying to get in and get in early."[54] Through these efforts, GE Healthcare sought to lay the foundation for future demand.

Microsoft's business is similarly dependent on shaping market context. By working to build the ecosystem of local partners—such as software developers and vendors, hardware producers, and systems integrators— the company sought to establish itself as a standard platform in emerging markets. Just as Google became dominant in online search engines by developing the ecosystem around its business, one Microsoft executive noted, multinationals in emerging markets can establish dominant positions by investing time and resources as early movers:

> You have to take a long-term view. The early years, it's about minimizing your losses while building the ecosystem and becoming the de facto standard. We're moving very fast in countries like India, China, Russia, to set up these ecosystems, which are still in their infancy. If you look at all multinationals that are successful in cracking emerging markets, that's one of the first things they do—set up that network of suppliers and distributors.[55]

As many of the examples in this chapter illustrate, institutional voids can be painful for developed market-based multinationals operating in emerging markets. Adaptation, collaboration, and context-changing initiatives to compensate for voids can be difficult and expensive propositions. Emphasizing opportunities elsewhere by waiting to enter or exiting an emerging market is an option for multinationals facing difficult institutional voids. We consider these options in the examples of The Home Depot in emerging markets and Tetra Pak in Argentina.

Enter, Wait, or Exit? The Home Depot in Emerging Markets

The Home Depot, the U.S.-based do-it-yourself home improvement retailer, has been cautious about entering emerging markets. The company offers a specific proposition to customers in the United States: low prices, great service, and good quality. To deliver on this proposition, The Home Depot relies on a variety of U.S.-specific institutions. It depends on U.S. highways and logistical management systems to minimize the amount of inventory it has to carry in its large, warehouse-style stores. It relies on employee stock ownership to motivate shop-level workers to offer top-notch service. And its value proposition takes advantage of the fact that high labor costs in the United States encourage homeowners to engage in do-it-yourself projects.

The absence of these contextual features in emerging markets challenged the company's ability to replicate its business model. In emerging markets with poorly developed capital markets, for example, the company might not have been able to use employee stock ownership as a compensation tool. Similarly, in markets with poorly developed physical infrastructure, The Home Depot might have had difficulty using its inventory management systems—a core competitive advantage in North American markets. In markets with relatively low labor costs, the target customer might not have been the homeowner but rather contractors serving as intermediaries between the store and the homeowner, requiring a different approach to marketing and other business operations.

The company made a tentative foray into emerging markets by setting up two stores in Chile in 1998 and another in Argentina in 2000. In 2001, however, the company sold those operations for a net loss of $14 million. At the time, the company's management emphasized that most of The Home Depot's future growth was likely to come from North America. After exiting the markets, The Home Depot switched from a greenfield strategy to an acquisition-led approach—discovering the value of collaboration after its failed initial attempts to compete alone. In 2001, The Home Depot entered Mexico by buying a home improvement retailer, Total Home, and the next year it acquired Del Norte, another small chain. By 2004, the company had forty-two stores in Mexico.

China presented tremendous opportunities for companies such as The Home Depot because of the country's fast-growing home improvement market. Perhaps chastened by its experience in Chile and Argentina, The

Home Depot took its time evaluating options to enter China. "We're going to make the prudent decision," said one company executive in 2006. "We're going to make sure we have the right business model."[56]

In addition to the general contextual challenges, The Home Depot would face other institutional voids in China. Housing in the country was sold as concrete shells, requiring more extensive home improvement than most of the do-it-yourself projects its U.S. customers pursued. B&Q of the United Kingdom and other home improvement stores in China were staffed with workers to install packages.[57] Replicating this model would have been difficult for The Home Depot in light of labor market institutional voids. In 2006, The Home Depot acquired Home Way, a chain in China that had replicated The Home Depot's model, even copying the company's familiar orange aprons.[58] Whether The Home Depot can catch up to B&Q, which entered China early and adapted its model aggressively, remains to be seen. The Home Depot's approach to emerging markets after its early stumbles illustrates that waiting is an option for developed market-based multinationals still looking for the right approach to match their business models and capabilities to the contextual challenges of emerging markets (see table 4-9).

Enter, Wait, or Exit? Tetra Pak in Argentina

In part because of institutional voids, such as regulatory voids and lack of information on the risk exposures of companies and of the broader

TABLE 4-9

The Home Depot in emerging markets: Responding to institutional voids

Spotting void question	Specific void	Response
How strong are the logistics and transportation infrastructures? Have global logistics companies set up local operations?	Underdeveloped hard and soft logistics and distribution infrastructure	Early: Waited: Emphasized opportunities elsewhere because unable to replicate Later: Collaborated: Shifted strategy to grow by acquisition

economy, emerging markets are particularly prone to financial, political, and other forms of crises.[59] Under these circumstances, some multinationals have simply emphasized opportunities elsewhere by beating a hasty retreat. However, multinationals are often better positioned to bear the pain of crises than domestic companies because of access to capital and other resources from headquarters. Multinationals with a long-term outlook on an emerging market in crisis can exploit relative advantage to sustain and build their operations in the midst of turmoil.

Consider the approach of Swiss firm Tetra Pak during the financial crisis in Argentina in 2001–2002. Tetra Pak sells aseptic packaging materials, and the machinery to fill them, for beverages (such as milk cartons and juice containers) and for other liquid foods (such as tomato paste and ice cream). Because the company's packaging enabled even perishable beverages to be transported and stored without refrigeration, its products helped fill the void of undeveloped cold chain distribution in developing countries. Tetra Pak offered world-class technology, scale, and a global supply chain to bring more efficiency to the food and beverage sector in Argentina, where agriculture and viticulture were major industries. The financial crisis strained the company's model, but Tetra Pak adapted to remain in the country, exploiting its capabilities as a multinational (see table 4-10).

Soon after Argentina went into sovereign default in December 2001, the Argentine government devalued the peso asymmetrically. As a result, receivables denominated in U.S. dollars were slashed to 30 percent of their previous U.S. dollar value, and the U.S. dollar value of import obligations was unchanged. Credit and consumption collapsed, and prices surged upward. In the midst of the crisis, 50 percent of Argentina's population had fallen below the poverty line and the unemployment rate had risen to more than 20 percent.

Tetra Pak had withstood macroeconomic crises in emerging markets before. The company had lost two-thirds of its business in Argentina when the country faced an earlier crisis in 1989, although Tetra Pak's operations in the country were small at the time. The lesson Tetra Pak drew from these crises, according to one company executive, was, "Don't

TABLE 4-10

Tetra Pak in Argentina: Responding to institutional voids

Spotting void question	Specific void	Response
How strong are the logistics and transportation infrastructures? Have global logistics companies set up local operations?	Absent cold chain distribution (product market aggregators and distributors)	Attempted to change market context: Sold goods that substituted for voids in cold chain
What kind of product-related environment and safety regulations are in place? How do the authorities enforce regulations?	Underdeveloped product safety regulatory regime (credibility enhancer)	Replicated: Brought world-class technology and global brand, signifying quality
Is it difficult for multi-nationals to collect receivables from local retailers?	Asymmetric devaluation and economic crisis rendered contracts unenforceable	Stayed: Renegotiated contracts with customers, substituting, in effect, for insurance companies

change your culture because it pays. We stayed in Mexico. We stayed in Russia. It pays, but let's try to manage it a bit more professionally to see how we can mitigate the losses. We will have losses, but we can mitigate them."[60]

The company first looked at the fundamentals of the market in Argentina—such as the fact that it is one of the lowest-cost milk producers in the world and among the highest per capita consumers of wine—and decided that it should stay in the market irrespective of the crisis. "Different from firms, countries may go bust, but they don't die," said one company executive. "They always come back again. A company can go bust, and then you lose all your money. Usually in a country, you always have a second chance. Up to now, it has always proved right for us."[61]

Beyond the losses from Argentina's general economic turmoil, the asymmetric devaluation put Tetra Pak in a particular pickle. Tetra Pak's business model globally was predicated on long-term relationships with suppliers as well as customers. To maintain its reputation for product safety and quality, Tetra Pak set strict specifications for its input supplies, and these were most easily and consistently met by long-term partners.

In all markets, Tetra Pak served as a credibility enhancer, substituting for underdeveloped product safety regimes.

For its customers, Tetra Pak was a packaging systems provider and not a producer of commoditized cartons. The company supplied sophisticated proprietary filling machines for processing and packaging liquid foods. Tetra Pak thus invested in customers' value chains but derived its real returns from sales of the packaging materials. The asymmetric devaluation cut Tetra Pak's receivables to one-third their value, in U.S. dollar terms. Tetra Pak's sales contracts contained a U.S. dollar conversion clause, but the clause was not practically enforceable in the midst of Argentina's crisis as the company's customers—with peso-denominated incomes but without currency-hedging contracts—struggled to keep their own businesses afloat. "Different from a country, a customer goes bust, and you can kill him. He can never come back," said one company executive. "So the important thing is to identify—the same way we identify the countries we want to stay in—which of the customers you want to protect."[62]

Within each category, Tetra Pak identified the customers and partners essential to its business and negotiated workable arrangements to continue their relationships. Payments owed to Tetra Pak were refinanced long term, an option enabled only by the company's financial position and support from headquarters.

Managing through the crisis in Argentina required Tetra Pak not only to reorient its financial bearings but also to conscientiously communicate to stakeholders—customers, suppliers, banks, employees—the company's commitment to remain in the country. The company did not lay off any employees, cancel any training programs, or alter its recruitment process through the crisis. "We bet on the country," said one company executive. "We knew we wanted to stay in the country, and the country would recover. We even moved to better offices. It was a strong message that we are here for the long term."[63]

Multinationals have unique capabilities that they often can exploit during times of crisis in emerging markets. Although exiting in the face of such contextual challenges is tempting, recommitting to markets undergoing strain can position multinationals for longer-term success.

Managing Voids and Growth in Emerging Markets

Developed market-based multinationals that enter and operate in emerging markets inevitably face institutional voids and have a range of choices to respond to them (see toolkit 4-1). None of the companies discussed in this chapter cracked emerging markets without difficulty, and all of them required experimentation to find the appropriate combination or sequence of approaches to align their businesses with the unique contexts of these markets. Multinationals should be open to and supportive of experimentation as they align themselves with institutional contexts and seek out competitive advantage in these markets.

In addition to these choices, multinationals must face the competitive challenge posed by what we call emerging giants: emerging market-based firms that have an intimate understanding of their home markets' institutional contexts and that are building globally competitive organizations—the subject of the next two chapters.

Toolkit 4-1
Toolkit for Multinationals in Emerging Markets

1. Self-Assessment

A. Business Model

What is the core of our business model?

What is changeable?

B. Home Market Institutions

What market institutions does my business model most depend on in my home market?

Which are core?

Which are transferable?

Taxonomy of institutional infrastructure	Function	Most critical market institutions for business model in home market		
		Capital market	Product market	Talent market
Credibility enhancers	Third-party certification of claims by suppliers or customers			
Information analyzers and advisers	Collect and analyze information on producers and consumers in a given market			
Aggregators and distributors	Provide low-cost matching and other value-added services for suppliers and customers through expertise and economies of scale			
Transaction facilitators	Provide a platform for exchange of information, goods, and services and provide support functions for consummating transactions			
Regulators and other public institutions	Create and enforce the appropriate regulatory and policy framework			
Adjudicators	Resolve disputes regarding law and private contracts			

2. Emerging market assessment

A. *Defining the opportunity*

What is the opportunity for us in this emerging market?

B. *Market segmentation*

What are the segments within this market opportunity?

What segments do we plan to target?

C. *Spotting institutional voids*

Using the "spotting institutional voids" toolkit, what are the institutional voids in this emerging market (and within these segments)?

Which institutional infrastructure that we identified as critical in our home market is missing in this emerging market?

How might this emerging market's institutional voids affect our ability to access our target market segments?

3. Responding to the institutional context

Using the following framework, how should we respond to the institutional voids we have identified in this emerging market?

Strategic choice	Options for multinationals from developed markets
Replicate or adapt?	• Replicate business model, exploiting relative advantage of global brand, credibility, know-how, talent, finance, and other factor inputs. • Adapt business models, products, or organizations to institutional voids.
Compete alone or collaborate?	• Compete alone. • Acquire capabilities to navigate institutional voids through local partnerships or JVs.
Accept or attempt to change market context?	• Take market context as given. • Fill institutional voids in service of own business.
Enter, wait, or exit?	• Enter or stay in market in spite of institutional voids. • Emphasize opportunities elsewhere.

Five

Emerging Giants: Competing at Home

UNSHACKLED BY economic liberalization, entrepreneurs and domestic companies in emerging markets are aggressively pursuing growth opportunities at home and overseas.[1] Alongside the fast economic growth of their home markets, successful emerging market-based companies are flourishing, regularly registering double-digit annual revenue growth and figuring prominently in global deal making.

Globalization and liberalization have also intensified competition in these firms' home markets as multinationals from developed markets enter with all the advantages outlined in chapter 4: established global scale, brands, technology, financial muscle, talent, and organizational capabilities. Beyond foreign competition, emerging market-based firms have faced each other in tough local competition and have confronted the challenges of institutional voids in their home markets—voids that frustrate their access to talent, technology, and capital. After establishing strong positions at home, some of these domestic firms have been able to access global capital, tap in to customer segments outside their home markets, make acquisitions overseas, and find new partners to develop their businesses.

A small but growing set of these companies has built world-class capabilities to challenge global rivals in their home countries and even in developed markets. Cemex (Mexico), Infosys (India), South African

Breweries (now SABMiller), and China's Haier Group are all making marks on international commerce by competing successfully worldwide. Other companies, such as Bharti Airtel (India), China Light and Power, Koç Group (Turkey), and Petrobras (Brazil), are viewed as worldclass companies because they have successfully grown their businesses and defended their turf domestically.

We use the term *emerging giants* to refer to these successful and globally competitive companies from emerging economies, which are thriving not as a result of protectionist regulatory barriers but on the basis of sustainable competitive advantage. This chapter looks at how emerging giants are confronting the strategic choices of responding to institutional voids as they look to acquire competitive advantage in their home markets.

In an absolute sense, institutional voids are an encumbrance. However, successful emerging market companies can use the fact that they are *comparatively* better placed to circumvent these voids—relative to incumbent multinationals—as the thin end of the wedge. Examining the origins of these firms is useful for developed market-based companies so that they can understand their rising competition, and for entrepreneurs in emerging markets to appreciate the models these companies have used to develop from small ventures into major global firms.

Facing Institutional Voids and Multinational Competition

How have emerging market-based companies grown beyond their still-developing home market contexts to become globally competitive? The rapid growth of their domestic markets has helped these firms fast-track their development, but they have been able to enter the competitive global arena only by first managing the prevalence of institutional voids and surviving the entry of multinationals into their home markets.

With the advantages of their global brands and resources, multinationals can quickly displace domestic companies from the global segment of emerging markets. Because of institutional voids, emerging market companies often cannot access risk capital and experienced research talent in their home markets. As a result, it is difficult for them to invest large sums in, for example, research and development—an investment that is critical if these companies are to compete effectively against global giants. In some emerging markets such as Brazil, India, or Russia, emerging market companies are also hampered by creaky domestic infrastructure and unreliable quality in their supply network. Even when emerging market-based firms are able to circumvent some of these hurdles and put themselves on a trajectory of rapid growth, they can be stymied by the shallow pool of domestic management talent.

Emerging market-based companies that choose to take on multinationals can potentially turn the disadvantage of operating in an emerging market into an advantage, or at least blunt multinationals' incumbency advantages of brand name and access to capital and technology. First, emerging market entrepreneurs have an advantage over foreign multinationals in dealing with local institutional voids because of their experience and cultural familiarity in dealing with these voids. Institutional voids hurt all firms operating in markets rife with them, but local firms often are better able to work around them.

Prospective emerging giants can exploit this relative advantage. Spoiled by their years of experience in environments having a well-developed institutional infrastructure, often multinational managers are ill equipped to deal with the institutional voids that make it difficult to access reliable market information or structure business partnerships based on reliable contracts.

Responding to Institutional Voids

Prospective emerging giants face a set of strategic choices to respond to institutional voids that mirror the choices faced by multinationals. Because of their home location and unique capabilities, however, emerging market-based companies have different options to respond (see table 5-1).

Replicate or Adapt?

Many emerging market-based companies have looked to developed market-based multinationals as exemplars and have attempted to replicate their models. But often, simply replicating these models does not

TABLE 5-1

Responding to institutional voids in emerging markets

Strategic choice	Options for emerging market-based companies
Replicate or adapt?	• Copy business model from developed markets. • Exploit local knowledge, capabilities, and ability to navigate institutional voids to build tailored business models.
Compete alone or collaborate?	• Compete alone. • Acquire capabilities from developed markets through partnerships or JVs with multinational companies to bypass institutional voids.
Accept or attempt to change market context?	• Take market context as given. • Fill institutional voids in service of own business.
Enter, wait, or exit?	• Build business in home market in spite of institutional voids. • Deemphasize home market early in corporate history if capabilities unrewarded there.

work. Companies that literally replicate business models developed in foreign contexts often end up paving the way for incoming multinationals from those foreign markets, which can then enter the market with more resources and worldwide economies of scale. Instead, success for emerging market-based companies is rooted in devising and implementing strategies that leverage their understanding of the local context, that find creative solutions to the challenges of undeveloped hard and soft infrastructure, and that use these solutions to blunt the edge of incumbent multinationals—in brief, adapting through local knowledge.

As described in chapter 4, adaptation is a difficult process, and multinational companies often are unable or unwilling to tailor their business models and strategies to the institutional context and local tastes of each developing market in which they operate. Local companies can often access and exploit diffuse local knowledge to tailor their offerings and operations to a much greater extent than multinationals.

Multinationals' incumbency advantages can be a disadvantage in localization because they might be particularly reluctant to modify brands, organizational cultures, and cost structures that were designed to derive strength from their global uniformity. Often less constricted by preexisting cost structures and organizational processes than developed market-based multinationals, local companies can often more nimbly incorporate local knowledge into their business models. Without adaptation, multinationals often have trouble reaching beyond the global market segment, as noted in chapter 4. Exploiting their relative advantage in local adaptation can enable emerging market-based companies to target the emerging middle class seeking global quality products and services with pared down features at local prices, the traditional segments that accept local quality at very low cost, and bottom-of-the-market segments that are looking for goods and services at extremely low cost.

Although replication is not a viable option for prospective emerging giants, these companies need to decide how to adapt their business models to the context of their home markets by exploiting local knowledge of product and factor markets. Product market knowledge is fundamentally about what goods local consumers need or want and how to produce and deliver them. Not surprisingly, consumers in emerging markets—particularly large markets with diverse populations and geographies—have localized preferences and unique needs. Indigenous companies can offer value by knowing local customers better and meeting their needs with desirable, affordable products through adaptation. This local knowledge is a substitute for market research and other intermediaries that are missing in emerging markets.

Some fast food companies in developing countries, for example, have built defensible businesses by understanding local tastes and providing more palatable menu selections than those offered by foreign competitors. Jollibee Foods in the Philippines emerged from the recognition that Filipinos liked their burgers to have a particular taste. Nando's started in South Africa by providing convenient cooked chicken that suited the local palate. Similarly, Pollo Campero, originating in Guatemala, has won domestic market share by providing locally palatable roast chicken.

These companies have done battle with larger multinationals and, to varying extents, have emerged victorious. Further, they have used their mastery of the unique tastes of their domestic market customers to expand globally. Jollibee Foods caters to the tastes of Filipino communities worldwide, Nando's can be seen in the United Kingdom and Malaysia (among other locations), and Pollo Campero has achieved growth throughout the Americas by targeting Latino communities in El Salvador, Honduras, Nicaragua, Ecuador, Peru, and Mexico as well as parts of the United States.

Domestic companies can also exploit their familiarity and experience with local product market infrastructure, such as unique distribution channels and logistics networks, that prevail in the absence of developed market infrastructure. The peculiarities of local product market infrastructure can be significant barriers to new competitors. Even if companies are able to introduce a product that consumers want, reaching them can be cost prohibitive and a business deterrent for foreign-based firms. South African Breweries (now SABMiller), for example, exploited its product market knowledge to build an efficient distribution system that could reach South Africa's traditional beer-drinking outlets—called *shebeens,* or backyard bars—and entrench its brand among local consumers. Developing this system would have been a difficult proposition for a multinational such as Heineken or Anheuser-Busch. Later in this chapter, we look at the ways in which India-based Tata Motors has exploited product market knowledge to adapt its business model in light of institutional voids.

Factor market knowledge is an understanding of the labor and supply chain inputs that enable companies to create products or services for the marketplace. Emerging market-based companies can exploit their superior ability to identify and manage local talent and resources or their experience with local supply chains to serve local as well as global customers.

Emerging markets boast high-quality talent and production resources, often at significantly cheaper rates than similar talent and resources in developed markets. Given the institutional voids in emerging markets, however, it can be difficult and costly for companies from developed markets to access talent and resources. Multinationals often have trouble sorting talent in markets where personnel quality and the reputations of educational institutions vary widely and where work experience and training may differ substantially from that available in developed markets. From a supply chain perspective, operating and managing remote sourcing and delivery services in regions with relatively poor infrastructure pose additional challenges to foreign companies.

Emerging market-based companies can leverage their expertise in factor markets in a number of ways. Later in this chapter, we look at how Cosan has successfully exploited its knowledge of factor markets in Brazil's sugar and ethanol sector.

Compete Alone or Collaborate?

Multinationals entering their home markets are powerful competitors, but they can also be valuable partners for prospective emerging giants. Emerging market-based companies face a choice parallel to the one faced by multinationals: compete alone or collaborate? Because many multinationals are required to collaborate with local firms when they enter emerging markets, collaboration is often more of a strategic choice for emerging market-based companies. Collaboration can help prospective emerging giants acquire new capabilities from developed markets and add credibility to their organizations, and that can be particularly valuable in light of institutional voids that challenge their ability to do so on their own. We look at how two emerging giants—Doğuş Group of Turkey and Bharti Airtel of India—approached their choices to collaborate with foreign partners.

Accept or Attempt to Change Market Context?

Beyond adapting to voids, prospective emerging giants are often compelled to invest in developing market infrastructure to fill voids. Filling voids can be a powerful source of competitive advantage, because foreign-based multinationals are often less willing to invest in the expensive proposition of changing the market context.[2] Chinese white goods firm Haier developed into a powerful brand in its home market by filling a number of institutional voids, as we discuss later in this chapter.

Enter, Wait, or Exit?

Developed market-based multinationals have clear exit options from emerging markets. These firms have the luxury of choosing among any number of markets in which to invest—and the resources to cover the cost of mistakes. Emphasizing opportunities elsewhere is a much more difficult option for entrepreneurs and domestic companies in emerging markets. Nonetheless, exiting early is an option for companies with mismatched and unrewarded capabilities that they cannot exploit amid the institutional voids of their home markets.

Emerging Giants Competing at Home: Examples

In the rest of this chapter, we look at examples of emerging giants that confronted these strategic choices in the face of institutional voids in their home markets (see table 5-2). As in chapter 4, even though each of these companies has confronted each of these strategic choices, we focus on the most salient choice for each example. Many emerging giants have organized themselves as business groups to help confront these choices in light of institutional voids. We consider the benefits and costs of business group organizations for emerging market-based firms at the end of this chapter.

TABLE 5-2

Case examples

Strategic choice	Examples
Replicate or adapt?	Tata Motors in India Cosan in Brazil
Compete alone or collaborate?	Doğuş Group in Turkey Bharti Airtel in India
Accept or attempt to change market context?	Haier in China
Enter, wait, or exit?	Software firms in India

Replicate or Adapt? Tata Motors

Tata Motors—part of India's Tata Group, one of the most successful emerging market-based business groups—has carefully adapted its offerings and organization based on institutional voids, particularly with the development of a new vehicle, the Ace.[3] By 2005, Tata Motors had become India's largest commercial truck maker but found itself squeezed amid growing foreign competition in its home market. At the top end of the market, major foreign truck manufacturers, such as Volvo, were challenging Tata Motors' supremacy in large trucks. Producers of pickup trucks from Japan, Korea, and other countries, meanwhile, were competing against Tata Motors' smaller commercial vehicles. The low end of India's commercial vehicle market was dominated by three-wheelers made by domestic and foreign companies.

Tata Motors responded to this competitive challenge by exploiting product market knowledge and adapting business processes with the development of the Ace, a four-wheeled mini-truck, to target a niche in the marketplace. The vehicle opened a new segment for Tata Motors, helping the company reduce the risk of dependence on its main commercial truck business, which was highly cyclical.

The Ace was designed in response to market conditions in India and an unmet consumer need identified by Tata Motors. Three-wheeled vehicles were pervasive as commercial vehicles in India, used to ferry produce and merchandise to rural markets and deliver goods in urban centers, some of which limited access to larger commercial trucks to ease congestion. Despite their low price and nimbleness, however, three-wheelers were unsafe, slow, and frequently overloaded. Reliance on the vehicles often resulted in damaged goods and delayed deliveries. Moreover, three-wheelers were barred from operating on India's "golden quadrilateral," the new expressway network that linked the country's largest cities.

The Ace was positioned as a replacement for three-wheelers. It had a comparable payload size and price point but offered many of the benefits of larger light commercial vehicles to serve the "last mile" of distribution in India's congested cities. The truck was designed to be the only vehicle in India allowed on all roads. Although the initial cost of the Ace—about $5,000—was higher than that of three-wheelers, the truck was designed to be more economical after accounting for its larger payload capacity and fuel costs. Tata Motors designed the Ace to meet higher safety standards than existing requirements and norms in India. The move put Tata Motors in a stronger position than competitors if higher standards were adopted by Indian regulators and would also facilitate the vehicle's entry into international markets having higher standards already on the books.

The Ace was unique not only in its concept but also in the ways in which Tata Motors adapted the execution of the project to meet the vehicle's target price point and reach its target customers. Tata Motors conducted extensive market research through interviews with potential customers to identify their needs and constraints, helping the company refine the Ace's design, pricing, and features—and substituting for absent market research intermediaries. The company looked at the product through the eyes of its customers, incorporating, for example, realistic expectations about overloading, a common practice in poor, populous countries.

Meeting the project's tight budget—to enable the Ace to be positioned at such a low price point—forced Tata Motors to be innovative in product development and procurement. The company employed a cross-functional team for product development and adopted a Japanese-style production preparation process (3P), which incorporated suppliers and other stakeholders earlier in the development process. Aggregate outsourcing, e-sourcing, and the use of existing production facilities also helped lower costs.

Because it blurred the lines of existing product segments, successfully introducing the Ace required Tata Motors to educate the marketplace. After listening to customer guidance through the product development process, the company needed to invest in customer education to stoke demand for the Ace, particularly because of the truck's operating economics. To ease concerns about the Ace's high initial cost, the company offered financing through its consumer finance arm. This action filled a void, because auto financing was a relatively new practice in India—and almost unknown among customers in the Ace's target market.

Tata Motors also adapted its distribution and after-sales service operations for the Ace to meet the needs of the vehicle's target customers. Many of the Ace's cost-conscious potential customers in rural areas might not be willing to travel long distances to see the vehicle, so the company deployed a new bare-bones dealership format that would bring the Ace closer to these customers without incurring the expense of a new network of full-service dealerships. Similarly, instead of building an expensive new network of service centers, the company trained local mechanics and gave them tools to take care of common problems. Vehicles would be sent to larger urban service centers only in the event of major repairs or accidents.

Less than a year after the Ace's introduction in May 2005, Tata Motors had already sold thirty thousand units even though the vehicle was available in only one-quarter of the country. A survey of Ace purchasers found that more than half were buying their first commercial vehicle, suggesting that the product had expanded the existing commercial vehicle market. "It is no more a niche product," said one company executive. "It has created a category by itself. What we are trying to create through this is . . . businessmen and entrepreneurs, who will come into the transportation business. That is the key driver of demand creation that we are looking at."[4]

Because demand surpassed the capacity of the existing plant where the Ace was initially produced, Tata Motors established a new plant in northern India to produce the Ace and related vehicles with a capacity of 250,000 vehicles. The company also introduced the vehicle in Sri Lanka, Nepal, and Bangladesh, with an eye to introducing the Ace in still other developing markets. Similarly, Tata Motors exploited local knowledge to target a difficult market segment with the development of the Nano, a $2,500 "people's car" introduced in 2008.

Tata Motors successfully exploited local knowledge in conceptualizing the Ace and adapted to institutional voids to deliver the product (see table 5-3). However, the company's market opportunity with this

TABLE 5-3

Tata Motors in India: Responding to institutional voids

Spotting voids question	Specific void	Response
Can companies easily obtain reliable data on customer tastes and purchase behaviors? Are there cultural barriers to market research? Do world-class market research firms operate in this country?	Underdeveloped sector of market research providers (product market information analyzers and advisers)	Adapted: Interviewed potential customers internally and incorporated results into Ace design and pricing
Do large retail chains exist in the country? If so, do they cover the entire country or only the major cities? Do they reach all consumers or only wealthy ones? How strong are the logistics and transportation infrastructures?	Underdeveloped dealer networks (product market aggregators and distributors); difficult for rural customers to travel to dealerships in urban centers (hard infrastructure)	Adapted: Established basic dealerships to bring Ace "showroom" closer to rural customers unwilling or unable to travel to cities to see Ace models
Are consumers willing to try new products and services? Do they trust goods from local companies? How about foreign companies?	Underdeveloped consumer information providers (product market information analyzers and advisers)	Adapted: Invested in customer education to show value proposition of the Ace
Do consumers use credit cards, or does cash dominate transactions? Can consumers get credit to make purchases? Is data on customer creditworthiness available?	Limited sources of capital for target customers (product market transaction facilitators)	Adapted: Offered financing for Ace through consumer finance arm
How do companies deliver after-sales service to consumers? Is it possible to set up a nationwide service network?	Underdeveloped vehicle service network (product market aggregators and distributors)	Adapted: Trained and provided tools to local mechanics for common problems

product was closely tied to the state of India's infrastructure at the time of its introduction. The company's success with the Ace soon attracted other companies—both foreign and domestic—to develop similar vehicles for India. By filling the void of India's underdeveloped market research intermediaries for its own product development, Tata Motors served as a market researcher for its competition.

Importantly, however, Tata Motors has a head start in the segment, and, perhaps more critically, execution was critical to the success of the Ace. The company's innovative procurement process and investments in developing the ecosystem for the vehicle through its distribution and service operations could help Tata Motors sustain competitive advantage.

Replicate or Adapt? Cosan

Cosan has exploited its ability to adapt to the institutional voids in the factor markets of Brazil to emerge as one of the world's leading sugar and ethanol producers. The Brazilian government had closely regulated prices, production, and purchase of sugar and ethanol, but after deregulation in the 1990s, the industry took off, enabling companies such as Cosan to exploit the country's inherent advantages in sugar and ethanol production conferred by its climate and soil.[5]

Cosan emerged from a competitive landscape in Brazil dominated by small and inefficient family-run businesses, particularly in the 1980s before deregulation.[6] The company had grown in the fragmented sugar and ethanol sectors mostly through acquisitions—particularly after deregulation—increasing its production efficiency through economies of scale.[7] With a 9 percent share of Brazil's sugar market and 7 percent of its ethanol market, Cosan was the country's largest producer of both as of June 2009.[8] (As of December 2007, Cosan's next-largest rival held a 4.3 percent share and others held shares of around 2 percent.)[9]

In 2007, Cosan raised more than $1 billion in an initial public offering (IPO) on the New York Stock Exchange, the first Brazilian biofuel firm to do so.[10] The company planned to use the proceeds of the public offering to continue expanding through acquisitions and some greenfield projects.[11] "The message they are giving now is they want to be consolidators, not acquired," said one stock analyst.[12]

More recently, foreign-based multinationals have been eager to tap in to the opportunities of Brazil's growing biofuel sector.[13] The attractiveness of the sector to large multinationals compelled Cosan to restructure its corporate organization to prevent an unwanted takeover, enabling founder Rubens Ometto Silveira Mello to maintain control of the company. "If he gave up voting control, boom, they would get taken out," one stock analyst said.[14] Cosan saw some benefits from the entry of large multinationals in consolidating the sector. As one company executive noted, "We have 350 players in Brazil. It would be better to have 20 of those companies expanding in the market because the discipline of those guys is so much better."[15]

Operational know-how and a willingness to invest in systems surrounding its production facilities were critical for Cosan to differentiate itself from its local and incoming foreign competition. "We manage the society around the mill, which is key," said one company executive. "We are an agricultural business. We plant, we fertilise, we raise cane, we cut cane, we operate the plants, we do everything. These major agribusinesses, they don't do agriculture. They buy and sell supplies."[16] Most of the institutional voids in Cosan's business remain upstream, so these capabilities have been persistent sources of competitive advantage vis-à-vis foreign agribusiness giants and oil companies targeting the biofuel market.

Cosan saw its investments in agricultural research and its use of technology to manage operations as other key sources of competitive advantage.[17] Through sophisticated monitoring of crops, production, and soil quality and process improvements such as in sugarcane washing, Cosan sought to maximize the efficiency of its operations. The company was able to bring these efficiency gains to the mills it acquired. Cosan increased production capacity at Da Barra from 79 tons of sugarcane at the time of acquisition in August 2002 to 894 tons in 2008–2009.[18] Cosan's expertise at managing acquisitions—developed amid myriad institutional voids immediately after deregulation—have remained a key source of competitive advantage for the company.

A large share of sugarcane production in Brazil relied on contracted labor to cut the sugarcane by hand. Working conditions for these laborers had been a frequent source of criticism. In 2007, Cosan became the largest producer—and among the first—to agree to eliminate outsourced labor in response to these concerns.[19]

In addition to acquisitions, Cosan pursued brownfield projects in the productive but competitively crowded São Paulo region, and greenfield developments inland. "[W]e need a place without sugar mills," one company executive explained, "a place where we can develop sugarcane fields surrounding the plants, to create clusters that act as a system. Having mills in a cluster reduces the cost of transportation to the mills and reduces the energy consumption."[20]

Some 85 percent of Brazil's ethanol production was sold through five distributors, giving these firms strong bargaining power.[21] Ethanol producers also bore the costs of transporting fuel from their facilities to distribution centers and then back to retail chains for final distribution.[22] As a result, Cosan sought to become the country's first integrated ethanol company.[23] Cosan bought a chain of fifteen hundred Esso filling stations from Exxon in 2008, making it the first major producer to move into retail distribution.[24] "We wanted to secure our access to consumers, and this deal gave us the necessary scale," said one company executive.[25]

The deal came as many major oil companies sought to move upstream into biofuel production.[26] Cosan saw its local knowledge and experience as key competitive advantages vis-à-vis incoming foreign multinationals. "[Y]ou have to deal with workers, unions, climate conditions, judges, cities and priests," one company executive said. "That is not very easy for any company to do, and it's an expertise that you have to develop over time. As a Brazilian, I can understand the culture better than an American or European. If I come to Europe to buy a wheat mill, it won't be easy either. I have to deal with the French Union that have a strong lobby. It requires experience."[27] Cosan's growth and development in Brazil illustrate how emerging market-based companies can exploit their ability to navigate factor markets to build competitive advantage against both local and foreign competition (see table 5-4).

Prospective emerging giants often face the question of whether to collaborate with multinationals or to compete against them alone. As we discuss next, Bharti Airtel of India and Turkey's Doğuş Group pursued collaborations with foreign firms at different stages of their corporate

TABLE 5-4

Cosan in Brazil: Responding to institutional voids

Spotting voids question	Specific void	Response
Can companies access raw materials and components of good quality? Is there a deep network of suppliers? Are there firms that assess suppliers' quality and reliability? Can companies enforce contracts with suppliers?	Limited ability to sort suppliers (factor market information analyzers and advisers; credibility enhancers)	Adapted: Invested in quality through technology and process improvements, and scale through acquisitions to differentiate business in fragmented sector
How strong are the logistics and transportation infrastructures? Have global logistics companies set up local operations?	Underdeveloped logistics and transportation infrastructure (product market aggregators and distributors)	Adapted: Sought to build out fully integrated operations
How are the rights of workers protected? If a company were to adopt its local rivals' or suppliers' business practices, such as the use of child labor, would that tarnish its image overseas?	Poor labor conditions in sugarcane production (labor market regulators and other public institutions)	Adapted: Signed contract to eliminate outsourced labor

histories. Their foreign partners provided capital, operational capabilities, strategic advice, and valuable connections to other global resources. The two companies sought partners that would also improve and signal the credibility of their organizations.

Compete Alone or Collaborate? Bharti Airtel in India

Established as a start-up by entrepreneur Sunil Mittal and with more than $5 million in annual sales by 1992, Bharti Airtel grew into one of India's largest telecommunications providers, with a market capitalization of $31.8 billion by 2008.[28] The company's partnerships with a range of foreign firms over the course of its history were central to Bharti Airtel's ability to grow in a capital-intensive industry and take on tough competition from state-owned enterprises and well-funded offshoots of powerful business groups. Foreign partners helped Bharti Airtel in its first bid for a cellular service license, and major equity investments by Singapore Telecom (SingTel) and U.S.-based private equity investor Warburg Pincus fueled the company's growth through acquisitions.

Bharti partnered first with Compagnie Générale des Eaux of France, Mauritian cell operator Emtel, and Mobile Systems International of the United Kingdom in a successful joint bid for India's first cellular service license. Soon after Bharti launched cellular service in Delhi in September 1995, it faced competition from Sterling Cellular, which was controlled by Indian steel giant Essar.

Bharti quickly learned how to compete against rivals having more resources. The company targeted small business owners and retail customers instead of the corporate market, where larger business groups would have an advantage. Although business group organizations can bring advantages to emerging market-based firms—as we discuss later in this chapter—Bharti exploited its focus. As a company executive noted, "We were lucky not to carry the baggage other players had of their existing businesses. I was often told this was a disadvantage, as I did not have the same resources as they. As you can see, that has been proved wrong. Often there were very strong temptations to start other businesses—we almost started an airline at one point. But every time we braced ourselves and said no. Today our focus has been our greatest asset."[29] (Bharti Enterprises, organized as a business group, later entered the retail, life insurance, and other sectors in India.)

Italian state-owned telecom operator STET invested $58 million in Bharti in 1996, and, from 1997 through 1999, British Telecom (BT) made $250 million in equity investments.[30] BT also helped Bharti improve its operations by providing assistance in corporate communication, lending technology support, and extending procurement benefits to Bharti through its own vendor network. Importantly, Bharti maintained management control in the partnership. "Despite its size, our partnership is one of equals and the inputs which we receive are tremendous," noted a Bharti executive.[31]

In 1995, a second tranche of cellular service licenses came up for auction, but Bharti did not bid high enough for the desirable locations. The winning bids turned out to be too high and unsustainable for some new entrants. Bharti wanted to expand through acquisitions, but it needed more capital. In 1999, Warburg Pincus purchased a 20 percent stake in Bharti for $60 million. The following year SingTel invested $400 million, and in 2001, Warburg Pincus and SingTel each invested an additional $200 million. Bharti received smaller investments from New York Life Insurance, Asian Infrastructure Fund Group, and International Finance Corporation.

Bharti was still a relatively small operation when it attracted these major investments. As the only profitable cellular service provider in a market tipped for stunning growth, Bharti presented investors with significant upside potential. An executive at Warburg Pincus also noted the quality of the company's management and the strength of its consumer-focused model compared with those of its competition:

> We were willing to bet big on Bharti because we saw the right strategy, the right team and the right focus. We were impressed by Sunil Mittal's vision, his deep domain expertise, and the quality of his management team. In spite of his accomplishments, we saw a man who was willing to learn, to listen, and to change—he does not pretend that he knows it all. It is not easy to find these qualities in an entrepreneur. Our business is about backing people, and Bharti is a very good example of this strategy.[32]

Partnering with investors such as Warburg Pincus and SingTel offered Bharti more than just capital. The business groups with which some of Bharti's toughest competitors were affiliated had access to capital, political support, and deeper wells of management talent, as well as valuable reputations. Investments from global players offered signals of credibility that helped Bharti neutralize some of these advantages.

Warburg Pincus and SingTel offered other resources and advice that helped Bharti build its business. Three representatives of SingTel and two Warburg Pincus partners sat on Bharti's thirteen-person board. Bharti and SingTel jointly built an underwater cable network linking

Bharti's domestic voice and data network to SingTel's global network. Warburg Pincus offered significant strategic advice on Bharti's geographic expansion, acquisition approach, financing, and operations. "Warburg Pincus let us think big," said a Bharti executive.[33] Warburg Pincus helped persuade Bharti to acquire existing operations—even those not fully meeting the company's high standards—and to look beyond northern India to craft a pan-India strategy to tap in to opportunities in the wealthier south.

Bharti went public in 2002, listing 10 percent of its shares on the National Stock Exchange, and subsequently has raised capital through loans and other facilities. By 2005, Warburg Pincus had earned $1.1 billion by selling two-thirds of its stake in Bharti—"one of the very best deals in the firm's history," according to a Warburg Pincus executive.[34]

Bharti's early foreign partnerships helped nurture its growth with much-needed capital, resources, and strategic advice. Risk capital is important to the development of any young company. Bharti's partnerships were particularly valuable because of the institutional voids in its home market and the deeper expertise and richer resources—such as the connection to SingTel's global network—it gained from foreign partners than would be possible to access locally (see table 5-5). These capabilities and resources helped Bharti combat the inherent advantages of state-owned and business group-affiliated rivals and grow into one of India's largest telecom service providers. These foreign partnerships signaled credibility to the outside world, but accessing them required Bharti to demonstrate not only a highly promising business model and successful track record but also credibility in its management and corporate governance—a lesson for any emerging market-based firm looking for help from overseas.

Compete Alone or Collaborate? Doğuş Group in Turkey

In 2005, Doğuş Group, one of Turkey's largest business groups, sought out a foreign partner to improve the competitiveness and capabilities of its flagship financial services company, Garanti Bank.[35] Doğuş Group had restructured itself in the early 2000s in response to economic

TABLE 5-5

Bharti Airtel in India: Responding to institutional voids

Spotting voids question	Specific void	Response
Does a venture capital industry exist? If so, does it allow individuals with good ideas to raise funds? Can companies raise large amounts of capital in the stock market? Is there a market for corporate debt?	Underdeveloped capital-providing intermediaries (capital market aggregators and distributors; transaction facilitators)	Collaborated: Sought out foreign partners for capital (as well as access to global resources and strategic advice)
Are consumers willing to try new products and services? Do they trust goods from local companies? How about foreign companies?	Underdeveloped consumer information providers (product market information analyzers and advisers)	Collaborated: Foreign partners helped build credibility for customers who might have opted for the reassurance of a business group brand name
Do independent financial analysts, ratings agencies, and the media offer unbiased information on companies? How effective are corporate governance norms and standards in protecting shareholder interests?	Underdeveloped capital market information providers and certifiers (capital market information analyzers and advisers; credibility enhancers)	Collaborated: Foreign partnerships helped build credibility for future investors when IPO was issued

crisis in its home market and incoming foreign competition. As part of the restructuring, the group streamlined its portfolio and worked to institutionalize standards across the fairly autonomous group operating companies.

Garanti Bank exemplified the restructured group's concentration on consumer- and marketing-focused businesses. Garanti had developed a strong brand and was a leader among Turkish banks in incorporating IT into its financial services offerings. By the time Garanti considered an international partnership in 2005, the bank had more than $20 billion in assets and was Turkey's third-largest private bank.[36] Foreign banks had a small but growing presence in Turkey at the time. As of June 2004, foreign-owned banks accounted for a 2.6 percent market share in assets, 4.1 percent of loans, and 2.5 percent of deposits.[37] In early 2005, BNP

Paribas of France and Fortis of Belgium separately bought stakes in Turkish banks.[38]

Doğuş sought out a foreign partner for Garanti for a number of reasons. The company hoped to reduce the debt on Garanti's balance sheet, join with a foreign entity to expand its business in the region, and institutionalize corporate governance and other best practices. This latter advantage of a partnership could bring to Doğuş operational know-how, such as lean management, and also enable the group to broach sensitive issues as the family business restructured itself, as a group executive noted: "Sometimes when you have a third party or a new shareholder, until that day, things that you couldn't converse or you couldn't discuss, now you can talk about this easier. In the family businesses in emerging markets, when the businesses are growing, the family, the owner, and the management become too much like the family and so any criticism or saying no is taken very much as a personal thing."[39]

However, while adding these capabilities Doğuş did not want to jeopardize its existing sources of competitive advantage, particularly Garanti's brand and a corporate culture of innovation and fast decision making. "Everybody was wondering what would be life after such a partnership. We had to convince them," said a group executive. "I didn't want to lose the culture of the institution."[40] The company also hoped to motivate employees through training and career development opportunities offered by a foreign partner.

Doğuş considered offers from multinational banks but ultimately partnered with GE Consumer Finance in an equal partnership. (Doğuş sold a 25.5 percent stake in Garanti to GE, half of the Doğuş holding in the bank.) The international banks that bid for stakes wanted to acquire majority holdings in Garanti and rebrand the bank.[41] "What they will do is simple," said a group executive. "They will put down the Garanti sign and they put up their sign . . . It's great that these guys have great programs all around the world, but those programs are one-size-fits-all programs."[42]

GE's bid was not the highest of the partnership contenders, but the organization offered other benefits to Garanti and Doğuş Group.[43] Because GE was not a bank, it would bring a different perspective to board discussions and would look at Garanti differently than would a multina-tional bank. "In a board, if you had a partnership with XYZ multinational bank, I think there will be nothing to talk about but the profitability," a group executive said.[44]

As a diversified multinational, GE also offered Doğuş the possibility of further cooperation in other sectors.[45] Doğuş had already partnered with GE's CNBC television network in Turkey starting in 1998, and with GE Real Estate in a joint venture in 2006. Because GE was not a full-service financial institution, however, the partnership would give Doğuş flexibil-ity to partner with different companies in other financial services; a group executive likened the deal to buying an individual vitamin at GNC with the possibility of buying others, instead of a single multivitamin.[46]

Since selling the stake to GE, Garanti has pursued regional growth in Romania while looking to expand in Ukraine, and the partners have transferred capabilities to each other. "The day after the relationship started, GE saw a lot more value that they did not see on the paper before," a group executive said. Examples of this value included Garanti's tech-nology, branding and marketing of credit cards, success with alternative distribution channels, and use of customer data to offer products through tellers.[47] The Garanti executive who spearheaded the merger of the three Doğuş-owned banks into Garanti has also transferred to GE as the company's head of operations for Europe.[48] Garanti has sent employ-ees to GE training facilities and learned operational capabilities from its partner. "We are now utilizing lean management, six sigma stuff. We already started getting results," said a group executive. "So maybe in cer-tain things we do not need the McKinseys of this world any more. We are taking it from our partner—with zero fee."[49]

Doğuş Group approached collaboration with a clear view of what it wanted from its partner. The company sought to preserve Garanti's brand—a valuable property in a market that lacked sophisticated product market information analyzers and advisers—but hoped to use the part-nership to compensate for other institutional voids in its home market (see table 5-6). Just as prospective emerging giants—like any company operating in an emerging market—need to match their capabilities to

TABLE 5-6

Doğuş Group in Turkey: Responding to institutional voids

Spotting voids question	Specific void	Response
Are consumers willing to try new products and services? Do they trust goods from local companies? How about foreign companies?	Underdeveloped consumer information providers (product market information analyzers and advisers)	Competed alone: Kept valuable brand, even within foreign partnership
How strong is the country's education infrastructure, especially for technical and management training?	Underdeveloped educational and training intermediaries (labor market aggregators and distributors)	Collaborated: Exploited opportunities for training exchanges with foreign partner
How effective are corporate governance norms and standards in protecting shareholder interests?	Underdeveloped corporate governance standards (capital market credibility enhancers)	Collaborated: Used foreign partnership to bring institutional best practices to restructuring family-owned company
Are corporate boards independent and empowered, and do they have independent directors?	Shallow pool of qualified independent directors (capital market information analyzers and advisers)	Collaborated: Sought out foreign partner that could provide strategic advice through seats on board

their home market contexts, these firms need to align their collaborations with the missing capabilities that could help them become more competitive in those contexts.

Accept or Attempt to Change Market Context? Haier in China

In the face of serious institutional voids, adaptation and collaboration are not enough for many prospective emerging giants.[50] Unwilling to accept the limitations on growth and corporate development imposed by institutional voids, these companies can work actively to fill these voids. Haier Group of China emerged as a globally competitive producer of household appliances by successfully exploiting product market knowledge and navigating the context of its home market by filling voids, particularly in distribution and service.

In December 1984, Haier—then named Qingdao Refrigerator Factory—was a debt-laden operation several months behind in paying its employees' salaries. At the time, only 6.6 percent of China's urban households had refrigerators, and the factory was one of China's three hundred refrigerator producers, most of whose products exhibited low standards of quality.[51] Despite robustly growing market demand for refrigerators as living standards improved in China, Haier resisted mass production and instead focused on quality and brand building—a valuable strategy in a market that lacked well-developed independent credibility-enhancing intermediaries.

By 2004, Haier dominated its home market with about a 30 percent share of China's white goods market and a growing presence in "black goods" sectors, such as televisions and personal computers. Amid industry consolidation, price wars, and the entry of powerful foreign brands, Haier built and sustained competitive advantage through innovative and rapid response to customer tastes and needs, by filling voids in after-sales service, and by employing efficient distribution.

Compared with foreign and domestic rivals, Haier was particularly responsive to market demands and was willing to offer differentiated products to meet customer needs. The company had some ninety-six product categories and 15,100 specifications, as a result of small feature innovations and tailored products that were inexpensive to produce—when incorporated modularly—and were highly valued by customers.

When a customer in a rural area of China's Sichuan province complained to Haier that his washing machine was breaking down, service technicians found the plumbing clogged with mud. Rural Chinese were using the Haier machines—designed to wash clothing—to clean sweet potatoes and other vegetables. Haier engineers then modified the washer design to accommodate this use. Since then, Haier washing machines sold in Sichuan have included a new label: "Mainly for washing clothes, sweet potatoes and peanuts."[52]

To accommodate summer lifestyles requiring frequent changes of clothing, Haier created a tiny washing machine that cleaned a single change of clothes. The model used less electricity and water than larger machines, making it an instant hit in Shanghai. Similarly, the company designed small refrigerators for urban households where space is at a premium. Haier's adaptation through market responsiveness was particularly valuable against foreign competition, which was less attuned to consumer preferences in a market that lacked sophisticated market research intermediaries.

Most critical to Haier's success in building a highly competitive business in its home market were the company's attempts to change the market context by filling institutional voids. In after-sales service, Haier established a service center in Qingdao in 1990 that featured a computerized system to track tens of thousands of customers.[53] By 2004, the company had a service network of fifty-five hundred independent contractors—one for each sales outlet—who made house calls from requests to a nationwide hotline. The company even provided temporary replacements for products undergoing repairs. Offering service that surpassed existing norms—and customer expectations—in China helped Haier differentiate itself and build brand loyalty.

Haier also built a unified, dedicated logistics operation to distribute its products. Chinese competitors such as Midea and TCL had separate logistics operations for each product line. Haier's scale and volume, coupled with consolidated distribution functions, gave the company one of the lowest logistics costs among competitors—a major advantage. Haier Logistics, an independently operated company created in 1999, was a national pioneer, offering just-in-time (JIT) purchasing, raw materials delivery, and product distribution. Five years after Haier established the logistics operation, the company had reduced the size of its main raw materials warehouse from a 200,000-square-meter facility with an inventory cycle of more than thirty days to a 20,000-square-meter distribution center with a seven-day inventory cycle, and the company reduced its roster of suppliers dramatically. Haier set up forty-two distribution centers across China, enabling the company to reach the country's interior, and cut the time from order to final product delivery by more than one-third through the unified operation and information systems of Haier Logistics.

Haier Logistics provided a critical competitive advantage because of the institutional voids in China. Establishing a logistics network was complicated by geographic and bureaucratic obstacles across China's varied terrain, unevenly developed roads and retail networks, and patchwork of local regulations. In large cities like Shanghai, it was difficult to find warehouse space large enough to accommodate the huge trucks required for white goods. In the most remote areas, it was a challenge to connect warehouses to a company's information network. Regulations affecting transportation, such as weight limits for trucks, varied across regions.

Foreign multinationals were forced to rely on Chinese distributors and faced high costs and limited coverage in the absence of national third-party logistics providers. These constraints limited many foreign brands to China's more developed eastern coast. Constructing a national network through multiple logistics providers was difficult and costly, and those that tried to run their own distribution networks often failed. Institutional voids made it difficult for Haier to build its business in China (see table 5-7), but, having circumvented them successfully, Haier found that voids served as barriers to the aspirations of its competitors.

Competitive advantage is dynamic—particularly competitive advantage built on local knowledge, which can be acquired by rivals over time, and institutional voids, which tend to be filled over time. Haier's early focus on product quality and service standards helped the company survive consolidation and price wars, but these propositions become comparatively less valuable as the competitive field is culled and surviving rivals catch up. Moreover, the development of market institutions that assess product quality—the equivalent of *Consumer Reports*—over time makes it easier for new firms to establish credibility that Haier was able to achieve only over time through significant investments in brand building. The value of local customer knowledge can diminish over time as competitors gain experience—particularly foreign firms with initially steep learning curves—or are able to acquire local expertise through emulation, partnerships, and use of sophisticated market research intermediaries. As regulations ease the entry and development of capable third-party logistics providers with national scope and as the retail sector matures, the value of dedicated logistics and distribution operations, such as Haier's, also can fall. (Chinese retailer Gome Electrical

TABLE 5-7

Haier in China: Responding to institutional voids

Spotting voids question	Specific void	Response
Can companies easily obtain reliable data on customer tastes and purchase behaviors? Do world-class market research firms operate in the country?	Underdeveloped market research intermediaries (product market information analyzers and advisers)	Adapted: Exploited access to local knowledge with responsiveness to customer needs in product development, gaining advantage over competitors lacking access to local knowledge
Can consumers easily obtain unbiased information on the quality of the goods and services they want to buy? Are there independent consumer organizations and publications that provide such information?	Underdeveloped product information and certification providers (product market information analyzers and advisers; credibility enhancers)	Adapted: Instilled focus on quality internally through worker accountability and focus of management
How strong are the logistics and transportation infrastructures? Have global logistics companies set up local operations? Do large retail chains exist in the country? If so, do they cover the entire country or only the major cities? Do they reach all consumers or only wealthy ones?	Underdeveloped third-party logistics and retail infrastructure (product market aggregators and distributors)	Attempted to change market context: Established dedicated logistics arm and network of distribution centers across China
How do companies deliver after-sales service to consumers? Is it possible to set up a nation-wide service network? Are third-party service providers reliable?	Underdeveloped after-sales service networks (product market aggregators and distributors)	Attempted to change market context: Established service center with customer tracking, customer service hotline, and network of independent contractors making house calls to customers

Appliances, for example, developed a nationwide footprint of 779 outlets across China as of mid-2009.)[54]

Emerging market-based companies can and should exploit their knowledge of local product markets and their ability to navigate the institutional context—even by filling institutional voids—but some of these advantages can become obsolete as home markets develop. (Indeed, Haier has seen its share of China's domestic refrigerator market fall from 29.1 percent in 2004 to 25.6 percent in 2006 as a result of rising domestic and foreign competitors, some of which returned to the country after learning from early mistakes.)[55]

Wait, Stay, or Exit? Software Firms in India

In the face of institutional voids or other contextual challenges, emerging market-based companies can deemphasize their home markets by avoiding particular sectors or focusing on building global operations relatively early in their corporate histories.[56] An entrepreneur might decide that a particular emerging market is not ready for a line of business if it will not be rewarded given the market's institutional context. A biotech firm might decide that regulations or other obstacles would stifle its business in an emerging market. Entrepreneurs or business groups weighing investments in a wide range of sectors might decide that a market's institutional context is not conducive to some investments—for example, the market simply might not be ready for private equity or big box retailing.

Software and IT consulting firms in India, such as Infosys Technologies, Tata Consultancy Services (TCS), and Wipro Technologies, have exploited India's labor force to offer IT services worldwide. These firms have developed globally competitive businesses based on their expertise and ability to identify, motivate, train, and manage talent. India boasts an abundance of software talent that is significantly cheaper than similar talent in developed markets. Given the institutional voids that pervade the Indian economy, however, it was difficult and costly for companies in developed markets to access this talent. Indian software companies developed business models and organizational capabilities that allowed them to match the talent in India with demand in developed markets.

Although these companies served domestic customers, early in their histories they focused on opportunities overseas, where these capabilities would be more highly rewarded. At the time that India's software and IT consulting firms emerged, most Indian companies were not using sophisticated IT systems to support their businesses. Moreover, most of the few Indian companies with IT systems had in-house IT departments and were not willing to consider outsourcing. Developed markets offered deeper pools of customers—and higher price points for IT services than those same services sold to Indian companies.

Established in India in 1981, Infosys Technologies opened its first foreign office in the United States only six years later. Ten years after that, the company opened additional development centers in India and offices in Canada and the United Kingdom. By 1999, Infosys had opened offices in Germany, Sweden, Belgium, and Australia as well as development centers in the United States. The company opened additional development centers in Canada, Japan, the United Kingdom, and the United States and, by 2001, offices in France, Hong Kong, the United Arab Emirates, and Argentina. In 2002–2003, Infosys established subsidiaries in China and Australia and offices in the Netherlands, Singapore, and Switzerland.

Given abundant access to cheap talent, an initial lack of reputation, and limited available hardware domestically, many Indian software providers started at the low end of the market with a "bodyshopping" model—sending talent into global markets to work on projects at client sites for significantly lower wages than local programmers. These companies gradually built reputations for reliability and high quality and began to provide more value-added services. Infosys, for example, reached a turning point in the mid-1990s when it began to initiate software development within India instead of exclusively at client sites. This was Infosys's first step toward generating more value for its clients and protecting its claim on this value.

Although the transition was subtle, the results were monumental. The company was able to differentiate itself by growing from its baseline labor-commodity model—selling qualified labor inputs at a low price to build value into other companies' businesses. Infosys successfully moved up the value chain by providing specialized services and solutions that were designed and managed by highly qualified technical engineers and programmers. Instead of simply offering cheap and talented—but increasingly replicable—labor input, the company offered valuable IT services to clients, moving further up the value chain to providing complete

TABLE 5-8

Software firms in India: Responding to institutional voids

Spotting voids question	Specific void	Response
How strong is the country's education infrastructure, especially for technical and management training? Is data available to help sort out the quality of the country's educational institutions?	Underdeveloped educational system beyond global tier (labor market aggregators and distributors); under-developed certification intermediaries (labor market credibility enhancers)	Adapted: Exploited local knowledge and developed ability to identify talent
Are consumers willing to try new products and services? Do they trust goods from local companies? How about foreign companies?	Limited business-to-business market for services because sophisticated IT systems not pervasive in India and outsourcing of IT not widely adopted practice	Exited: Sought out customers in developed markets early in corporate histories

turnkey solutions for *Fortune* 500 companies, most of them based outside India (see table 5-8).

Business Groups

While executing any of the strategies discussed here, many prospective emerging giants have adopted business group organizations to reduce the costs of institutional voids in their home markets.[57] The Ayala Group in the Philippines, the Koç Group in Turkey, the Tata Group in India, Luksic Group in Chile, and Grupo Carso in Mexico are among the many successful emerging market-based business groups that have developed internal capabilities to deal with institutional voids in their respective countries. Think of business groups as agglomerations of firms that typically are legally independent, often diversified across a range of industries, and tied together to varying extents by formal links (equity ties, common board members, common brand names) and informal links, such as control by various members of a family.

As a form of organization, business groups are considered by many observers in developed Western markets to be anachronistic. This form of organization, however, makes sense in emerging markets in light of institutional voids. When entering a new line of business, group organizations often can bypass the voids faced by another start-up by using the capital, talent, or reputation built by another business in the group. The business group can thus serve as a private equity firm, executive search firm, and branding consultant in a market that lacks a sophisticated network of these intermediaries.

Ayala Corporation of the Philippines, for example, grew from a family real estate company into a highly diversified business group with holdings in telecommunications, financial services, IT, and other sectors (see figure 5-1 for the structure of major Ayala companies). Some of these firms were publicly traded (shaded gray in the figure).

To oversee the unlisted group companies, Ayala established AC Capital in 2002. AC Capital functioned somewhat like an internal venture capital or active investment management firm, filling an institutional void in

FIGURE 5-1

Ayala Corporation business group structure

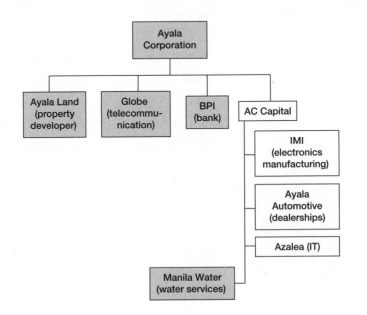

Source: Ayala Corporation Annual Report 2007.

risk capital provision. "AC Capital has a distinct mandate, which is to have a more active management of the emergent businesses," said Ayala treasurer Ramón Opulencia. "AC Capital plays the role of an investment company for them, deciding whether to nurture them or to harvest value for the corporation."[58] Manila Water Company, one of the companies nurtured under AC Capital, went public in 2005.[59] Ayala's group resources and time horizon enabled it to launch Globe Telecom in the face of steep challenges—high costs, sometimes contentious government relations, entrenched incumbents—that would have been much more difficult for a new entrepreneur to manage.[60]

A group structure can enable emerging market firms to develop a corporate brand name that signifies quality, trust, and transparency. Business groups can help defray the cost of building and maintaining a brand by spreading it across multiple arms of their businesses. The business media in emerging market countries abound with advertisements that promote group identity rather than merely emphasize the products or services of individual companies within a group. Once established, these brands wield tremendous power. Consumers in these countries value group brands; these groups have an incentive not to damage brand quality in any one business, because they will pay the price in other businesses as well.

A business group with a reputation for quality products and services can use its group name to enter new businesses, even if those businesses are unrelated to its current product lines. The Korean *chaebols* are perhaps most well known for extending their group identity over multiple product categories. The Samsung brand, for instance, emerged quickly worldwide as Samsung affiliates produced goods as wide ranging as televisions, commercial ships, chemicals, mobile phones, and microwave ovens.[61] Many groups in Brazil, China, India, Malaysia, and Turkey have successfully employed similar strategies of diversification.

Business groups can also exploit their reputations to raise capital in local stock markets. Diversified groups can point to their track record of returns to raise money from investors for new ventures. Business groups also can use their own internally generated capital to grow existing businesses, including those too small to obtain capital from financial institutions, or to enter new industries—in effect acting as venture capitalists.

Additionally, because of their ability to circumvent local institutional voids, established local business groups often become partners of choice for multinationals when they enter emerging markets. Group structures can also make emerging market companies more attractive to foreign investors eager to tap in to these fast-growth markets. With few reliable financial analysts and knowledgeable mutual fund managers to guide them, outsiders instead turn to diversified groups, which, in turn, invest in a wide range of industries. Investors trust groups to evaluate new opportunities and to exercise an auditing and supervisory function—in effect serving as quasi-mutual funds.

The groups thus become the conduit for large amounts of investment in their capital-starved countries. When Jardine Matheson—a business group based in Hong Kong—sought to invest in India, it purchased a 20 percent stake in Tata Industries (the Tata Group's new business development arm) in 1996, giving it exposure to a wide swath of industries in the country.

Group structures can also help emerging market firms access, attract, and develop management talent in the still-developing labor markets of their home countries. Management training intermediaries, such as business schools, are not well established in emerging markets, and conglomerate organizations can spread the fixed costs of professional development over the businesses in the group.

Many of the large groups in India, for example, have internal management development programs, often with dedicated facilities. These programs typically are geared toward developing the skills of experienced managers. Some groups, however, have instituted training programs for all levels of employees in an attempt to develop a broad range of human capital. Some of the Korean *chaebols* have set up special training programs in collaboration with top U.S. business schools.

The mobility of talent across industries in emerging markets is hindered by the absence of executive search firms in these countries. By offering opportunities and exposure to management challenges in a variety of industries, business group affiliates can attract managerial talent that they would not be able to do as stand-alone entities.

Finally, governments in emerging markets usually make it difficult for companies to adjust their workforces to changing economic conditions. Rigid laws often prevent companies from laying off employees, and labor unions insist on job security in the absence of government-provided unemployment benefits. The internal labor markets of business groups can help counteract these rigidities and offer job security in economies that have few safety nets. When one company in a group faces declining prospects, its employees can be transferred to other group companies that are on the rise—even to companies in otherwise undesirable locations.

Some Indian business groups, for example, have built communities around their production facilities in remote parts of the country. Because the group provides services such as schools, hospitals, and places of worship, and because there will eventually be career options in more attractive locations when the group is present, managers and other trained employees are more willing to relocate. The growing companies benefit by receiving a ready source of reliable employees.[62]

Groups are also able to put new talent to good use. By allocating talent to where it is most needed, conglomerates gain a head start in beginning new activities. Wipro Technologies in India, for example, successfully moved beyond computers into financial services by relocating skilled engineers first to computer-leasing services that would make use of their technical know-how and then to a broad range of financial services. In contrast, to build their operations, unaffiliated companies usually need to recruit publicly—a difficult proposition in countries where labor varies widely in quality and lacks certification from respected institutions.

There are risks, however, for emerging market-based companies that organize themselves as business groups. Even though internal financing within business groups offers the obvious advantage of its low cost relative to funding available through external arms-length sources in markets that lack specialized financial intermediaries, this funding method comes at a potential price. Without the external monitoring provided by arms-length investors, internal cash flows are more easily diverted to ill-advised investments.

Consider the experience of Sime Darby, a Malaysian group with interests spread across Southeast Asia in plantations, manufacturing, consumer products, financial services, and construction.[63] In the late 1990s, Sime Darby expanded into the banking sector, a fast-growing industry in which the company had relatively little expertise, in a move that arguably overstretched the group's competence.[64] Group structures can also add to the cost of raising external financing. The opaqueness of emerging market companies with complex organizational structures, particularly those with densely interlocking equity relationships between group companies, can deter external—particularly foreign—financiers.

In mature markets, conglomerates trade at a discount. The empirical evidence gathered to date seems to suggest that the benefits of group affiliation outweigh the costs in many emerging markets because of institutional voids, although the variance can be quite high.[65] Whether the benefits of a group structure outweigh the potential costs is a function of the quality of the group management. Adapting organizational form through business group organizations is one way in which prospective emerging giants can compensate for institutional voids.

Becoming an Emerging Giant

Prospective emerging giants face a raft of challenges as they navigate the growth opportunities of their home markets, the pressure of new foreign competition, and the obstacles of institutional contexts (see toolkit 5-1). Managing institutional voids is tough for prospective emerging giants, but they are better positioned to manage them than are multinationals. Moreover, multinationals often are not willing to invest in developing institutional infrastructure outside their home markets. Prospective emerging giants can use their ability to identify and manage institutional voids—and their willingness to invest in filling them—to gain competitive advantage.[66]

Collaboration can enable prospective emerging giants to acquire new capabilities, but these companies should be clear about which capabilities will add value to the company in light of the institutional context in their home markets. Business group organizations can help emerging market-based companies execute any response to institutional voids, but groups present challenges and sometimes costs. After establishing viable business models, prospective emerging giants face a new set of challenges as they globalize their businesses, as we discuss in the next chapter.

Toolkit 5-1
Toolkit for Emerging Giants Competing at Home

1. Self-Assessment

A. Business Model

What is the core of our business model?

2. Home Market Assessment

A. Defining the Opportunity

What is the opportunity for us in this emerging market?

What pieces of our business model are uniquely defensible from global competition?

B. Market Segmentation

What are the segments within this market opportunity?

What segments do we plan to target?

C. Spotting Institutional Voids

Using the "spotting institutional voids" toolkit, what are the institutional voids in this emerging market (and in these segments)?

How might this emerging market's institutional voids affect our ability to access our target market segments, particularly vis-à-vis foreign competition?

3. Responding to the Institutional Context

Using the following framework, how should we respond to the institutional voids we have identified in this emerging market?

Strategic choice	Options for emerging market-based companies
Replicate or adapt?	• Copy business model from developed markets. • Exploit local knowledge, capabilities, and ability to navigate institutional voids to build tailored business models.
Compete alone or collaborate?	• Compete alone. • Acquire capabilities from developed markets through partnerships or JVs with multinational companies to bypass institutional voids.
Accept or attempt to change market context?	• Take market context as given. • Fill institutional voids in service of own business.
Enter, wait, or exit?	• Build business in home market in spite of institutional voids. • Exit home market early in corporate history if capabilities unrewarded at home.

Six

Emerging Giants: Going Global

AFTER IDENTIFYING UNIQUE value propositions and establishing strong competitive positions in their home markets,
prospective emerging giants face a new set of challenges as they try to
develop into multinationals in their own right.[1] These companies aspire
to be world-class competitors, but how can they develop world-class
capabilities? They would like to be true global players operating in all
geographies, but the range of opportunities available to them is daunting. How should these firms think about globalizing their businesses?

Just as the home country origins of developed market-based multinationals matter as they enter emerging markets, the home country origins
of emerging giants matter as they globalize their businesses. It is difficult
for emerging giants to compete against world-leading players, particularly in developed markets, in part because of institutional voids in their
home markets that limit their access to, for example, expansion capital,
sophisticated R&D capabilities, and top-quality talent. Moreover, because
the unique institutional contexts of emerging markets demand custom-
tailored business models, these models need to be adapted to new markets having different contextual features. This chapter focuses on how
successful emerging giants manage these challenges as they move out of
their home markets.

Strategies for Going Global

Why are emerging giants going global? Global markets can offer these companies new customer bases, production platforms, or innovation centers. Emerging giants can expand beyond their borders for reasons of scale—enlarging their businesses and building cash flow or brand—or stretch, learning to do new things that their local environment may not facilitate.

Many emerging market-based companies were limited in the extent to which they could globalize until regulatory constraints, such as foreign exchange and capital controls, were gradually loosened during liberalization in the 1990s. As these emerging economies and stock markets surged and their attractiveness increased in the eyes of foreign portfolio investors, more resources were available for prospective emerging giants to invest in building international businesses.[2]

Some business models are intrinsically global, such as those that seek to use cheaper factor inputs in one part of the world to serve a demand in another region; examples are Indian software and IT consulting firms, or Chinese manufacturers. These companies are often global from their inception. Other business models can be contained entirely within country boundaries, particularly within large markets where companies can exploit economies of scale domestically. Not every emerging market-based firm can or should build a global footprint. If a particular company's inherent capabilities will not be rewarded outside its home market and if it lacks the resources or management bandwidth to adapt or acquire new capabilities in foreign markets, then delaying globalization—emphasizing opportunities elsewhere, including in their home markets—is often a smart approach.

For example, after a brief, unsuccessful entry into Western European markets in the 1990s, Titan—the watch and jewelry brand of India's Tata Group—chose to maintain a largely domestic focus. The brand succeeded in the Middle East, particularly among nonresident Indian populations, and developed a small retail presence in the United States. It also globalized part of its supply chain to Hong Kong. But by 2008, it had not yet sought to challenge the world's major watch and jewelry brands.[3] "To be a global watch player, you've got to have a Swiss brand," said one Tata Group executive. "Titan realizes that to become a serious watch player sometime they have to make a Swiss acquisition. Given its existing scale and given its existing resources, it says, 'Listen, until I get the financial muscle to take the big plunge, I will primarily be a domestic player.' So it dominates the domestic watch segment, dominates it."[4] Given the fast growth in these markets and the competitiveness of incoming multinationals, remaining exclusively domestic makes sense for many emerging giants. There are many world-class emerging market-based companies that are not quite as global as one might expect.[5]

Encouraged by flush balance sheets, enabled by regulatory changes, and compelled by home market overreliance and institutional voids as well as the globalization of industries, however, many emerging market-based companies have turned their attention overseas. Market selection is a critical strategic decision for these companies. Unlike many developed market-based companies that can afford to fail, companies from emerging markets with relatively limited resources and access to capital may have a one-shot opportunity to launch internationally.

Prospective emerging giants that decide to go global need to think systematically about how they should grow their businesses outside their home markets and which capabilities they need to seek out. Both of these decisions—where to go and what to acquire—should be related to these firms' initial sources of competitive advantage. The journeys of emerging giants that move into foreign markets vary widely, but they often reflect core capabilities developed in the companies' home markets. The origins of emerging giants in market contexts rife with institutional voids can hamper their globalization, but their ability to negotiate institutional voids can enable globalization to other markets having similar market structures. Emerging giants can also compensate for the institutional voids in their home markets through globalization by borrowing global market institutions to help build global capabilities.

Replicate Business Models in Markets with Structural Similarities

Experience operating amid institutional voids can position emerging giants to establish operations in other emerging markets having similar structural impediments—mirroring developed market-based multinationals that replicate their business models in the segments of emerging markets most similar to those in their home markets. To build scale, emerging giants can extend the models developed in their home markets into new markets. Companies whose business models focus on unique customer knowledge can expand to similar market segments in other emerging market countries.

Many companies based in emerging markets simply do not have the resources to launch a product or operational initiative in a developed market. However, experience meeting emerging market consumer needs, particularly at low price points, is an advantage for emerging market-based firms competing against mature market-based multinationals in developing markets. Similarly, emerging market-based companies whose business models are based on unique local factor markets can replicate their models in other emerging markets having factor inputs similar to their home markets. For example, after seeking out customers in developed markets early in their corporate histories, many Indian IT firms later developed software development centers in other emerging markets like China and some countries in Eastern Europe.

Adapt Business Models to Developed Markets

To be truly global companies, many emerging market-based companies aspire to operate and be competitive in the world's most developed markets. Entering these markets can enable emerging giants to learn how to compete amid developed market infrastructure, such as sophisticated retail channels, and cater to highly demanding customers. This experience can help prepare emerging giants to compete in their home markets as more developed market-based competition enters and as more sophisticated market infrastructure and more demanding customers emerge. Some emerging giants have targeted developed markets in part to build their brands and credibility in their home markets, which lack many of the market institutions that can provide credible market information and certify quality. Entering developed markets is a costly venture for emerging giants, particularly as they look to move up the value chain, but it can serve as a valuable long-term investment in building capabilities.

Like multinationals looking to establish a presence outside the global segment in emerging markets, emerging giants need to adapt to the market contexts of developed economies. Although these companies do not encounter institutional voids in developed economies to the extent they do at home, they need to compensate for the institutional voids of their home markets. Voids make it difficult for prospective emerging giants to rival the resources and capabilities of global multinationals in developed markets. Some emerging market-based firms have successfully adapted to developed markets and have compensated for home market voids by targeting underserved niches where their home market-developed capabilities will be rewarded as a point of entry.

Acquire Global Capabilities Through Global Institutions

For emerging giants, going global is a matter not only of entering new markets outside their borders but also of building global capabilities. To develop their capabilities, access capital, or build credibility, prospective emerging giants can access global institutions from developed markets to compensate for local institutional voids. Borrowing global institutions can take the form of listing on U.S. or other foreign stock exchanges (the approach of Indian IT firms Infosys and Wipro, among many others), seeking protections from developed market patent systems for their intellectual property (such as Korea's Samsung, one of the world's top patent holders), or acquiring companies in developed markets (the approach of Chinese firms Lenovo and TCL and several companies in India's Tata Group).

Most of these global institutions are available only to those prospective emerging giants that have identified and successfully exploited business models amid the institutional voids in their home markets. Global share listings will attract investors only if an emerging market-based company brings something new to the investor's proverbial table, through an established position in the home market, for example, and global acquisitions require prospective emerging giants to have amassed sufficient capital.

Although many of these initiatives are aimed at adding direct and tangible capabilities, such as capital, brands, or other resources, borrowing global institutions can be a particularly valuable tool for prospective emerging giants to improve their governance and build credibility.

In the rest of this chapter, we look at examples of emerging giants that have pursued these approaches as they have globalized their businesses (see table 6-1). Kuwait-based Zain grew into one of the world's largest telecommunications providers by targeting developing markets, particularly in Africa—exploiting its ability to cater to segments and manage voids in emerging product markets. India-based IT firm Tata Consultancy Services used its experience exploiting emerging factor markets in its operations in Latin America. China's Haier, Israel's Teva Pharmaceutical Industries, and ICICI Bank of India each adapted to developed markets by entering through niches that both avoided incumbent competition and exploited capabilities developed in their home markets. A number of emerging giants have globalized their capabilities by seeking out foreign capital markets, acquisition targets, and other institutions, in effect

TABLE 6-1

Case examples

Strategic challenge	Examples
Replicate business models in markets having structural similarities	Zain Tata Consultancy Services Iberoamerica
Adapt business models to developed markets	Haier Teva Pharmaceutical Industries ICICI Bank
Acquire global capabilities through global institutions to compensate for voids	Overseas listings Overseas acquisitions

borrowing developed market institutions to compensate for institutional voids in their home markets.

Replicate Business Models in Markets with Structural Similarities: Zain

Kuwait-based telecommunications provider Zain knew that it would need to extend its footprint beyond its home region to attain global scale and capabilities.[6] Unlike some emerging giants, however, Zain saw entering developed markets relatively early in its globalization as a stretch. Zain "wanted to go grow internationally and we knew that we had to look at developing markets or else pay a lot," said one company executive. "We saw a lot of potential in Africa—but it was a big gamble."[7] Zain had been a pioneer in developing mobile telephony service in Kuwait and the Gulf region and was similarly intrepid as it invested in the development of mobile communications in sub-Saharan Africa.

The company saw its familiarity with the region as an advantage. "Being adjacent to Africa, being people that have long historical ties, whether it's geographical, cultural, religious, and other ties with Africa . . . we think we know Africa and we are more concerned with Africa than others," said one company executive.[8] Zain quickly grew its business in Africa and across the Middle East by replicating its ability to manage institutional and infrastructural voids in developing markets and to reach the local and bottom-of-the-market customer segments. The institutional voids in African markets—and the perceptions thereof—were barriers to entry for many large global multinationals. Exploiting these untapped opportunities—actively identifying and filling infrastructural and institutional voids—enabled Zain to differentiate itself from competitors and globalize its business.

Zain, then called MTC, had moved into sub-Saharan Africa by acquiring Celtel in 2005, a $3.4 billion deal that was, at the time, the largest investment from the Middle East in Africa.[9] Established with the assistance of development organizations in 1999, Celtel had grown its footprint quickly by purchasing affordably priced mobile licenses from African governments eager to increase telecommunications penetration rates, which were among the lowest in the world.[10]

By the time of the acquisition, Celtel had established a successful brand in Africa, but Zain faced a number of challenges in adapting to and expanding in the continent's markets. Although Celtel's business in Africa was predicated on filling voids through its development of telecommunications infrastructure, Zain found that it needed to fill other voids in these markets to grow its business there, particularly as a first mover in many markets. In addition to the absent physical telecommunications infrastructure that the company had to develop, other voids ranged from the absence of banks—requiring the company to collect cash—to inadequate electricity supply for its base stations. In Nigeria, for example, the company purchased five thousand generators in a single day. In some of the markets in which it operated, Zain produced more electricity than the country's power company.[11] (In Iraq, Zain similarly built four thousand kilometers of transmission lines in two years by mid-2008 and employed a "small army" of eleven hundred security guards to protect employees and network base stations and switches.)[12]

Zain's move into Africa was bold in its scale and attracted attention from large competitors from the Middle East and multinationals based in more developed markets. "I used to tell the people at [Zain] when we came to Africa that we had a two-year window before we generate attractiveness to this region," said a company executive. "The challenge is how we fill up these two years in the best possible way."[13] Relentless focus on differentiation from existing and potential competitors by filling voids was critical to Zain's approach in Africa.

Zain looked beyond differentiation by products and prices and saw that its biggest advantage—or potential advantage—vis-à-vis its competitors was its large regional footprint. Zain leveraged this presence with the introduction of One Network in Kenya, Tanzania, Uganda, the Democratic Republic of the Congo, Republic of the Congo, and Gabon in September 2006. One Network made mobile phone service borderless across the six countries. Under the service, customers could make calls and send text messages at local rates without roaming charges and, in the case of prepaid subscribers, add minutes to accounts in any of the countries. When One Network debuted, the *Economist* noted, "Celtel has, in effect, created a unified market of the kind that regulators can only dream about in Europe."[14] The initiative was targeted at the local and bottom-of-the-market segments. "The rich have no problem with roaming," said one company executive. "It's the poor that [have] a problem with roaming. We created it for the prepaid cards."[15]

The successful offering resulted from an organizational openness to innovation. "We have not asked for the One Network," said a company executive. "It's an initiative that has come up from the field. It's not us as management, [saying,] 'Please look for a strategic competitive advantage for us.' Our people thought of it out of experimenting [in] the field, and when it was proposed, we went for it."[16] A company executive describes the company's approach to differentiation, not in terms of strategy or value proposition but in terms of organization and ethic:

> We all buy the networks from the same great suppliers, and any product and service you can produce in no time. That's why we opted to differentiate ourselves on the community level . . . style of leadership, HR, the way we organize ourselves, the way we manage ourselves, our outlook to the world, our attitude . . . Could [One Network] be copied? Yes, but by the time it is copied, we will have something else. That's the whole point—a string of sustainable advantages. It's easy to clone any product, service, or technology. It's not easy to clone a community.[17]

Like many successful multinationals from developed markets operating in emerging markets, Zain was able to grow quickly by positioning itself as a partner in progress. "A great asset is your relationship with the communities you serve and how you position yourself to the world," said a company executive. "That is the differentiation we seek."[18] Zain invested $14 billion in its first two-and-a-half years in Africa, making it the continent's largest-ever investor, and created eight jobs in support services outside the company for every job it created inside the company.[19] The company became the largest taxpayer in many of the markets in which it operated in Africa.[20] "So of course people love us," said a company executive. "You have to invest in the future of this continent. This is turning around the whole continent, not a country. That's the history-making mission we are in."[21]

Unlike many emerging giants, which have rushed to enter developed markets, Zain was holding off as of 2008—emphasizing opportunities elsewhere. This strategy could be attributed in part to the nature of the telecommunications industry in these markets, such as high penetration and costly service and asset prices in Europe. "We want to apply our limited resources wherever it brings us the maximum value right in the beginning, because that's growth," a company executive said. "The strategy is to hurry—first-mover advantage—in an untapped market . . . and then become bigger and stronger in many ways and then refine yourself and reposition . . . for the next stage."[22]

At the prospect of facing more squarely the large developed market-based providers, such as Vodafone and Telefónica, Zain saw its origins as an advantage. Having operated in markets rife with institutional and other infrastructural voids, Zain had been, in the words of a company executive, prepared "to be more effective, more agile, and more capable than the larger companies in the long run. This is what we are betting on."[23] Zain was more worried about other large emerging market-based firms, such as Bharti Airtel and China Mobile, which emerged from similar contexts.[24]

Zain transformed itself from a government-controlled monopoly with only 600,000 customers in Kuwait in 2002 into the world's fastest-growing wireless telecommunications provider with 32 million customers in twenty-two countries across the Middle East and Africa by 2008. By buying Celtel, Zain quickly acquired a significant footprint in Africa. Replicating its ability to operate in developing markets by investing in filling market voids, targeting poorer customers, and serving as a partner in progress, Zain was able to stay ahead of incoming competitors (see table 6-2).

Replicate Business Models in Markets with Structural Similarities: Tata Consultancy Services Iberoamerica

Tata Consultancy Services (TCS), the Tata Group's IT consulting and software services firm, developed into an emerging giant by exploiting

TABLE 6-2

Zain: Responding to contextual challenges in globalization

Contextual challenge	Response
Underdeveloped soft and hard infrastructure in developing markets	Replicated: Managed and filled voids in energy supply, banking system, telecommunications infrastructure, and security (in Iraq)
Difficult to reach local and bottom market segments	Replicated: Applied experience targeting poorer customers with prepaid cards and developed One Network

the high quality and cost advantages of Indian technical talent and the company's privileged ability to identify, sort, and manage that talent amid the institutional voids in its home market. Later in its journey, like many other factor market-based emerging giants, TCS sought to replicate its model to deliver services from other developing markets having factor market characteristics similar to those of India. Building a "global network delivery model" across other emerging markets compelled TCS—like Zain—to fill institutional voids as a source of differentiation and competitive advantage, as illustrated by the development of Tata Consultancy Services Iberoamerica (TCSI), the company's subsidiary covering Latin America, Spain, and Portugal.

Developing operations in Latin America offered several advantages to TCS. The region was an additional source of talent at a time when salaries for technical workers in India had increased on demand from the outsourcing boom there.[25] Beyond salaries, the growth of the outsourcing industry meant that the best technical talent in India could find positions in desirable shifts, so the overnight shift posed staffing challenges to TCS.[26] "The third shift in India, which is our main shift in the United States, is chaos," said one company executive. "Forty percent turnover."[27] Latin American operations could help TCS cover this shift. As one TCS executive noted, "When [a customer] has a problem, he doesn't want to wait for India to wake up and all that. He wants that solved today."[28] As part of the TCS global model, TCSI sought to complement, not try to replace, its operations in India.[29]

TCSI established operations in Uruguay, a decision based in large part on features of the country's institutional context, such as its political stability and high level of education. Uruguay's small size and the government's desire to create jobs in a country with high unemployment meant that TCSI could be influential in its government relations. An arrangement with Uruguay's Ministry of Foreign Relations enabled TCSI to secure a business visa for a foreign TCS employee to come to the country within twenty-four hours, a process that would take four months, on average, in Brazil, and eight weeks in Mexico.[30] TCSI both brought in employees to Latin America from India and trained its first local hires at training centers in India so that it could replicate its home market model.[31] "We tried to do India in Latin America," said one company executive. "Everything has been invented in India. Bring it here, we'll localize somewhat, but let's be another India."[32]

TCSI faced both local and multinational competition and was wary of possible entry by its Indian rivals, such as Infosys and Wipro. The local competition was "mostly bodyshopping," according to one company executive, with Accenture and IBM dominating the top end of the market. "They had owned the market, and they still own the market, never paid any attention because they owned the market anyhow."[33]

TCSI sought to differentiate itself from the current competition by focusing on quality. The firm exploited a global credibility enhancer to attest to the quality of its capabilities by becoming the first firm in Latin America with Capability Maturity Model Integration (CMMI) level 5 certification.[34] TCSI also sought to raise a barrier to entry to potential competition from India by establishing scale quickly and quietly. "If I have a hundred and somebody else comes in with forty, I mean, there's no difference," said one company executive. "[But] if I have a thousand, they're going to have to make a major investment."[35]

Institutional voids in education—missing labor market aggregators, distributors, and credibility enhancers—hampered TCSI's ability to grow in the region. "'Right now I have five hundred job openings I can't fill, and the problem is education,'" a company executive told *New York Times* columnist Thomas Friedman in 2006. "'The prestige career to follow in

India is engineering, and in Latin America it is [still] law or being a notary public.'"[36] TCSI's early success attracted rivals to the region, further stretching the talent pool, so the company decided to fill the institutional void by establishing a regional training center in Uruguay in 2007.[37] TCSI sees this strategy also as a way in which the firm can move up the value chain, according to a company executive:

> We had something called outsourcing 1.0: let's try to get the costs down and send everything to India. Now outsourcing looks strategic. [W]e have squeezed everything we could from the technical [people]. We're very efficient in the systems. The maintenance is good. I think the next wave of outsourcing is giving business value. For me it's easier to get a guy who is ten years in banking and teach him some technology so he knows how to apply the technology than to get someone who knows Java very well and teach him banking. It would take me years to do. So I am betting that the next wave of outsourcing is going to be more about business knowledge than about technical knowledge. And I have lots of people that I can tap—even in a place like Uruguay—who are accountants, who are bankers, who are all kinds of professions—who I can bring in and teach them technology. So that's why I am setting up my own university—because I cannot wait for the education system to change.[38]

Just as Haier developed its own distribution network in China, McDonald's cultivated suppliers in Russia, and Zain offered One Network in sub-Saharan Africa, TCSI bet on filling institutional voids as a source of differentiation and competitive advantage, replicating its success at home (see table 6-3). By 2007, TCSI had grown to five thousand employees in fourteen countries, accounting for 4 percent of TCS worldwide revenues.[39] As the financial crisis and global recession of 2008–2009 pushes companies to pare back on costs even more, outsourcing to Latin America is tipped to increase further, bringing TCSI more opportunities but likely also more competition.[40]

TABLE 6-3

TCS Iberoamerica: Responding to contextual challenges in globalization

Contextual challenge	Response
Underdeveloped training and certification intermediaries to build operations in Uruguay	Replicated: Exploited talent and training from operations in India; attained CMMI level 5 certification; established technology training institution

Adapt Business Models to Developed Markets: Haier

Through its early development—as described in chapter 5—Haier engaged foreign multinationals as contract manufacturing customers and joint venture partners and competed against global brands as they entered China.[41] By 1997, Haier had established itself as a dominant brand in China but faced the prospect of intensifying foreign competition and slimmer profit margins.[42] In that year, the company began charting a strategy to become a multinational organization and global brand in its own right.

Starting in the mid-1990s, the company had opened production facilities in other emerging markets—Indonesia, Malaysia, and the Philippines—not unlike the replication strategies of Zain and TCSI. To be a global company beyond emerging markets, Haier needed to adapt its portfolio of offerings, most importantly by targeting a niche in the U.S. market, enabling the company to learn about the market and develop relationships with major retailers.

Developed markets were home to Haier's largest global competitors. By playing in their backyards, Haier hoped to learn better how to compete against the brands that posed the most serious long-term threat to its market position in China. By gaining experience in navigating the mature distribution networks and discerning retail channels of developed markets, Haier could be better prepared to compete at home and in other maturing markets where the institutional voids that the company had exploited—missing product market aggregators and distributors—would lose relevance over time.

Although building a brand organically in developed markets can be a costly approach for emerging market-based companies, the premium attached to such a brand can be valuable in other, particularly emerging, markets (as a substitute for product market information analyzers and advisers). Haier was able to leverage its experience and reputation in developed markets to access prized distribution channels in other emerging markets. Moreover, Haier hoped that having even a few successful products in developed markets would burnish the brand's reputation, enabling the company to introduce the full line of products to developing markets immediately upon market entry. In addition to serving as a credibility enhancer, operating in developed markets forced Haier to uphold high standards of quality that might be rewarded by customers at home as they increasingly demanded global-level quality.

Haier brought own-branded products to developed markets only after establishing competitive standards of quality. Among its early foreign contract manufacturing ventures, the company had partnered with appliance company Liebherr to sell refrigerators in Germany under the Blue Line brand. After a German magazine awarded eight top rankings to Blue Line—more than the seven awarded to Liebherr—Haier decided to bring own-branded products to developed markets. The foreign market intermediary served as a credibility enhancer, giving Haier confidence that it could hold its own in these markets.

Haier emerged from a crucible of competition in China by exploiting its product market expertise and by quick reaction and experimentation to meet local customer needs. The company transferred this capability as it globalized. When it entered the U.S. market in 1999, Haier initially focused on unpopulated niche segments in the white goods market to avoid directly competing against the market's dominant brands. Haier started by selling compact refrigerators, such as those used in offices, hotels, and college dorm rooms—a segment eschewed by many large U.S. manufacturers because of its low volumes and low prices. Electric wine cellars—inexpensive stand-alone refrigerated cabinets for storing bottles of wine—were another niche successfully exploited by Haier in the United States. "We started on the fringe, building more the niche products for the market," said one company executive. "Wine cellars can't be considered a core appliance, yet it is a big business."[43] With minimal competition, such niche products initially brought in high margins.

The company did not see Chinese personnel or low prices as sources of competitive advantage. Haier relied on an almost exclusively American staff for its U.S. operations.[44] "We behave as if we are Haier America," said one company executive. "We don't behave as if we're Chinese."[45] Although based in a low-cost market, the company knew that cost alone was not a sustainable competitive advantage and sought to differentiate itself on quality, innovation, and service—several of the key ways in which the company differentiated itself from competition in China.[46]

Haier continued to work for developed market-based companies, even competitors, as a contract manufacturer to build global-level quality and capabilities. This work helped Haier acquire not only know-how but also credibility, as one company executive related. Speaking of Haier's work on commercial air conditioners with U.S.-based heating and cooling equipment producer Trane, he noted, "Trane sent a team of engineers into our plant to help us develop an air conditioner that we really didn't know how to build . . . That's really made us a better company . . . from a man-ufacturing standpoint. It also earned us a lot of credit in the market because it's sort of an open secret that we manufacture for Trane. So by default, our product[s] must be very good if it's good enough for Trane."[47]

Haier's other key competitive advantage at home—its willingness to invest in market infrastructure in logistics and distribution—would not transfer to developed markets that did not feature such voids. Instead, Haier needed to access the prime U.S. product market aggregators and distributors—big box retailers. It took Haier one year to arrange an appointment with Walmart, but by demonstrating product quality and success with its few initial niche products, Haier convinced retailers to stock a wide range of its appliances. "We have to take all the barriers away," said one company executive. "We have to be better from a quality standpoint. We have to offer a better warranty. We have to offer a better price. We have to offer better aesthetics. That's a tremendous challenge. And then, after we do all of that, we have to convince the person on the floor who is selling the product that we're right."[48] Establishing strong relationships with retailers such as Walmart and Best Buy in the United States not only offered Haier access to important U.S. distribution channels but also had the potential to help the company in China as foreign retailers established themselves there.

Exploiting niches enabled Haier to establish a presence in a highly competitive market such as the United States and build relations with some of the country's major retailers. Focusing on niche products also introduced the risk of being pigeonholed, leaving Haier unable to move into major appliances. "As a brand, Haier doesn't work," noted one U.S.-based industry analyst in 2002. "People may buy a dorm refrigerator from Haier, but I don't think they'll spend a lot of money on an appliance from a company they've never heard of."[49]

When Haier attempted to match the quality—and price—of the highest-end refrigerators on the U.S. market in 2007, it faced difficulties. The company introduced a $2,000 refrigerator that was developed and manufactured at its production facility in South Carolina, reportedly at a cost ten times the equivalent development costs in China.[50] The product was slow to sell because of the U.S. economic downturn, coupled with Haier's limited brand recognition in that product segment.[51] Haier had previously targeted the equivalent of the "local" market segment in the United States with compact refrigerators and rapidly moved to target the top market segment. This jump proved challenging.

As an emerging market-based company looking to compete in the world's most competitive market against powerful, established brands, Haier faced a number of challenges in the United States (see table 6-4). To avoid the brunt of the market's largest brands, Haier adapted its product portfolio, identifying and exploiting niches that were underserved by the major U.S. competitors. To compensate for the low recognition of its brand, Haier needed to pursue big box retailers aggressively, both to stock and to publicize its products. Even after finding early success through these strategies, Haier faced an uphill climb in high-end product segments.

Haier hoped its brand-building efforts in developed markets would allow it to reap advantages in other emerging markets, but in India, the

TABLE 6-4

Haier: Responding to contextual challenges in globalization

Contextual challenge	Response
Limited local knowledge in developed market	Adapted: Hired local management and staff
Limited ability to build brand in developed market	Adapted: Targeted underserved niche product segments
Limited ability to access big box retail distribution channels	Adapted: Used niche products to establish reputation for quality with retailers

company discovered the challenges of that market's institutional voids. "In the United States you can easily find the top 10 chain stores," noted one company executive. "But in India, you cannot find them" because of missing product market information analyzers and advisers.[52]

Building a powerful brand and organization based on institutional voids in the face of the tough competition in China was a significant challenge for Haier. To build a business in the United States, Haier needed to adapt to a different competitive and institutional context. Even after establishing a successful track record in the U.S. market, however, Haier—like other multinationals—encountered new institutional voids in other emerging markets.

Adapt Business Models to Developed Markets: Teva Pharmaceutical Industries

Teva Pharmaceutical Industries developed from a small foundation in Israel by effectively exploiting the factor market advantages in its home market—the deep pool of scientific expertise in Israel.[53] "I used to say in the early days that we have more PhDs per square inch than any other country," a company executive said.[54] To enter foreign markets and grow to become the world's largest producer of generic pharmaceuticals, the company, like Haier, needed to adapt to the contexts and competition of developed markets.

Teva began charting a strategy for globalization with the realization that it had the capabilities of a full-sized company—capabilities that would, if brought to bear in a large developed market, make Teva a billion-dollar company. Teva's growth targets had always been incremental, but this "billion-dollar theory" recalibrated these goals.

Geographic proximity and cultural familiarity suggested Europe as a natural first destination for Teva's international business, but the region's institutional context suggested otherwise. Price controls and the wide variation in the regulatory environments in different European markets would have made the region particularly challenging as Teva's first major foray outside Israel. The United States, by contrast, offered a uniform and liberalizing market for generic pharmaceuticals. Although emerging giants will not encounter institutional voids in developed markets as pervasive as those in their home markets, the most successful of these companies have aligned their business models with the institutional contexts of foreign markets.

Entering as large and competitive a market as the United States was a risky move for a relatively small, emerging market-based enterprise such as Teva in the mid-1980s. To minimize risk and acquire expertise in the new market, Teva sought out a joint venture with W. R. Grace & Company. "You start from a local company understanding the local environment," a Teva executive noted. "We had an advantage that the health-care system in Israel is very advanced, but at the same time, when we came to the States I said, 'Maybe we know English, but we don't know American.'"[55]

Teva said that it would contribute to the partnership whatever resources it could marshal—except significant capital. A member of the board of Teva's North America business recalled, "Here comes Teva, a nothing company from a tiny country . . . and somehow, [Eli] Hurvitz [Teva's chairman] manages to structure a deal where Grace puts in over 90% of the capital for 50% of the joint venture. Who else could negotiate that kind of deal? . . . Grace was so much bigger than us at the time, and yet Mr. Grace himself used to come to the office just to spend time with Eli. He viewed him as an equal. That was part of the genius of Hurvitz."[56]

Mastering the U.S. regulatory environment was critical to Teva's success in the market. The company was able to execute applications to

U.S. regulators to produce generic drugs more quickly than competitors, helping the company attain permission to produce during a coveted exclusivity period. The scope of Teva's operation was also critical. Teva's entry and expansion in the market coincided with the expansion of U.S. national pharmacy chains. By enlisting Teva, with its wide scope of products, the chains reduced their sourcing costs—cutting out wholesalers and distributors—and took advantage of Teva's volume-based discounts and inventory management. Teva filled a void for these growing chains.

Teva successfully established itself as a top generic pharmaceuticals firm in the U.S. market. In 2006, every American consumed, on average, more than one hundred tablets per year produced by Teva.[57] As a generics producer, however, Teva's profits were a fraction of those of innovative pharmaceutical producers.[58]

Teva was tempted to move up the value chain and enter the innovative pharmaceuticals business—just as Haier took on the top U.S. brands in high-end products—but such a strategy posed serious challenges, particularly in research and marketing. The innovative pharmaceutical industry was dominated by a few firms—Big Pharma—with massive R&D budgets that even a highly successful generics producer such as Teva could not match. The innovative business also required a different approach to marketing. Teva's customers in a market like the United States were pharmacists who could substitute generic alternatives for more expensive branded options at their discretion. The development of national pharmacy chains in effect consolidated Teva's customer base in the market. In the innovative business, however, physicians—and not pharmacists—were the customers, and reaching them entailed much more substantial investments in marketing.

Teva circumvented these challenges and moved into the innovative pharmaceuticals business by identifying a niche where it could exploit its inherent capabilities. The company minimized its R&D disadvantage vis-à-vis Big Pharma by exploiting its relationships with the scientific research community in Israel to build on original research instead of developing drugs on its own. In terms of marketing, the company avoided incurring the costs of expensive marketing by bringing an innovative drug to market that would not require such a significant investment. A company executive explained Teva's approach:

> Niches usually are a small product. We said no. Our limitation is not that we don't know [how] to count a lot of money. Just try me. Our problem is that we don't have the marketing power to reach tens of thousands or hundreds of thousands of doctors. And that's why we have chosen a niche of neurologists that are dealing with [multiple sclerosis]— . . . 1,500 doctors [in the United States]. With 1,500 doctors, we know how to deal much better than the Big Pharma because that's what we have in Israel . . . if you take specialists. That's a number . . . we know how to deal with.[59]

Teva's first innovative drug, Copaxone, became a blockbuster treatment for multiple sclerosis, generating worldwide sales of $1.2 billion in 2005 and contributing significantly to Teva's profits.

As Teva moved into the innovative pharmaceuticals space, Big Pharma pursued the generics business more aggressively. Facing such competition, Teva—not unlike Zain—saw its origins as an advantage. "It is very easy to manage a generic company when you are poor," a company executive noted. "It becomes very complicated when you are rich. It is impossible for a rich company to act poor. As long as we remember this equation, and we do not become bureaucrats, and as long as we fight the fat culture, we will succeed."[60]

When Teva looked to globalize its business, it sought out the market having an institutional context most amenable to its model and adapted to it (see table 6-5). To establish itself in the United States, Teva needed to acquire capabilities through its partnership with W. R. Grace. As the company expanded into the higher-value innovative pharmaceuticals, it exploited the capabilities to which it had privileged access—the scientific research community in Israel—to target an accessible niche. Later in its corporate history, Teva expanded its footprint through major acquisitions of Ivax and Barr Pharmaceuticals and managed well through the global recession of 2008–2009 as cost cutting made generics all the more attractive.[61]

TABLE 6-5

Teva Pharmaceutical Industries: Responding to contextual challenges in globalization

Contextual challenge	Response
Limited local knowledge in developed market	Adapted: Partnered with W. R. Grace
Limited ability to market in large developed market	Adapted: Targeted underserved niche product segment
Limited ability to rival Big Pharma R&D	Adapted: Exploited relationships with research institutes in Israel

Adapt Business Models to Developed Markets: ICICI Bank

Both Haier and Teva developed global strategies that leveraged capabilities they developed in their home markets. Part of Haier's success in China can be attributed to its willingness and ability to adapt products to local needs. Similarly, the company identified local product segments to establish a foothold in the United States. Teva drew on its relationship with external research institutes in Israel to compete against the large R&D budgets of Big Pharma in a portion of the U.S. market similar in scale to Teva's home market. Similarly, Indian bank ICICI identified niches in developed markets to establish a global business, limiting its ambition early on to segments of foreign markets where its home market capabilities would be rewarded.[62] ICICI built a global business by following Indian companies as they expanded overseas and filling a cross-border institutional void of offering seamless remittances and other financial services for nonresident Indians (NRIs).

Born with a mandate to fill institutional voids in India's capital markets by providing development finance, ICICI developed into a large, full-service financial institution, offering corporate banking, retail banking, insurance, asset management, venture capital, and other financial services. Whereas larger rivals already had significant branch networks, ICICI focused on alternative distribution channels, such as ATMs and Internet banking. The bank began installing three ATMs per day—at a time when India had only forty ATMs. In 2001, retail banking was a growing but still small share of ICICI's overall business. Unable to match the branch infrastructure of rivals in India, ICICI looked for ways to leverage its domestic strengths in the international marketplace.

ICICI viewed globalizing its business as a strong imperative for a number of reasons.[63] First, as the Indian corporations that were ICICI customers in India globalized their own businesses, it was important for ICICI to follow them for offensive and defensive reasons. The globalization of Indian business meant new opportunities in a wider range of corporate banking activities, such as trade finance, treasury and corporate lending, and investment banking. Although ICICI still had untapped—and insecure—opportunities in India, the bank was vulnerable to foreign competition expanding its presence in the country. ICICI could deepen existing business relationships by gaining the international business of these clients (who might otherwise work with foreign banks overseas) but also protect its business from foreign competition already operating in India—competitors that offered ICICI's clients more seamless service offerings for both domestic and international financial needs.

Second, pursuing international business might help ICICI diversify its risk and access new pools of capital. International business might reduce ICICI's country and credit risk of dependence on the Indian market, particularly domestic corporations. Finally, going global would give the bank exposure to best practices in foreign markets, experience that would help ICICI build its capabilities and, defensively, help it compete against foreign banks in India.

The large state-run Indian banks had built international presence, but none were particularly successful. The banks staffed their branches outside India with Indian personnel who had little exposure to or experience in the business environments in which they were posted. Marketing and product innovation by these foreign branches were minimal. Poor technology in these operations—and loan approval processes that were routed through India—slowed credit decisions. Nonperforming asset levels were high, and profitability was low in these international operations, leading to high closure rates.

ICICI's globalization strategy exploited its domestic success in catering to Indian companies and, in its retail business, in sidestepping expensive branch networks through alternative distribution channels. The bank targeted Indian companies expanding overseas and NRIs for remittances and other financial services. The Indian diaspora, from blue-collar workers in the Middle East to wealthy professionals in the United States, United Kingdom, and other developed countries, numbered 20 million in 130 countries and held a huge amount of wealth. Remittances were a large source of capital in India—three times the total foreign direct investment in India in 2001—and NRIs were promising potential customers for deposits, mutual funds, wealth management, other financial services, and even real estate services for those returning to India for short stints or purchasing real estate as an investment. ICICI filled cross-border capital market voids for the Indian diaspora, as a transaction facilitator for remittances and real estate transactions and as an information analyzer and adviser for NRIs looking to invest in India. ICICI's brand and experience in India gave the bank a relative advantage in filling this void compared with foreign competitors.

ICICI succeeded where the large state-run Indian banks failed, and it did so through sharp execution and by leveraging partnerships to enter new markets. ICICI sought out partners that were leading players in target markets but were not already present in India. Partnerships enabled ICICI to expand into new markets more quickly and less expensively than it could independently. Partnerships might also serve as opportunities for ICICI to build capabilities and gain local expertise and, because its partners were not already present in India, pitch ventures as symbiotic relationships through which ICICI could exploit its strong brand name to bring wealthy NRIs into the foreign partner bank's client ranks.

ICICI elected to enter the Gulf states first through a partnership with Emirates Bank in Dubai, offering dual accounts—one in Dubai and one in India—through which customers could seamlessly transfer funds. Later, ICICI joined with Lloyds TSB in the United Kingdom. In addition to dual accounts and seamless transfer, ICICI placed a service desk within Lloyds branches, particularly to handle mortgage services.

ICICI built a valuable brand in India and sought to exploit it to build its international business. The bank targeted its marketing at specific communities within the Indian diaspora through ethnic Indian media and events held in regions that were common destinations of those communities.[64] ICICI's international business broke even in its first year, and by 2005, international operations contributed more than 10 percent of the bank's profits. ICICI's share of the remittance market increased from 3 percent in FY 2002 to 15 percent in FY 2005. The bank's market share in India, meanwhile, increased from 10 percent to 35 percent from 2001 to 2005.

ICICI had only a limited presence in developed markets, and its international exposure took a toll in the midst of the global financial crisis in 2008–2009.[65] Nevertheless, its approach to globalization illustrates how emerging giants can adapt their models to serviceable niches that leverage home market capabilities. Like Haier's contract manufacturing and Teva's joint venture with W. R. Grace, ICICI's partnerships show the value of collaboration as emerging giants enter developed market contexts (see table 6-6).

Acquire Global Capabilities Through Global Institutions

To compensate for home market voids and to fast-track entry into foreign markets, emerging giants can look to acquire global capabilities through global institutions. For example, Zain leapt into Africa with its acquisition

TABLE 6-6

ICICI Bank: Responding to contextual challenges in globalization

Contextual challenge	Response
Expense and regulatory constraints on building branch network in developed markets	Adapted: Partnered with local banks
Limited ability to build brand in developed market	Adapted: Targeted Indian corporate customers and NRI populations in developed markets

of Celtel. The acquisition gave Zain an established brand, substituting for the absence of information analyzers and advisers. Tata Consultancy Services Iberoamerica borrowed global credibility when it sought to establish itself by attaining CMMI level 5 certification. The German product rating publication certified the quality of Haier's Blue Line products, instilling confidence that the company was ready to enter developed markets on its own. Teva and ICICI both borrowed through their partnerships in developed markets.

In some cases, emerging market firms do not need to seek out foreign institutional intermediaries overseas. Many developed market intermediaries, such as management consulting firms and investment banks, have set up shop in these emerging markets to profit from filling institutional voids not only for existing multinational clients but also for prospective emerging giants. In the talent market, many U.S. business schools have launched educational programs in Singapore, Thailand, and China, enabling emerging market companies to train and recruit employees whose skills are comparable to those working for multinationals. World-class emerging market companies with sound business propositions can therefore access levels of capital and talent that are somewhat similar to those available to multinationals in developed markets, although in practice various hurdles of regulation and reputation often make this option hard to exercise.

Overseas stock market listings and foreign acquisitions are two common ways in which emerging giants can seek out new capabilities from developed markets, but neither is a panacea, as we discuss next.

Listing Overseas

Listing overseas can help emerging market-based firms circumvent the institutional voids and other limitations of financial markets in their home countries.[66] South African Breweries (SAB), for example, moved its headquarters to London and pursued a listing on the London Stock Exchange in 1999 in part because of the state of its home market's capital markets. South Africa generated more than half of SAB's profits at the time, but the South African rand was depreciating. The company turned to global capital markets to circumvent the costs of raising capital in the underdeveloped South African capital markets. Another example is Mexico-based cement producer Cemex. As it expanded into other emerging markets, it raised debt through a subsidiary in Spain starting in 1996 to avoid a "Mexico discount" and raised equity through an American depository receipt (ADR) issue in New York. Cemex leveraged its home market business capabilities to enter other markets, many of which were similarly emerging, but simultaneously raised expansion capital in developed markets.[67]

However, incurring the costs of accessing institutions in developed markets usually is worthwhile only for high-quality firms. Overseas listings require the implementation of changes in financial reporting and attendant internal organizational changes, which can be significant and costly. Lower-quality firms face steeper costs when listing overseas, but successful overseas listings can serve as credible signals of quality to potential customers and factor market providers.[68]

For example, leading Indian software companies, such as Infosys Technologies and Wipro Technologies, have listed on U.S. stock markets in large part to help attract customers as well as talent. These listings allow firms to offer dollar-denominated stock options, something that can be critical to attract software programmers in the competitive worldwide market. By listing on the New York Stock Exchange or NASDAQ, emerging market firms subject themselves to rigorous disclosure requirements and other norms that offer a measure of credibility and reassurance to potential customers, which might otherwise be concerned about doing business with an entity based in a market having weak contractual enforcement.

Infosys, for example, was among the Indian software firms least in need of capital when it listed on NASDAQ, our research has found, although it was at the forefront of Indian software firms establishing international corporate governance standards. In fact, Infosys adopted these standards long before it listed internationally, and, when it did list on NASDAQ in March 1999, it voluntarily subjected itself to the more rigorous standards required of domestic companies listed on the exchange instead of the standards for foreign firms.[69] Reflecting on the overseas listing of Indian software firms, a member of the Securities and Exchange Board of India said, "The industry that probably needs capital the least, went after the international capital markets most aggressively . . . In fact many of these companies don't know what to do with the capital they raised."[70] These companies have pursued listings on international capital markets largely for other reasons, such as building credibility and developing mechanisms to retain employees.

Institutional voids often compel emerging market-based firms to list overseas, but they also raise the costs for firms to do so. When Compañía de Teléfonos de Chile (CTC) issued Chile's first ADR in 1990, it faced the challenge of overcoming the perceptions of political and financial risk held by international institutional investors who would be evaluating a firm from that country for the first time.[71] "We had to go through an education process within Chile and with foreign investors," recalled an executive who successfully orchestrated the ADR issue for CTC. "We have definitely done the Chilean corporate sector a favor."[72]

The "favor" done by the first ADR for Chilean businesses was not only in laying the groundwork for future ADRs. ADRs also furthered the development of financial intermediaries in Chile, most significantly by further deepening the pool of capital market information analyzers and advisers. New York–based analysts initially covered the Chilean companies issuing ADRs, but this attention to Chilean equities spurred the development of the domestic analyst sector. U.S. investor interest in Chilean companies stoked demand for domestic Chilean analysts, who learned first through imitation and the dissemination of financial analysis techniques and technologies from foreign analysts. "The quality of information available in the financial markets has improved radically," noted one executive. "Before 1990, the information was primarily distributed through word-of-mouth, or through rudimentary newsletters issued by some domestic stockbrokers' offices. Analysts became a part of the landscape only after the internationalization of the Chilean stock market."[73]

Foreign Acquisitions: Tata Motors

Acquisitions can enable emerging market-based companies to leapfrog into new markets and up the value chain, but they pose challenges as well. Companies often take on burdensome debt to finance the acquisition and must integrate diverse corporate cultures. The decision to acquire poses a strategic choice similar to the "compete alone or collaborate" choice facing multinationals in emerging markets and emerging giants competing at home. Like those other actors, emerging giants going global need to approach the decision to acquire with clear objectives and an appreciation of the risks involved.

Tata Motors, as described in chapter 5, was a leading producer of commercial trucks and a significant player in passenger cars in its home market, India.[74] The company differentiated itself at home through its sturdy, reliable vehicles—a ubiquitous presence on India's highways and rural roads—and an intimate understanding of local product markets. Tata Motors invested in product development initiatives such as the Ace and the Nano in part to outmaneuver incoming foreign competition. This competition also pushed Tata Motors to build a foreign presence for reasons of stretch—to learn about more-developed markets (and competition and customers therein) and to build global capabilities. Acquisitions were a key vehicle for the company to globalize its presence and capabilities.

As of the early 2000s, Tata Motors' international business had consisted of exports sold to a wide range of countries without much consideration for global strategy. As part of a plan to diversify the company's business after an economic downturn in India exposed the vulnerability of its reliance on highly cyclical commercial truck sales, Tata Motors conceived a more focused global strategy. Like other product market-based emerging giants, the company targeted developing markets where it could exploit its home market capabilities. In South Africa, Korea, and markets in the Middle East, Tata Motors invested in developing an ecosystem of service, spare parts, and branding to support and help grow its business.

Tata Motors was able to compete against major multinational competitors such as Mercedes and the large Japanese brands outside India in part through an approach similar to its success with the Tata Ace at home. The company had heard customers complain about the high maintenance costs associated with the major global brands. Tata Motors saw an opportunity to price its spare parts strategically and sell customers on the total life-cycle cost of its trucks. The company needed to prove this proposition to customers, as it had with the Ace as a replacement for the three-wheelers that predominated as small commercial vehicles in India. "I'm upgrading myself, so I will give all that comfort that Mercedes is giving . . . I will take these people along with me once I've hooked them on the business," said one company executive. "Then I'm able to satisfy both his commercial desire and his psychological desire. And that's the philosophy that we're trying to follow in other countries."[75]

To accelerate this upgrading, Tata Motors sought out acquisitions and partnerships in markets more developed than India's. A 2003 attempt to bring Tata-produced passenger cars to the United Kingdom through a partnership with MG Rover failed to produce expected sales, but other efforts were more fruitful.[76] In 2004, Tata Motors bought Daewoo Commercial Vehicle Company of Korea. The acquisition complemented Tata Motors' existing portfolio because Daewoo Commercial produced heavier trucks than any Tata Motors produced. "It was not M&A in the classical sense. It is not so much to get scale," one company executive said. "Our thing was, how do I close the gap [with foreign competition] as quickly as possible? One was through these acquisitions."[77] Similarly, Tata Motors bought a 21 percent stake in Hispano Carrocero, a Spanish busmaker, in 2005. The company has also "borrowed" global institutions by partnering with Fiat of Italy and building a product development technical center in the United Kingdom.

Challenges in the institutional context of China and the United States prevented Tata Motors from attempting to enter either market on its own. "I have not given up on China," one company executive said, "but I think because of the restrictive nature of doing business there, it has certainly made us take a step back, and I don't want to commit money for which I don't see a return. We are not General Motors, and we are not Daimler Chrysler that you throw $2 billion or $3 billion. We have to be very prudent and cautious."[78] Meeting the standards of demanding customers and the product liability regime posed a different set of challenges in the

United States. "The only way I can enter the U.S. market is through mergers and acquisitions," said one company executive. "So if I get an opportunity, then I will look at it very actively."[79]

In 2008, Tata Motors seized an opportunity for a major acquisition into developed markets with its $2.3 billion purchase of Jaguar and Land Rover from U.S.-based Ford Motor Company. The purchase gave Tata Motors access to global brands, technology, and distribution channels in developed markets, particularly in Western Europe and the United States. The acquisition, however, was completed just as the global recession hit car markets in the developed world.[80] Losses at Jaguar and Land Rover forced Tata Motors to inject more than $1 billion into the two brands.[81] With its credit ratings downgraded, Tata Motors had difficulty refinancing its outstanding loans for the deal. The company was close to defaulting on a portion of its debt when the State Bank of India and other institutions guaranteed a bond for Tata Motors.[82]

The global financial crisis and recession of 2008–2009 are rare circumstances—particularly given how acutely the world's automotive industry was affected—but the experience of Tata Motors illustrates the risks of audacious globalization by emerging giants. The company sought out a global footprint because of vulnerabilities at home, but global acquisitions expose emerging market-based companies to a different set of vulnerabilities that they need to appreciate and take into account.

Foreign Acquisitions: Nicholas Piramal India Limited

Emerging giants also face acute challenges as they look to integrate acquisitions, particularly those from developed markets, into their fold. Consider the example of pharmaceutical manufacturer Nicholas Piramal India Limited (NPIL).[83] NPIL itself was created by the acquisition of the Indian operations of Australian pharmaceutical firm Nicholas Laboratories by family-owned textile firm Piramal. NPIL offered outsourced pharmaceutical development and production, largely for foreign firms and start-ups that lacked the capabilities to produce on their own. In a bid to position itself closer to clients in developed markets, NPIL acquired Avecia, with operations in the United Kingdom and Canada, in

2005. Avecia seemed to complement NPIL's business model and aspirations perfectly.

The acquisition featured tensions common in many such deals by prospective emerging giants. Corporate cultures clash in any acquisition, particularly any cross-border acquisition, but these clashes are accentuated when the two companies emerge from sharply differing market contexts. One company executive described the tension at NPIL between "Indian action-oriented style versus the English plan/do/review style."[84] Such acquisitions can create tensions of identity among employees. Employees of the acquired developed market-based firm simultaneously wear the hats of their former company (the acquisition target), their new employer (the emerging market-based acquirer), and as citizens of their home country, which often loses jobs as a result of the acquisition. This tension of identity can complicate and challenge efforts to integrate developed market-based acquisitions into the organizations of emerging giants.

Foreign Acquisitions: TCL

The experience of China-based TCL's acquisition of Thomson of France—one of the most high-profile early emerging giant acquisitions of a developed market-based firm—starkly illustrates the challenges of acquisition by emerging giants.[85] Consumer electronics firm TCL's early globalization journey was very similar to that of Haier. TCL established joint ventures in other emerging markets and, like many prospective emerging giants, differentiated itself in these markets by filling institutional voids of product market aggregators, distributors, information analyzers, and advisers.

One company executive described the company's operations in Vietnam: "The distribution system was still weak, so it made sense to develop our own marketing and sales channels. We did a market survey to get a sense of how Vietnam was different from China . . . We were so busy with these markets that none of us were worrying about entering the U.S. or Europe."[86] Like Haier, TCL had trouble cracking the distribution channels in developed markets. In 2002, TCL acquired German firm Schneider, a television manufacturer that had recently shuttered production in the face of high costs. TCL hoped to rekindle the operations by maintaining the Schneider brand and design—everything visible to consumers—while cutting costs on the rest. The venture failed, however, because of high production costs for the portions of operations still conducted in Germany.

In 2004, TCL tried again—but with a much bigger target. TCL joined with Thomson to create TCL Thomson Enterprise (TTE), a joint venture that combined the television production assets of the two companies, making it the world's largest television manufacturer. The venture, 67 percent owned by TCL, gave TCL instant global scale and the opportunity to exploit the Thomson brand in Europe and the Thomson-owned RCA brand in the United States.

The acquisition was seen as a watershed moment in the emergence of emerging market-based firms in global business. "TCL Thomson Enterprise is a milestone for China," said one TTE executive. "If it succeeds, all the Chinese companies will follow. If we have trouble, they will not."[87] Wary of the high costs of investing in LCD or plasma displays, TTE planned to focus on reducing costs and increasing the efficiency of the supply chain in the production of cathode ray tube (CRT) televisions. As one company executive described TCL's view of the venture, "Chinese companies are still behind in technology, but our biggest advantage is our flexibility and finesse. We find Thomson a bit slow in reacting. So now we have to see whether we can infuse TCL's flexibility into TTE to make it a strong organization. We already contribute our low-cost structure to Thomson, but can we bring TCL supply-chain efficiency to Thomson?"[88]

High costs in Europe, linguistic barriers, and compensation discrepancies between Chinese and European employees challenged the venture early on.[89] Less than three years after TTE was established, TCL announced that it would close most of its European operations amid tough losses from the venture as the television market demand shifted to the LCD and plasma displays that TTE had eschewed.[90] The failed venture became a cautionary tale. "While going global is a must rather than a choice for many companies, they often underestimate the difficulties of managing a global organisation, when you don't have the global expertise and the global sales channels," said one analyst. "They think it is very easy to be a hero, but it is not."[91]

Acquisitions are tempting avenues for emerging giants to use in fast-tracking their global growth, and many have succeeded, including Teva, Zain, and China-based Lenovo, which acquired the PC business of U.S.-based IBM in 2004. Executing acquisitions by emerging market-based firms, particularly of developed market-based companies, is more difficult than many anticipate, however, requiring clear objectives, truly complementary models, and a great deal of sensitivity.

Globalizing Emerging Giants

Emerging giants can extend their reach beyond their home markets by replicating their models in similarly structured markets, or by adapting to the contexts of developed markets. They can also build capabilities through global institutions once they have established value propositions in their home markets. Often, emerging market-based firms built on exploiting product market knowledge find success by targeting other emerging markets first and then attempting to tackle advanced markets. Firms built on exploiting factor market knowledge can often best exploit their capabilities by first seeking out customers in developed markets and later establishing operations in emerging markets where they can replicate models amid similar factor market features. As emerging market-based firms move into developed markets and compete even more squarely against world-leading multinationals, they need to adapt to the different competitive and institutional contexts of these markets. Acquiring new capabilities is often necessary if prospective emerging giants are to access resources and capabilities to improve their competitiveness in the global marketplace.

Although we have focused on individual initiatives of particular emerging giants, most successful emerging giants have pursued a combination of these strategies. Emerging market-based firms can extend the capabilities they have developed in their home markets into other emerging markets for scale while simultaneously stepping into developed markets for stretch and learning. As ICICI globalized its business, it targeted markets in the Middle East and developed markets in the United Kingdom and Canada. Although we focus on Haier's entry into the United States in this chapter, the company also has built large businesses in emerging markets in the Middle East and Southeast Asia.

Globalization is not a straightforward process for emerging giants. Market selection is a difficult proposition. It is not always clear which markets will be easy for such firms to enter, as Haier found in India. Given the challenges for emerging market-based firms to establish themselves successfully as multinationals and the growth opportunities in their home markets, cautious globalization is often well advised. Execution is critical if such firms are to succeed outside their home markets, particularly in more developed markets.

By taking stock of their inherent capabilities and the context of new markets, emerging giants can establish an international presence (see toolkit 6-1). Many of these firms have successfully identified and exploited niches as foundations for larger global businesses. Like multinationals establishing themselves in emerging markets, emerging giants can reach deeper into foreign—and particularly developed—markets only by adapting to institutional and competitive contexts and acquiring new capabilities. Multinationals from developed markets that have succeeded in emerging markets have been willing to experiment, and so too have emerging giants that have become successful multinational enterprises.

To manage growth and globalization successfully, emerging giants need to cultivate a range of capabilities. These firms need to maintain the entrepreneurial drive that enabled them to distinguish themselves in their home markets while instilling a global mind-set not only among top managers but also among rank-and-file employees. Innovation is critical for any company to sustain competitive advantage. It is critical for emerging giants to develop and manage innovation as they begin to move into higher-value products and processes.

These firms need to identify not only sources of capital but also world-class talent and board members from within and outside their home markets, and they need to establish a leadership pipeline to manage and develop this talent. Establishing or acquiring businesses in foreign markets can add great value to emerging giants, but they need not globalize to become globally competitive. Many emerging market-based firms have become world-class companies without aggressively moving outside their home markets. Many of these companies have looked to borrow institutions beyond their borders, however, to build their resources and improve their capabilities.

As several of the examples in this chapter show, borrowing global institutions also can help build credibility. Accessing these institutions requires that prospective emerging giants not only have strong value propositions in their home markets but also high standards in their management and corporate governance. Corporate cleanup may be the best preparatory step that an emerging market company can take to bolster its positioning against multinational rivals. Even small efforts can be a major source of differentiation in emerging markets. By focusing on cleaning up its corporate structure to maximize efficiencies and support good business practices, a prospective emerging giant can build confidence and social capital in consumer, supplier, and investor circles, contributing to its competitive advantage. The chief executive of one emerging giant described his company's objective:

> We are a company that has come from a very small country. We come from areas that are described by poverty and corruption and dictatorships and the absence of human rights and so on. It is our dream that we want a global company—which is a human company that belongs to the whole human community. That's what global means to us. It means the universe is our homeland. The more we humanize business and make it a mission with values and ideals, the better we do. If you look at the history of all the great companies in the world, they were great in their values and their ideals and their ethical and moral standards and what they stand for to advance the human cause and that's how they become great even commercially and competitively.[92]

Toolkit 6-1
Toolkit for Emerging Giants Going Global

1. Self-Assessment

A. Business Model

What is the core of our business model?

B. Home Market Context

What key constraints do we face from institutional voids?

2. Opportunity Assessment

How can we extend our business model into new markets for scale (particularly in other developing countries)?

How can we transcend our home market contexts by operating in markets for stretch (particularly in developed markets)?

What global capabilities can we borrow from developed markets to compensate for institutional voids in our home market?

- Product markets: Branding and advertising intermediaries; patent protections

- Capital markets: Overseas listings; global private equity

- Labor markets: Talent from world-leading business schools and universities

Given our capabilities, domestic opportunities, and the state of foreign competition, does it make sense to go global now or later?

Seven

The Emerging Arena

EMERGING MARKETS HAVE GARNERED news headlines and have figured prominently in the strategies of companies and investment funds of all stripes because of their emergence. The liberalization, growth, and development of these economies have lifted millions out of poverty and have created attractive new markets for firms and investors. Many of these markets are already among the world's largest economies and are poised to be critical drivers of the world economy in coming decades. The current economic crisis engulfing the United States, Europe, and Japan has only strengthened the potential attractiveness of emerging markets as a source of growth for many Western multinationals and investors.

Noting the emergence of these economies is important and interesting but not particularly actionable. Throughout this book, we have tried to show that companies need to understand and respond to the emergingness of emerging markets—the persistent institutional voids embedded in their market structures—to craft strategies and operate successfully in these economies. Whether filling voids as entrepreneurial opportunities, moving from a developed market base into an emerging market, building a company based in an emerging market, or building a multinational from a base in an emerging market, companies operating in or out of emerging markets need to match their strategies to the markets' institutional contexts.

This structural view of emerging markets has different implications for entrepreneurs, for multinationals based in developed markets, and for domestic companies looking to position themselves in their home markets and build themselves into multinationals in their own right. As a first step, however, all these companies need to audit the institutional context of the emerging markets in which they operate or invest. Chapter 2 and toolkit 2-3 point to many of these voids. Voids exist in the product, labor, and capital markets of emerging economies—and different emerging markets feature different combinations of voids. Politics, history, and culture undergird and shape both the nature and stickiness of institutional voids. Businesses need to understand the role these forces play in determining institutional context.

The process of identifying voids also points to entrepreneurial opportunities to fill those voids, as we discuss in chapter 3. Because institutional voids carry costs for companies operating in emerging markets, filling them adds value. Developed markets rely on a wide range of intermediaries, many of which are private sector entities. Transactions in developed product, capital, and labor markets are facilitated by information analyzers and advisers, aggregators and distributors, transaction facilitators, credibility enhancers, regulators, and adjudicators. Local and foreign companies have built significant businesses by filling these intermediary roles in emerging markets.

This taxonomy of market intermediaries can help entrepreneurs and companies identify opportunities to fill voids. Intermediary-based businesses face a set of questions as they execute these opportunities:

- *What segment can we reach?* Institutional voids present tremendous opportunities to entrepreneurs in theory, and these opportunities attract competition. Blue River Capital differentiated itself from other risk capital providers in India by targeting what it identified as an underserved segment—middle-market family- and entrepreneur-run businesses. As in many examples in this book, the institutional voids in the segment were also a source of opportunity. Serving the segment required Blue River to tailor its investment process and even fill voids in service of its business.

- *How do we need to adapt this intermediary-based business to the local context?* The experience of online auction site Deremate in Argentina illustrates the challenges of transferring intermediary concepts from developed to emerging markets. Deremate sought to replicate eBay's model, but that model was built on a market infrastructure that was not as well developed in Argentina when Deremate debuted, forcing Deremate to adapt its model.

- *How can we expand into adjacent intermediary services and move up the intermediation value chain?* Intermediaries can evolve their models into related opportunities. After starting out as a deal-brokering transaction facilitator between Chinese factories and Western firms, Li & Fung grew to take on a wide range of intermediary functions, enabling the firm to move up the value chain as it offered more value-added services to its clients.

- *What vested interests are we displacing or might we encounter as we seek to fill this void?* Intermediaries need to be conscious of stakeholders that might be displaced by their efforts to change market context, as Metro Cash & Carry found when it brought its wholesale model to India. Filling voids rarely means filling a vacuum, and the entities pushed aside by such initiatives can also push back by mobilizing popular and political support.

Institutional voids can prevent multinationals based in the developed world from replicating their models in emerging markets and can stifle the ability of domestic companies to develop and compete against those incoming multinationals. Voids present foreign-based and domestic companies with a common set of strategic choices. Because of their different origins and sources of competitive advantage, these choices lead to different sets of options for these actors (see table 7-1).

As we discuss in chapter 4, multinationals based in mature markets can build emerging market strategies on their core capabilities—access to global capital, resources, technology, and talent—but exploiting these

TABLE 7-1

Responding to institutional voids

Strategic choice	Options for multinationals from developed markets	Options for emerging market-based companies
Replicate or adapt?	• Replicate business model, exploiting relative advantage of global brand, credibility, know-how, talent, finance, and other factor inputs. • Adapt business models, products, or organizations to institutional voids.	• Copy business model from developed markets. • Exploit local knowledge, capabilities, and ability to navigate institutional voids to build tailored business models.
Compete alone or collaborate?	• Compete alone. • Acquire capabilities to navigate institutional voids through local partnerships or JVs.	• Compete alone. • Acquire capabilities from developed markets through partnerships or JVs with multinational companies to bypass institutional voids.
Accept or attempt to change market context?	• Take market context as given. • Fill institutional voids in service of own business.	• Take market context as given. • Fill institutional voids in service of own business.
Enter, wait, or exit?	• Enter or stay in market in spite of institutional voids. • Emphasize opportunities elsewhere.	• Build business in home market in spite of institutional voids. • Exit home market early in corporate history if capabilities unrewarded at home.

capabilities without adaptation often limits these companies to the narrow global market segment (see table 7-2 for an overview of the features of different market segments in emerging economies).

GM successfully transplanted its global model when it entered China while targeting the country's wealthy elite with its Buick brand. The company later adapted to reach deeper into the market. Similarly, L'Oréal exploited its global quality and brand but only after a failed attempt to target the local market segment.

Stepping outside their comfort zone in the global segment brings greater opportunities and challenges to multinationals in emerging markets. Adaptation to the contextual challenges in other segments of

TABLE 7-2

Market segments in emerging economies

Segment	Global	Emerging middle class		Local	Bottom
Price	Global	Global	Local	Local	Lowest
Quality	Global	Global	Global	Local	Lowest
Features	Global	Local	Local	Local	Fewest
Advantage	Multinationals	Battleground	Battleground	Domestic	Domestic

emerging markets can take a number of forms. Multinationals can modify their models, product offerings, or organizations. Adaptation can be a difficult, expensive process for developed market-based multinationals, particularly because of the institutional voids in emerging markets, such as the absence of third-party market research or product design firms that could contribute to product adaptation. Moreover, the different forms of adaptation needed in different emerging markets pose challenges to coordination among subsidiaries.

Given the limits of replication and the challenges of adaptation in emerging markets, multinationals need to consider collaborations, such as joint ventures or other local partnerships, to help them acquire local knowledge and navigate institutional voids. Collaboration is often mandated as a price of admission into emerging markets, but partnerships are often the best way for multinationals to equip themselves to manage institutional voids. Microsoft attempted to enter China by adapting its software largely on its own but successfully established a business in the market only after it collaborated with local players and invested in the development of the local software industry. To produce sophisticated medical equipment in emerging markets to the standards of its global line, GE Healthcare needed to work closely with supply chain partners in emerging markets. Both multinationals acquired local capabilities through their partnerships, but they also filled voids for their partners by bringing technology and global standards to the emerging markets in which they invested.

When adaptation and collaboration are not sufficient, multinationals can look to fill voids in service of their businesses. To deliver fast food in Russia of comparable quality to that in the United States, McDonald's invested heavily in filling voids in its supply chain. Faced with intellectual property rights violations that threatened to undermine its business in Brazil, Monsanto "borrowed" global market institutions to press for contextual change. Filling institutional voids is difficult and expensive, so multinationals need to weigh the importance of particular emerging markets, the extent to which voids undermine their businesses, and their ability to change institutional context.

In the face of pervasive institutional voids that are too difficult to adapt to, navigate with partners, or fill on their own, multinationals can decide to exit or to emphasize opportunities elsewhere. Multinationals are in a privileged position to choose the markets in which they operate. Forswearing particular markets or waiting until the institutional context changes can be a wise strategy for multinationals when voids raise doubts about building viable businesses or suggest the prospect of significant investments in filling voids. The Home Depot retreated from some emerging markets when it found it could not replicate its U.S. business model in Chile and Argentina because of voids and only later expanded into developing economies through collaboration that mitigated these costs.

Waiting can carry costs for multinationals in emerging markets. While The Home Depot waited in China, for example, competitors established significant presence—and acquired valuable local knowledge. Waiting can be particularly problematic for companies in industries where first-mover advantage is highly valuable. Microsoft, for example, persisted in China in the face of painful voids in intellectual property rights because of the long-term value in establishing its software as a standard platform. Some multinationals have exited emerging markets in the face of financial and other crises. Tetra Pak's example shows how multinationals can exploit the relative advantages of their global capabilities to recommit to emerging markets undergoing crisis in light of the markets' long-term potential.

Domestic companies in emerging markets have a different set of responses to these strategic choices because of their origins in developing amidst institutional voids. Some emerging market-based companies have sought to build businesses by replicating models from the developed world. Many of the most successful emerging giants have devised and executed strategies that are tailored to the institutional contexts of their home markets. As with multinationals, this adaptation can come in different forms. Tata Motors created a truly local product (the Ace) as it worked around institutional voids in market research, dealer and service networks, and credit providers. India's IT giants have become emerging giants by exploiting their ability to adapt to labor market voids in their home market.

Facing foreign competition and unable to access global-caliber capabilities because of institutional voids, prospective emerging giants have the option of collaboration with foreign firms. The successful partnerships of India's Bharti Airtel and Turkey's Doğuş Group illustrate how emerging market-based companies can match their collaboration with the capabilities they cannot access at home. Beyond capital and technology, foreign collaborations can help prospective emerging giants build credibility—a highly valuable commodity in emerging markets that lack well-developed forms of quality certification.

Institutional voids are obstacles for prospective emerging giants, but efforts to fill voids can be powerful sources of differentiation and competitive advantage vis-à-vis domestic and foreign rivals. Haier's success in China through its investments in distribution and after-sales service illustrates how emerging market-based companies can differentiate themselves by filling voids.

Although emerging market-based companies do not have as straightforward an exit option as multinationals, these firms can choose to emphasize opportunities elsewhere. A prospective emerging giant choosing among sectors in which to invest in its home market might opt to wait before moving into a particular sector because the institutional context is not conducive to its development. Some emerging giants have exited their home markets relatively early in their corporate histories. Indian software and IT consulting firms developed strong capabilities in talent markets—identifying, training, and managing talent—but the customer market in India was simply not developed enough to reward those capabilities. Early on, these firms sought out customers in the United States and other developed markets.

The institutional contexts of emerging markets shape the globalization journeys of emerging giants in other ways, as we discuss in chapter 6. We describe how emerging giants can build global businesses by extending their home market models in markets having similar institutional contexts—replicating in other emerging markets—or transcending their origins by adapting to developed markets. Zain has developed into a telecommunications giant by targeting emerging markets, where it exploits its ability to manage voids and reach customers in underdeveloped product markets. The company's investments in hard and soft infrastructure in sub-Saharan Africa facilitated its growth in much the same way Haier built competitive advantage in China. After initially targeting customers in developed markets—like other Indian IT firms—Tata Consultancy Services replicated its ability to manage and fill labor market voids in emerging markets, as in its operations in Latin America.

Emerging giants have gained prominence in the developed world in large part through headlines of their entry and acquisitions in developed markets. The examples of Haier, Teva Pharmaceutical Industries, and ICICI Bank illustrate the challenges for emerging market-based firms in adapting to developed market contexts. Somewhat like developed market-based multinationals entering emerging markets, these firms are operating outside their comfort zone when they enter developed markets. Learning about these markets, though costly, can serve prospective emerging giants in their home markets by equipping them to compete against multinationals more squarely and meet more demanding customer needs as their home markets develop. Overseas listings and acquisitions are two critical tools of globalization for prospective emerging giants, but—as we describe in several examples—securing and instilling global standards and capabilities throughout an emerging market-based organization is a difficult, long-term task.

Emerging Market Action Items

The frameworks and examples in this book point to several key action items for companies operating in and out of emerging markets.

Experiment to Fit Business Models to Emerging Markets

Institutional voids can frustrate, stifle, and undermine the business models and operations of any company doing business in emerging markets. In light of these contextual challenges, some companies choose to exit or avoid emerging markets. Those companies that decide that the opportunities in emerging markets are too great to pass up or delay need to appreciate and respond to the challenges posed by institutional voids.

Emerging markets are so tough to crack that companies are highly unlikely to get their strategies right the first time out. Companies of all stripes need to experiment to fit their strategies to the unique contexts of emerging markets—and instill in their organizations an organizational openness to experiments. Zain's One Network and Microsoft's FonePlus are only two examples of successful emerging market experiments.

Position Your Business as a Partner in Progress

Foreign as well as domestic companies have found success in emerging markets by positioning themselves as partners in progress—building businesses that also advance market development. Initiatives along these lines can take a number of forms—from advancing traditional corporate social responsibility to filling institutional voids—in service of businesses or as stand-alone projects.

Microsoft's investments in the development of China's software industry facilitated the development of its own business in the country. The job creation and tax revenue produced by Zain's business in African countries facilitated its government relations and operations. Similarly, the employment Tata Consultancy Services brought to Uruguay enabled the company to receive fast-tracked visas for employees traveling from India. At home, Tata Group filled voids in social services for employees in Tata Steel's company town Jamshedpur. Metro Cash & Carry's primary business filled voids in the food supply chains in emerging markets, reducing waste and bringing more transactions into the tax net, although this argument could not overcome entrenched opposition in Bangalore. Nonetheless, working to be—and to be seen as—a partner in progress can help companies in emerging markets, particularly multinationals coming in from more developed markets.

Balance Ambition with Humility in Emerging Markets

Multinationals based in developed countries as well as emerging market-based companies face a tension between ambition and humility. Multinationals want to exploit the tremendous opportunities in emerging markets, but they need to carefully evaluate the extent to which they have the local knowledge and capacity to fully exploit those opportunities. Segmenting these markets and carefully aligning ambitions and capabilities can help multinationals avoid costly mistakes. Multinationals need the humility not only to gauge their own capabilities in relation to the institutional context of emerging markets but also in terms of their position in emerging markets. As one multinational executive explained, "Most emerging markets are highly sensitive. They're emerging because for years, they've been colonized. That has left its own suspicions, distrust, et cetera of foreigners. It's certainly true in China. It's certainly true in India. It's probably true in many other places. So people want the benefits of globalization and development, but they want to know that they're not being exploited."[1]

Emerging market-based companies also need to weigh their ambitions with their capabilities, particularly as they consider approaches to globalization. Teva Pharmaceutical's "billion-dollar theory" exemplifies emerging giant audacity. As one company executive explained, "Many companies pass the same way in Israel. The difference is really not personal. The difference is in the recognition that going the path that history wrote for us, we will remain a small Israeli company that will not have any influence on anything. If you want to do something, try to do something very different. What we did was something that, at that time, was very different."[2]

India's Tata Group, among the most audacious emerging market-based globalizers, has faced organizational strains in its globalization, as one company executive described:

> [B]ecause we are starting fresh, we don't have the collective memory of mistakes. [B]ecause India is booming, because our balance sheet is strong, people don't see risk in the same way they would do if they were working in [a multinational company] where growth rates are high at 10 percent. That balance of risk versus ambition: How fast can we go? What's our capability? How far can you test people who've never done it? We've got lots of smart people whose experience is very limited in international business. So that's the balance between throwing people in versus holding people back because you don't have the bench strength to do it.[3]

Just as any company operating in an emerging market needs to audit its institutional context in relation to its own capabilities, multinationals and emerging market-based companies need to audit their management capabilities and bandwidth as they weigh how far they can go in emerging markets and, in the case of emerging giants, how ambitious they can be in their globalization. As the example of TCL shows, audacious moves into new market contexts and attempts to integrate widely different corporate cultures through acquisitions can be particularly challenging.

Appreciate the Inherent Risks of Emerging Markets

To many observers, the emerging market story is largely one of growth and opportunity. This euphoria can quickly end when companies are burned by corruption, abrogation of contracts, wanton expropriation, or other risks in these markets. These risks are inherent in emerging markets, but in light of them, what should firms do? Companies can exit these markets, limit their ambition so as not to encounter them squarely, limit their exposure by operating through an agent or other party, or build in mechanisms, such as audits and internal vigilance, to deal with corruption.

Infosys and Tata Group set high standards for their organizations in light of corruption in India. As illustrated by the experience of Siemens—which agreed to pay $1.36 billion to U.S. and German authorities in 2008 to settle corruption charges—not maintaining such high standards can impact not only a multinational's business in an emerging market but also its wider business.[4] In mid-2009, it was reported that more than 120 companies were under investigation by the U.S. Department of Justice for potential violations of the Foreign Corrupt Practices Act.[5] Specialized antibribery compliance firms—credibility enhancers, in our taxonomy of market intermediaries—have sprouted up to help firms manage these issues.[6]

The chief executive of one emerging giant active in many emerging markets described how his firm has managed the corruption issue:

> How do we survive? It's like many of the great companies who survive corruption in their own countries. For us, the challenge is how to conduct our business in the most ethical way and according to the highest standards, moral standards. That is something we will not give up. And that's a choice because we have the whole world to go after. We have more than 220 countries worldwide. Therefore we have a choice. If we go to a country where we are asked to do something which is corrupt, we will just withdraw. We just don't do business there. And that happened a number of times, so we accept only to work in areas where we will not be forced in any degree of corruption, whether directly or indirectly.[7]

The Emerging Future

The story of emerging markets presented in this book is incomplete. These dynamic economies—and the strategies of companies operating within them—continue to evolve. One ongoing question and avenue for future research is the extent to which models built for emerging markets will migrate to developed markets, either through multinationals based in developed markets or through emerging giants becoming even more significant players in developed markets.

The growth in emerging markets has made them prime grounds for innovation and experimentation, as many of the examples in this book illustrate. Ideas and models born in emerging markets will continue to shape industries in the developed world. Indian automotive company Mahindra plans to bring low-cost diesel pickup trucks into the United States by 2010.[8] The Tata Nano might arrive in the United States not long after.[9] Partnerships between developed market-based multinationals and emerging giants are also a key vehicle for the transfer of ideas between market contexts. GE and Garanti Bank, for example, are learning a great deal from each other.

Another key question is how emerging giants can manage the strains to their organizations as they manage growth, go global, and try to move up the value chain. Instilling global mind-sets through their organizations, managing talent, creating leadership pipelines, developing and managing innovation, and integrating acquisitions are all key challenges for these companies.

In the wake of the financial crisis and recession of 2008–2009, emerging markets have, in the eyes of many observers, taken on an even more important role in the global economy. Some emerging markets have been havens of growth and opportunity as many developed economies struggle. Other emerging economies have been hit hard by the crisis, their trajectories of growth seriously disrupted. The persisting importance of emerging markets behooves executives, policy makers, and citizens to better understand these markets. The frameworks and examples in this book are intended to offer a start.

Notes

Introduction

1. Portions of this introduction have been adapted from Tarun Khanna, Krishna Palepu, and Kjell Carlsson, "Why Study Emerging Markets," Note 5-706-422 (Boston: Harvard Business School, 2007).

2. David Oakley, "Emerging Market Equities Outperform West," *Financial Times* (FT.com), June 7, 2009.

3. "Emerging-Market Indicators," *The Economist*, January 8, 1994, 102.

4. "Economic and Financial Indicators," *The Economist*, January 6, 2007, 81.

5. "The World This Week," *The Economist*, January 8, 1994, 5.

6. "The New World Order: Back to the Future," *The Economist*, January 8, 1994, 21.

7. *The Economist*, January 8, 1994, 52.

8. *Standard & Poor's Global Industry Surveys*, "Computers: Hardware: Asia," October 2006, 20.

9. Antoine van Agtmael coined the term. See Antoine van Agtmael, *The Emerging Markets Century: How a New Breed of World-Class Companies Is Overtaking the World* (New York: Free Press, 2007), 1–6. Mark Mobius of Franklin Templeton Investments pioneered equity investing in emerging markets.

10. International outsourcing, or offshoring, has not and may not result in widespread unemployment in the United States and other developed markets compared with the normal churn of jobs in the hurly-burly of competitive, technologically dynamic market economies. It may nonetheless have a transformative impact on the labor markets of developed economies, as Alan Blinder has argued. The accessibility of labor in emerging markets is likely to reshape different service industries in different ways in developed economies, because some highly skilled workers will be vulnerable to emerging market competition while some low-skilled workers in personal services will be less vulnerable. Offshoring to emerging markets could have a profound impact on the educational systems and social safety nets of developed economies as these countries come to terms with preparing their youth to compete in this new landscape and support those who lose out to labor competition based overseas. See Alan S. Blinder, "Offshoring: The Next Industrial Revolution?" *Foreign Affairs*, March/April 2006, http://www.foreignaffairs.org/20060301faessay85209/alan-s-blinder/offshoring-the-next-industrial-revolution.html.

11. Dominic Wilson and Roopa Purushothaman, *Dreaming with BRICs: The Path to 2050*, Goldman Sachs Economics Paper No. 99, October 1, 2003.

12. Fareed Zakaria, *The Post-American World* (New York: W.W. Norton & Company, 2008).

13. As of April 2009, 168 listings on the New York Stock Exchange were based in countries included in the Morgan Stanley Capital International (MSCI) Emerging Markets

Index; New York Stock Exchange, http://www.nyse.com/about/listed/lc_ny_region.html. The MSCI Emerging Markets Index included 24 countries as of January 2009: Argentina, Brazil, Chile, China, Colombia, Czech Republic, Egypt, Hungary, India, Indonesia, Israel, Jordan, Korea, Malaysia, Mexico, Morocco, Peru, Philippines, Poland, Russia, South Africa, Taiwan, Thailand, and Turkey. In 2008, 300 of the 1,125 billionaires identified by *Forbes* on its annual list resided in countries included in this index. *Forbes* identified only 83 billionaires from those countries in 2001 (out of 538) and only 13 in 1987 (out of 141); Luisa Kroll, ed., "The World's Billionaires," *Forbes*, March 5, 2008, http://www.forbes.com/2008/03/05/richest-people-billionaires-billionaires08-cx_lk_0305billie_land.html. See also "The World's Richest People," *Forbes*, July 9, 2001, 110–124; and Harold Seneker, "The World's Billionaires," *Forbes*, October 5, 1987, 82.

14. Adapted from Tarun Khanna and Krishna Palepu, "Why Focused Strategies May Be Wrong for Emerging Markets," *Harvard Business Review*, July–August 1997, 41–51.

15. We use the terms *emerging* and *developing* interchangeably throughout this book to refer to economies having a variety of transactional challenges or institutional voids.

Chapter 1

1. Portions of this chapter have been adapted from Tarun Khanna and Krishna Palepu, "Spotting Institutional Voids in Emerging Markets," Note 106-014 (Boston: Harvard Business School Publishing, 2005); and Tarun Khanna, Krishna Palepu, and Kjell Carlsson, "Why Study Emerging Markets," Note 706-422 (Boston: Harvard Business School Publishing, 2007).

2. Thomas L. Friedman, *The World Is Flat: A Brief History of the Twenty-First Century* (New York: Farrar, Strauss & Giroux, 2005).

3. Amarchand & Mangaldas & Suresh A. Shroff & Co., quoted in Kian Ganz, "India Special Report: Hard Court Battle," *The Lawyer*, June 8, 2009, http://www.thelawyer.com/india-special-report-hard-court-battle/1000999.article.

4. Ibid.

5. Tarun Khanna and Krishna Palepu, "Why Focused Strategies May Be Wrong for Emerging Markets," *Harvard Business Review*, July–August 1997, 41–51.

6. Eric Bellman, "The Infomercial Comes to Life in India's Remotest Villages: Traveling Salesman Mr. Sharma Sings, Jokes to Spread Gospel of Global Consumerism," *Wall Street Journal*, June 10, 2009, A1.

7. "Company profile," Ctrip.com, http://pages.english.ctrip.com/webhome/purehtml/en/footer/CompanyProfile.html.

8. Capital IQ, https://www.capitaliq.com/main.asp.

9. Ibid.

10. George A. Akerlof, "The Market for 'Lemons': Quality Uncertainty and the Market Mechanism," *Quarterly Journal of Economics* 84, no. 3 (August 1970): 488–500.

11. Economists call this an *adverse selection problem*.

12. Khanna and Palepu, "Why Focused Strategies May Be Wrong for Emerging Markets."

Chapter 2

1. Portions of this chapter have been adapted from Tarun Khanna and Krishna G. Palepu, "Spotting Institutional Voids in Emerging Markets," Note 106-014 (Boston: Harvard Business School Publishing, 2005).

2. Paragraph adapted from Tarun Khanna, "Local Institutions and Global Strategy," Note 702-475 (Boston: Harvard Business School Publishing, 2002).

3. The four-context framework, the application of the "spotting institutional voids" questions, and the full list of questions in the toolkit are drawn from Tarun Khanna, Krishna G. Palepu, and Jayant Sinha, "Strategies That Fit Emerging Markets," *Harvard Business Review*, June 2005, 63–76.

4. See C. K. Prahalad and Allen Hammond, "Serving the World's Poor, Profitably," *Harvard Business Review*, September 2002, 48–57.

5. This section has been adapted from Tarun Khanna, Krishna G. Palepu, and Kjell Carlsson, "Why Study Emerging Markets," Note 706-422 (Boston: Harvard Business School Publishing, 2007).

Chapter 3

1. Portions of this chapter have been adapted from Tarun Khanna and Krishna G. Palepu, "Spotting Institutional Voids in Emerging Markets," Note 9-106-014 (Boston: Harvard Business School Publishing, 2005).

2. Informed by Tarun Khanna, "Local Institutions and Global Strategy," Note 9-702-475 (Boston: Harvard Business School Publishing, 2002).

3. John Joseph Wallis and Douglass C. North, "Measuring the Transaction Sector in the American Economy, 1870–1970," in *Long-Term Factors in American Economic Growth*, ed. Stanley L. Engerman and Robert E. Gallman (Chicago: The University of Chicago Press, 1986), 121.

4. Tarun Khanna, Rakesh Khurana, and Krishna G. Palepu, "Russell Reynolds Associates, 1999," Case 9-100-039 (Boston: Harvard Business School, 2001); and Tarun Khanna, "Russell Reynolds Associates, 1999: Teaching Note," Note 5-701-115 (Boston: Harvard Business School Publishing, 2001).

5. Steve Scroggins, managing director (head of Asia-Pacific operations), "Russell Reynolds Associates," Video 9-701-804 (Boston: Harvard Business School Publishing, 2001).

6. Heidrick & Struggles International, Inc., "Heidrick & Struggles Opens Office in Chongqing, China," press release, PRNewswire-FirstCall, November 28, 2006, http://phx.corporate-ir.net/phoenix.zhtml?c=91196&p=irol-newsArticle&ID=936669&highlight=.

7. Heidrick & Struggles International, Inc., "Heidrick & Struggles and Jobkoo Form Strategic Partnership to Reinvent Career Management Platform," press release, GlobeNewswire, February 24, 2009, http://finance.yahoo.com/news/Heidrick-amp-Struggles-and-pz-14458625.html.

8. Kevin Kelly, CEO, Heidrick & Struggles, quoted in Robert G. Eccles and David Lane, "Heidrick & Struggles International, Inc.," Case 9-408-066 (Boston: Harvard Business School Publishing, 2008), 14.

9. Blue River Capital example derived from Krishna G. Palepu, Tarun Khanna, and Richard J. Bullock, "Blue River Capital," Case 9-708-448 (Boston: Harvard Business School Publishing, 2007); and Shujaat Khan, managing director, Blue River Capital, presentation by teleconference at Harvard Business School, October 12, 2007.

10. Khan, presentation by teleconference at Harvard Business School.

11. Ibid.

12. Khan, quoted in Palepu, Khanna, and Bullock, "Blue River Capital," 8.

13. Khan, presentation by teleconference at Harvard Business School.

14. Khan, quoted in Palepu, Khanna, and Bullock, "Blue River Capital," 8.

15. Ibid.

16. Ibid.

17. M. Chandrasekaran, quoted in Palepu, Khanna, and Bullock, "Blue River Capital," 9.

18. Khan, quoted in ibid., 7.

19. Portions of Deremate example informed by Michael G. Rukstad and David Collis, "Deremate.com: Building a Latin American Internet Auction Site," Case 9-702-454 (Boston: Harvard Business School Publishing, 2002).

20. Ibid., 3, 5–6.

21. Ibid., 7.

22. Ibid., 11.

23. Alec Oxenford, CEO, Deremate.com, presentation at Harvard Business School, April 23, 2003.

24. Ibid.

25. Ibid.

26. Roger Kenney, CFO, Deremate.com, quoted in Rukstad and Collis, "Deremate.com: Building a Latin American Internet Auction Site," 12.

27. Oxenford, presentation at Harvard Business School.

28. Ibid.

29. Ibid.

30. F. Asis Martinez-Jerez, "MercadoLibre.com," Case 9-106-057 (Boston: Harvard Business School Publishing, 2007), 3; Shane Romig, Dow Jones Newswires, "Mercadolibre Tightens Grip on Lat Am Mkt Amid Online Boom," September 10, 2008.

31. Romig, "Mercadolibre Tightens Grip On Lat Am Mkt Amid Online Boom"; "Argentina: La Nacion launches demotores.com.ar," *La Nacion*, August 16, 2006.

32. Oxenford, presentation at Harvard Business School.

33. Example informed by Joan Magretta, "Fast, Global, and Entrepreneurial: Supply Chain Management, Hong Kong Style," *Harvard Business Review* OnPoint, product number 2020 (Boston: Harvard Business School Publishing, 2002); Joan Magretta, "Fast, Global, and Entrepreneurial: Supply Chain Management, Hong Kong Style: An Interview with Victor Fung," *Harvard Business Review*, September–October 1998, 102–114; Antony St. George, Carin-Isabel Knoop, and Michael Y. Yoshino, "Li & Fung: Beyond 'Filling in the Mosaic': 1995–1998," Case 9-398-092 (Boston: Harvard Business School Publishing, 1998); F. Warren McFarlan, William C. Kirby, and Tracy Yuen Manty, "Li & Fung 2006," Case 9-307-077 (Boston: Harvard Business School Publishing, 2007); Bang-yan Feng, *100 Years of Li & Fung: Rise from Family Business to Multinational* (Singapore: Thomson Learning, 2007); and Tarun Khanna and Krishna G. Palepu, "Emerging Giants: Building World-Class Companies in Emerging Markets," Note 9-703-431 (Boston: Harvard Business School Publishing, 2005).

34. Victor Fung, quoted in Joan Magretta, "Fast, Global, and Entrepreneurial: Supply Chain Management, Hong Kong Style: An Interview with Victor Fung," 104.

35. Ibid., 105, 106.

36. Ibid., 104.

37. Ibid., 108.

38. Ibid., 109.

39. Ibid., 110.

40. Ibid.

41. Danny Lau, Li & Fung executive director of sales, quoted in Jason Booth, "Value Creators: Outsell, Outlast, Outclass—Going the Last Mile—Li & Fung Takes Its Middleman Role to Extremes," *Asian Wall Street Journal*, December 14, 2001, W5.

42. Bruce Einhorn, with Aili McConnon, "How Not to Sweat the Retail Details: Hong Kong's Li & Fung Takes On All the Manufacturing Headaches for Big Brands," *BusinessWeek*, May 25, 2009, 52.

43. William L. McComb, CEO, Liz Claiborne, quoted in ibid., 52.

44. Ibid., 52; Frank Longid and Wing-Gar Cheng, "Li & Fung Seeks 'Major' Deal to Meet 3-Year Targets (Update 1)," Bloomberg, May 13, 2009, http://www.bloomberg.com/apps/news?pid=email_en&sid=aO8EqIqt9h0E.

45. Metro example adapted from Tarun Khanna, Krishna G. Palepu, Carin-Isabel Knoop, and David Lane, "Metro Cash & Carry," Case 9-707-505 (Boston: Harvard Business School, 2007); and "Metro Cash & Carry," Note 5-707-464 (Boston: Harvard Business School, 2007); and Thomas Hübner, James Scott, and Michael Wiedman, "Metro Cash & Carry," Video 9-707-812 (Boston: Harvard Business School Publishing, 2007).

46. James Scott, regional operating officer, Metro Cash & Carry Asia, "Metro Cash & Carry," video.

47. Michael Wiedman, general manager, Metro Cash & Carry International, ibid.

48. Thomas Hübner, CEO, Metro Cash & Carry, ibid.

49. James Scott, regional operating officer, Metro Cash & Carry Asia, ibid.

50. Ibid.

Chapter 4

1. Portions of this chapter have been adapted from Tarun Khanna, Krishna G. Palepu, and Jayant Sinha, "Strategies That Fit Emerging Markets," *Harvard Business Review*, June 2005, 63–76.

2. Procter & Gamble, 2004 Annual Report, 33; Procter & Gamble, 2008 Annual Report, 43, www.pg.com.

3. Martin Fackler, "In India, a New Detroit," *New York Times*, June 26, 2008, 1.

4. Ericsson Annual Report 2008, 15.

5. "Nokia Unveils Four New Devices and Local Email Solution Aimed at 'Replacement Buyers' in Emerging Markets," Nokia, press release, April 2, 2008, http://www.nokia.com/A4971206; Jack Ewing, "Nokia Brings the Web to Emerging Markets," *BusinessWeek*, November 4, 2008, http://www.businessweek.com/globalbiz/content/nov2008/gb2008114_268373.htm.

6. *Nokia in 2008: Review by the Board of Directors and Nokia Annual Accounts 2008*, 2.

7. Tarun Khanna and Krishna G. Palepu, "Multinationals as Global Intermediaries," Note 9-703-428 (Boston: Harvard Business School Publishing, 2002), 15.

8. Calculated by authors from data as of December 1997 from Ministry of Communications, January 12, 1998, via CEIC Data, China Premium Database.

9. "Investing in China: Testing GM's Shock Absorbers," *The Economist*, May 1, 1999, 64.

10. Peter Wonacott, "China's Buick Infatuation: The Stodgy American Auto Is a Pre-revolutionary Icon for Booming Middle Class," *Wall Street Journal*, July 22, 2004, B1.

11. Rick Wagoner, "Carmakers Are Vying to Meet China's Needs," *Financial Times*, November 4, 2003, 19.

12. Rahul Jacob, "Inside Track: Racing Start for Buicks in China," *Financial Times*, April 25, 2000, 18.

13. "Investing in China: Testing GM's Shock Absorbers," 64.

14. Raymond Bierzynski, quoted in Gordon Fairclough, "Chinese Cadillac Offers a Glimpse of GM's Future," *Wall Street Journal*, November 17, 2006, B1.

15. Fairclough, ibid., B1.

16. Ibid.

17. "Investing in China: Testing GM's Shock Absorbers," 64.

18. http://www.gmchina.com/english/corporate_info2/company_operations_sgm.jsp.

19. http://www.gmchina.com/english/corporate_info2/company_operations_patac.jsp.

20. http://www.gmchina.com/english/corporate_info2/company_operations_gmw.jsp.

21. http://www.gmchina.com/english/corporate_info2/company_operations_gmcsaic.jsp.

22. http://www.gmchina.com/english/corporate_info2/company_gmchina.jsp.

23. William C. Durant, quoted in Alfred P. Sloan, Jr., edited by John McDonald with Catharine Stevens, *My Years with General Motors* (New York: Doubleday, 1963), 303.

24. Gordon Fairclough, "Passing Lane: GM's Chinese Partner Looms as a New Rival—Learning from Detroit, Shanghai Automotive Pushes Its Own Cars," *Wall Street Journal*, April 20, 2007, A1.

25. Calculated from data in General Motors Corporation 2007 Annual Report, 16, 47.

26. Heather Timmons, "In Overhaul, G.M. May Look to Its Far-Flung Arms," *New York Times*, June 3, 2009, http://www.nytimes.com/2009/06/04/business/global/04overseas.html?emc=eta1.

27. Nick Reilly, president, GM Asia-Pacific, quoted in Bill Powell, "The Other GM," *Time*, May 18, 2009, http://www.time.com/time/magazine/article/0,9171,1896626,00.html. Model introduction figure from same article.

28. Timmons, "In Overhaul, G.M. May Look to Its Far-Flung Arms."

29. L'Oréal discussion derived from Christina Passariello, "Beauty Fix: Behind L'Oréal's Makeover in India: Going Upscale—When Cheap Shampoo Didn't Sell, Company Tapped Rising Class," *Wall Street Journal*, July 13, 2007, A1.

30. Alain Evrard, quoted in Passariello, "Beauty Fix: Behind L'Oréal's Makeover in India: Going Upscale—When Cheap Shampoo Didn't Sell, Company Tapped Rising Class."

31. Tarun Khanna, *Billions of Entrepreneurs: How China and India Are Reshaping Their Futures—and Yours* (Boston: Harvard Business Press, 2008), 22–23.

32. Tarun Khanna and Prithwiraj Choudhury, "Microsoft in China and India, 1993–2007," Case 9-708-444 (Boston: Harvard Business School Publishing, 2007).

33. Amy Yee, "Cisco Invests in Lavish Campus to Lure the Local Talent," *Financial Times*, January 25, 2008, 4.

34. Peter Löscher, CEO, Siemens, quoted in Richard Milne, "Siemens Too White, German and Male, Says Chief," *Financial Times*, June 25, 2008, 18.

35. Ravi Venkatesan, chairman, Microsoft India, "Ravi Venkatesan, Chairman, Microsoft India," Video 9-708-804 (Boston: Harvard Business School Publishing, 2007).

36. Thomas Hübner, CEO, Metro Cash & Carry, "Metro Cash & Carry," Video 9-707-812 (Boston: Harvard Business School Publishing, 2007).

37. Microsoft example informed by Tarun Khanna and Prithwiraj Choudhury, "Microsoft in China and India, 1993–2007," Case 9-708-444 (Boston: Harvard Business School Publishing, 2007); Tarun Khanna, "Microsoft in the People's Republic of China—1993" Case 9-795-115 (Boston: Harvard Business School Publishing, 1995); Khanna, "Microsoft in the People's Republic of China—1993 & 2005 Update," Note 5-796-072 (Boston: Harvard Business School Publishing, 2005); Khanna, "Microsoft in the People's Republic of China: 2005 Update," Case Supplement 706-429 (Boston: Harvard Business School Publishing, 2005); and Khanna, "Microsoft in the People's Republic of China: 1998 Update," Case Supplement 797-107 (Boston: Harvard Business School Publishing, 2001).

38. Sarah Schafer, "Microsoft's Cultural Revolution: How the Software Giant Is Rethinking the Way It Does Business in the World's Largest Market," *Newsweek*, June 28, 2004, 36.

39. Ravi Venkatesan, "Ravi Venkatesan, Chairman, Microsoft India."

40. Ibid.

41. Ibid.

42. Tarun Khanna and Elizabeth Raabe, "General Electric Healthcare, 2006," Case 9-706-478 (Boston: Harvard Business School Publishing, 2006); and Tarun Khanna and James Weber, "General Electric Medical Systems 2002," Case 9-702-428 (Boston: Harvard Business School Publishing, 2002).

43. Marc Onetto, who served as vice president of GEMS's global supply chain, quoted in Tarun Khanna and James Weber, "General Electric Medical Systems 2002," Case 9-702-428 (Boston: Harvard Business School Publishing, 2002), 8.

44. Ibid.

45. Reinaldo Garcia, head of GEMS Europe, quoted in ibid., 11.

46. Chih Chen, head of GEMS China, quoted in ibid., 14–15.

47. Joe Hogan, "Joe Hogan, President & CEO, GE Healthcare," Video 9-708-801 (Boston: Harvard Business School Publishing, 2007).

48. Mike Jones, who served as GEMS's global business and market development manager, quoted in Khanna and Weber, "General Electric Medical Systems 2002," 11.

49. Jena McGregor, "GE Plans a Big Health-Care Push: To Spark Growth, the Conglomerate Will Spend $6 Billion on Lower-Cost Equipment for Underserved Markets," BusinessWeek.com, May 7, 2009.

50. McDonald's example from Tarun Khanna, Krishna G. Palepu, and Jayant Sinha, "Strategies That Fit Emerging Markets," 73–74; Niraj Kaji and Max Yacoub provided research assistance for the example. See also George Cohon with David Macfarlane, To Russia with Fries (Toronto: McClelland & Stewart, 1997).

51. Ferit Sahenk, chairman, Doğuş Group, "Doğuş Group: Weighing Partners for Garanti Bank," Video 9-709-807 (Boston: Harvard Business School Publishing, 2008).

52. Monsanto example informed by David E. Bell and Mary Shelman, "Monsanto: Realizing Biotech Value in Brazil," Case 9-507-018 (Boston: Harvard Business School Publishing, 2006).

53. Rick Greubel, president, Monsanto Brazil, quoted in ibid., 8.

54. Greg Lucier, CEO, GEMS-IT, "General Electric Medical Systems" Video 9-703-904 (Boston: Harvard Business School Publishing, 2003).

55. Ravi Venkatesan, "Ravi Venkatesan, Chairman, Microsoft India."

56. Chuck Elias, head of The Home Depot China, quoted in Frederik Balfour with Brian Grow, "Home Depot: One Foot in China," BusinessWeek, May 1, 2006, 44–45, http://www.businessweek.com/print/magazine/content/06_18/b3982066.htm?chan=gl.

57. Balfour with Grow, ibid.

58. Vivian Wai-yin Kwok, "Home Depot Buys China Clone," Forbes.com, December 13, 2006, http://www.forbes.com/2006/12/13/home-depot-china-markets-emerge-cx_vk_1213markets01.html?partner=email; and Balfour with Grow, "Home Depot: One Foot in China."

59. Derived from Tarun Khanna, Krishna G. Palepu, and Gustavo Herrero, "Tetra Pak Argentina," Case 9-708-402 (Boston: Harvard Business School Publishing, 2007); and Alex Anavi, Tetra Pak senior vice president for business development and previously head of Tetra Pak Argentina, presentation at Harvard Business School, September 12, 2007.

60. Alex Anavi, presentation at Harvard Business School.

61. Ibid.

62. Ibid.

63. Ibid.

Chapter 5

1. This chapter is adapted in part from Tarun Khanna and Krishna G. Palepu, "Emerging Giants: Building World-Class Companies in Emerging Markets," Note 9-703-431 (Boston: Harvard Business School Publishing, 2005); and Tarun Khanna and Krishna G. Palepu, "Emerging Giants: Building World-Class Companies in Developing Countries," *Harvard Business Review*, October 2006, 60–69.

2. See Tarun Khanna, "At Home, It's Not Just Profits That Matter: The Case for National Ownership," *International Herald Tribune*, February 22, 2006, 8.

3. Krishna G. Palepu and Vishnu Srinivasan, "Tata Motors: The Tata Ace," Case N2-108-011 (Boston: Harvard Business School Publishing, 2008).

4. Ravi Kant, managing director, Tata Motors, presentation via teleconference to Harvard Business School, September 26, 2007.

5. Jonathan Wheatley, "Brazil Prepares to Grow the Next World Fuel—Moves to Increase the Proportion of Ethanol in Petrol Would Generate a Surge in Sugar Demand, Writes Jonathan Wheatley," *Financial Times*, March 9, 2006, 7.

6. Cosan, "Strategy and Competitive Advantages," http://www.cosan.com.br/en/ir.

7. Ibid.

8. Ibid.

9. "Cosan's Strategy for Future Growth," *Ethanol Statistics*, www.ethanolstatistics.com, December 10, 2007.

10. Antonio Regalado, "Deals and Dealmakers: Cosan Raises $1.05 Billion in Trading Debut on NYSE," *Wall Street Journal*, August 17, 2007, C5.

11. Antonio Regalado, "Cosan to List Stock in Bid for Growth," *Wall Street Journal*, June 26, 2007, C12.

12. Marcos Paulo, stock analyst with Banco Fator, quoted in ibid.

13. Antonio Regalado and Grace Fan, "Sugar Rush: Ethanol Giants Struggle to Crack Brazil Market: Family Owners Hesitate to Sell Out to Big Players; Visit from Google Guys," *Wall Street Journal*, September 10, 2007, A1.

14. Marc McCarthy, Bear Stearns, quoted in ibid.

15. Marcos Lutz, chief commercial officer, Cosan, quoted in "Cosan's Strategy for Future Growth."

16. Ibid.

17. Cosan, "Strategy and Competitive Advantages."

18. Ibid.

19. Kenneth Rapoza, "Brazil Sugar Cos Taking Steps to Improve Labor Conditions," *Dow Jones International News*, April 11, 2007.

20. "Cosan's Strategy for Future Growth," *Ethanol Statistics*.

21. Cosan, "Strategy and Competitive Advantages."

22. Antonio Regalado, "Corporate News: Ethanol Maker Buys Exxon's Brazil Outlets," *Wall Street Journal*, April 25, 2008, B4.

23. Cosan, "Strategy and Competitive Advantages."

24. Jonathan Wheatley, "Cosan Buys Filling Station Chain for $826m," *Financial Times* (FT.Com), April 24, 2008.

25. Paulo Diniz, chief financial officer, Cosan, quoted in Regalado, "Corporate News: Ethanol Maker Buys Exxon's Brazil Outlets."

26. Regalado, ibid.

27. Marcos Lutz, quoted in "Cosan's Strategy for Future Growth."

28. Bharti Airtel example derived from Tarun Khanna, Krishna G. Palepu, and Ingrid Vargas, "Bharti Tele-Ventures," Case 9-704-426 (Boston: Harvard Business School Pub-

lishing, 2004); and Tarun Khanna and Krishna G. Palepu, "Teaching Note: Bharti Tele-Ventures," Teaching Note 5-707-467 (Boston: Harvard Business School Publishing, 2007). Data converted from data at the Bharti Airtel Web site, http://www.airtel.in/wps/wcm/connect/About%20Bharti%20Airtel/bharti+airtel/investor+relations/overview/.

29. Sunil Mittal, quoted in Indranil Ghosh, "Casting a Wide Net," *Business India*, April 3, 2000, 54.

30. "Another First for the Leader," *Business India*, June 1, 1998; Amy Louise Kazmin, "Why Phones Are Ringing for Sunil Mittal," *BusinessWeek*, December 27, 1999.

31. Sunil Mittal, quoted in Indranil Ghosh, "Casting a Wide Net."

32. Pulak Prasad, managing director, Warburg Pincus, quoted in Khanna, Palepu, and Vargas, "Bharti Tele-Ventures," Case 9-704-426.

33. Sunil Mittal, quoted in Henry Sender, "Bharti's Stock Price May Not Show Potential," *Wall Street Journal Europe*, April 30, 2002.

34. Dalip Pathak, quoted in Manjeet Kripalani, "Private Equity Pours into India," *BusinessWeek*, June 20, 2005, http://www.businessweek.com/print/magazine/content/05_25/b3938158_mz035.htm?chan=gl.

35. Example informed by Tarun Khanna, Krishna G. Palepu, and Richard J. Bullock, "Doğuş Group: Weighing Partners for Garanti Bank," Case N9-709-401 (Boston: Harvard Business School Publishing, 2008); Rakesh Khurana, Simon Johnson, and Gina Carioggia, "Taking Charge at Doğuş Holding (A)," Case 9-402-009 (Boston: Harvard Business School Publishing, 2002); and "Doğuş Group: Weighing Partners for Garanti Bank," Video 9-709-807 (Boston: Harvard Business School Publishing, 2008).

36. Garanti Consolidated Financial Statements, 2005H1, June 30, 2005, http://www.garantibank.com/download/investor_relations/investor/pre_ifrs_h1_05.pdf; BRSA Earnings Presentation, July 22, 2005, www.garantibank.com/download/investor_relations/presentations/brsa_pres_05_q2.pdf.

37. ING Sector Review Turkish Banks, December 3, 2004.

38. Piraye Kuranei, "Foreign Banks Poised to Invest in Turkish Banking Sector," Mondaq Business Briefing, March 2, 2005; "Fortis to Acquire Turkey's Disbank," Reuters News, April 12, 2005.

39. Ferit Şahenk, chairman, Doğuş Group, interview with author, April 10, 2008.

40. Ibid.

41. Ibid.

42. Ferit Şahenk, "Doğuş Group: Weighing Partners for Garanti Bank," video.

43. Ibid.

44. Ibid.

45. Ferit Şahenk, interview with author.

46. Ferit Şahenk, presentation at Harvard Business School.

47. Ferit Şahenk, interview with author.

48. Ibid.

49. Ferit Şahenk, "Doğuş Group: Weighing Partners for Garanti Bank," video.

50. Haier example derived from Tarun Khanna, Krishna G. Palepu, and Ingrid Vargas, "Haier: Taking a Chinese Company Global," Case N2-706-401 (Boston: Harvard Business School Publishing, 2005); and Tarun Khanna and Krishna G. Palepu, "Haier: Taking a Chinese Company Global, Teaching Note," Note No. 707-459 (Boston: Harvard Business School Publishing, 2006).

51. Penetration figure from Graham Ormerod, G. K. Goh Research, "Guangdong Kelon: A White Good Comeback Play," August 29, 2003, available from The Investext Group, http://www.investext.com.

52. Andrew Browne, "Haier Group Never Says 'No,'" Reuters News, December 9, 1997.

53. Pamela Yatsko, "To Serve and Profit: A Chinese Fridge-Maker Wows Customers with Service," *Far Eastern Economic Review*, October 17, 1996.

54. http://www.gome.com.hk/businessoverview.php.

55. Russell Flannery, "Watch Your Back: China's Haier Got So Good at Selling Appliances Abroad That It Underestimated the Threat at Home," *Forbes*, April 23, 2007, 104.

56. This section has been adapted from Tarun Khanna and Krishna G. Palepu, "Globalization and Convergence in Corporate Governance: Evidence from Infosys and the Indian Software Industry," *Journal of International Business Studies* 35, no. 6 (November 2004): 484–507.

57. This section has been adapted from Tarun Khanna and Krishna G. Palepu, "Why Focused Strategies May Be Wrong for Emerging Markets," *Harvard Business Review*, July–August 1997, 41–51; Tarun Khanna and Krishna G. Palepu, "The Right Way to Restructure Conglomerates in Emerging Markets," *Harvard Business Review*, July–August 1999, 125–134; and Tarun Khanna, "Local Institutions and Global Strategy," Note 702-475 (Boston: Harvard Business School Publishing, 2002).

58. Ramón Opulencia, quoted in Belen Villalonga and Raphael Amit, "Ayala Corporation," Case 9-207-041 (Boston: Harvard Business School Publishing, 2007), 6.

59. Villalonga and Amit, ibid.

60. Tarun Khanna, Krishna G. Palepu, and Ingrid Vargas, "Globe Telecom," Case 9-704-505 (Boston: Harvard Business School Publishing, 2004).

61. John A. Quelch and Anna Harrington, "Samsung Electronics Co.: Global Marketing Operations," Case 9-504-051 (Boston: Harvard Business School Publishing, 2008).

62. Raymond J. Fisman and Tarun Khanna, "Facilitating Development: The Role of Business Groups," *World Development* 32, no. 4 (April 2004): 609–628.

63. Tarun Khanna, Robert Pekannen, and Michael Yoshino, "Sime Darby Berhad (A)—1995," Case 9-797-017 (Boston: Harvard Business School Publishing, 2001).

64. Ibid.

65. Tarun Khanna and Yishay Yafeh, "Business Groups in Emerging Markets: Paragons or Parasites?" *Journal of Economic Literature* 45, no. 2 (June 2007): 331–372.

66. See Tarun Khanna, "At Home, It's Not Just Profits That Matter: The Case for National Ownership," 8.

Chapter 6

1. This chapter is adapted in part from Tarun Khanna and Krishna G. Palepu, "Emerging Giants: Building World-Class Companies in Emerging Markets," Note 9-703-431 (Boston: Harvard Business School Publishing, 2005); and Tarun Khanna and Krishna G. Palepu, "Emerging Giants: Building World-Class Companies in Developing Countries," *Harvard Business Review*, October 2006, 60–69.

2. Tarun Khanna, Krishna G. Palepu, and Richard J. Bullock, "House of Tata: Acquiring a Global Footprint," Case 9-708-446 (Boston: Harvard Business School Publishing, 2008), 3–4.

3. Ibid., 5.

4. Ishaat Hussain, finance director, Tata Sons, interview with author, April 2007.

5. The raw correlation between size and degree of globalization in the United Nations Conference on Trade and Development (UNCTAD) list of top fifty (by market valuation of assets) companies based in these markets was only 0.4 in 2006.

Khanna and Palepu, "Emerging Giants: Building World-Class Companies in Developing Countries."

6. Tarun Khanna and Ayesha Khan, "Crossing Borders: Notes on a Middle Eastern Journey Through Africa," Case 1-708-477 (Boston: Harvard Business School Publishing, 2008); Saad Al-Barrak, "Zain (MTC) Pre-Class," Video 9-709-803 (Boston: Harvard Business School Publishing, 2008); Saad Al-Barrak, "Zain (MTC) Post-Class," Video 9-709-805 (Boston: Harvard Business School Publishing, 2008).

7. Haitham Al Khaled, COO, Zain (MTC) Middle East quoted in Khanna and Khan, "Crossing Borders: Notes on a Middle Eastern Journey Through Africa."

8. Saad Al-Barrak, "Zain (MTC) Pre-Class."

9. AMEinfo.com, "African Leaders Keen to Attract More Middle East Investment," press release, November 25, 2007, http://www.ameinfo.com/139706.html.

10. "Africa—Telecoms, Mobile and Broadband Overview and Analysis," Paul Budde Communication Pty Ltd., 2007.

11. Saad Al-Barrak, CEO, Zain Group, presentation at Harvard Business School, May 1, 2008.

12. Saad Al-Barrak, "Zain (MTC) Post-Class."

13. Saad Al-Barrak, presentation at Harvard Business School.

14. "Out of Africa—Mobile Telecoms," *The Economist*, December 9, 2006, 67–68.

15. Saad Al-Barrak, "Zain (MTC) Post-Class."

16. Ibid.

17. Ibid.

18. Ibid.

19. Saad Al-Barrak, presentation at Harvard Business School; and Saad Al-Barrak, "Zain (MTC) Pre-Class."

20. Saad Al-Barrak, "Zain (MTC) Pre-Class."

21. Saad Al-Barrak, presentation at Harvard Business School.

22. Saad Al-Barrak, "Zain (MTC) Post-Class."

23. Ibid.

24. Ibid.

25. Michael Chu and Gustavo Herrero, "Tata Consultancy Services Iberoamerica," Case 9-705-020 (Boston: Harvard Business School Publishing, 2005), 5.

26. Gabriel Rozman, CEO, Tata Consultancy Services Iberoamerica, presentation at Harvard Business School, September 25, 2006.

27. Ibid.

28. Ibid.

29. Ibid.

30. Chu and Herrero, "Tata Consultancy Services Iberoamerica," 8.

31. Ibid., 9.

32. Gabriel Rozman, presentation at Harvard Business School.

33. Ibid.

34. Tata Consultancy Services, http://www.tcs.com/worldwide/s_america/locations/5x5/Pages/default.aspx.

35. Gabriel Rozman, presentation at Harvard Business School.

36. Gabriel Rozman, quoted in Thomas L. Friedman, "Latin America's Choice," *New York Times*, June 21, 2006.

37. Gabriel Rozman, presentation at Harvard Business School; and Tata Consultancy Services, http://www.tcs.com/worldwide/s_america/locations/5x5/Pages/default.aspx.

38. Gabriel Rozman, presentation at Harvard Business School.

39. Tata Consultancy Services, http://www.tcs.com/worldwide/s_america/locations/5x5/Pages/default.aspx.

40. Theresa Bradley, "Offshoring Booms in Latin America as Crisis Pushes Companies to Cut Costs—Closer to Home," Associated Press Newswires, April 12, 2009.

41. Tarun Khanna, Krishna G. Palepu, and Ingrid Vargas, "Haier: Taking a Chinese Company Global," Case N2-706-401 (Boston: Harvard Business School Publishing, 2005); and Tarun Khanna and Krishna G. Palepu, "Haier: Taking a Chinese Company Global, Teaching Note," Note 5-707-459 (Boston: Harvard Business School Publishing, 2006).

42. Mei Fong, "Chinese Refrigerator Maker Finds U.S. Chilly," Wall Street Journal, March 18, 2008.

43. Michael Jemal, "Michael Jemal, CEO, Haier America," Video 9-707-801 (Boston: Harvard Business School Publishing, 2006).

44. Jeannie J. Yi and Shawn X. Ye, The Haier Way: The Making of a Chinese Business Leader and a Global Brand (Dumont, New Jersey: Homa & Sekey Books, 2003), 205–225; and Michael Jemal, "Michael Jemal, CEO, Haier America."

45. Michael Jemal, "Michael Jemal, CEO, Haier America."

46. Ibid.

47. Ibid.

48. Ibid.

49. Nicholas P. Heymann, appliance industry analyst, Prudential Securities, quoted in Michael Arndt, "Can Haier Freeze Out Whirlpool and GE?" BusinessWeek Online, April 11, 2002.

50. Fong, "Chinese Refrigerator Maker Finds U.S. Chilly."

51. Ibid.

52. Li Pan, quoted in Tarun Khanna, Krishna G. Palepu, and Ingrid Vargas, "Haier: Taking a Chinese Company Global," Case N2-706-401.

53. Derived from Tarun Khanna, Krishna G. Palepu, and Claudine Madras, "Teva Pharmaceutical Industries, Ltd.," Case 9-707-441 (Boston: Harvard Business School Publishing, 2006); and Tarun Khanna and Krishna G. Palepu, "Teva Pharmaceutical Industries, Ltd., Teaching Note," Note 5-708-419 (Boston: Harvard Business School Publishing, 2007.)

54. Eli Hurvitz, chairman, Teva Pharmaceutical Industries, "Teva Pharmaceutical Industries, Ltd.," Video 9-708-806 (Boston: Harvard Business School Publishing, 2007).

55. Eli Hurvitz, presentation at Harvard Business School, September 26, 2006.

56. Elon Kohlberg, quoted in Tarun Khanna, Krishna G. Palepu, and Claudine Madras, "Teva Pharmaceutical Industries, Ltd.," Case 9-707-441, 8.

57. Eli Hurvitz, "Teva Pharmaceutical Industries, Ltd.," video.

58. Ibid.

59. Ibid.

60. Eli Hurvitz, quoted in Tarun Khanna, Krishna G. Palepu, and Claudine Madras, "Teva Pharmaceutical Industries, Ltd.," Case 9-707-441, 13.

61. "Generic Drugmakers Teva and Barr Show Earnings Resilience amid Economic Downturn," Associated Press Newswires, November 6, 2008.

62. This example derived from Tarun Khanna and Ramana Nanda, "ICICI's Global Expansion," Case 9-706-426 (Boston: Harvard Business School Publishing, 2005); Tarun Khanna, "ICICI's Global Expansion, Teaching Note," Note 5-707-483 (Boston: Harvard Business School Publishing, 2007); and Lalita Gupte and Bhargav Dasgupta, presentation at Harvard Business School, September 26, 2005.

63. This section based on Bhargav Dasgupta, who spearheaded ICICI's international business, presentation at Harvard Business School, September 26, 2005.

64. ICICI Bank, presentation at Harvard Business School, September 26, 2005.

65. Nandini Lakshman, "Credit Chatter Snares India's ICICI Bank: Despite Nasty Rumors, the Bank's Health Is Good, But Anxieties About the World Economy and Future Loans Cast a Dark Shadow," *BusinessWeek.com*, October 1, 2008.

66. Tarun Khanna and Krishna G. Palepu, "Globalization and Convergence in Corporate Governance: Evidence from Infosys and the Indian Software Industry," *Journal of International Business Studies* 35 (2004), online publication date October 21, 2004.

67. See Pankaj Ghemawat and Jamie L. Matthews, "The Globalization of CEMEX," Case 9-701-017 (Boston: Harvard Business School Publishing, 2004).

68. This is exactly the logic of Michael Spence's famous signaling model for which he was awarded the Nobel Memorial Prize in Economic Sciences in 2001. See Michael Spence, "Job Market Signaling," *Quarterly Journal of Economics* 87 (1973): 355–374. See also Asher Blass and Yishay Yafeh, "Vagabond Shoes Longing to Stray: Why Foreign Firms List in the United States," *Journal of Banking and Finance* 25, no. 3 (2001): 555–572.

69. Tarun Khanna and Krishna G. Palepu, "Globalization and Convergence in Corporate Governance," 491–492.

70. Jayanth Verma, quoted in Tarun Khanna and Krishna G. Palepu, "Globalization and Convergence in Corporate Governance," 492.

71. Discussion of Chilean capital market development and Empresas CAP is derived from Tarun Khanna and Danielle Melito Wu, "Empresas CAP," Case 9-798-053 (Boston: Harvard Business School Publishing, 1998); and Tarun Khanna, "Empresas CAP—1994, Teaching Note," Note 5-701-038 (Boston: Harvard Business School Publishing, 2001).

72. Jaime Charles, quoted in Tarun Khanna and Danielle Melito Wu, "Empresas CAP," Case 9-798-053, 6.

73. Ibid.

74. Example adapted from Tarun Khanna, Krishna G. Palepu, and Richard J. Bullock, "House of Tata: Acquiring a Global Footprint," Case 9-708-446 (Boston: Harvard Business School Publishing, 2008), 10–14.

75. Ravi Kant, managing director, Tata Motors, quoted in ibid., 11.

76. "MG Rover Mulls Tata Indica Diesel Sourcing Too," *Business Standard*, September 17, 2003, http://www.tata.com/tata_motors/media/20030917_indica.htm; and "Tata's Grand Vision," *Autocar Professional*, January 15, 2006, http://www.tata.com/tata_sons/-media/20060115.htm.

77. Ravi Kant, managing director, Tata Motors, quoted in Khanna, Palepu, and Bullock, "House of Tata: Acquiring a Global Footprint," 11.

78. Ibid., 12.

79. Ibid.

80. "The New People's Car," *The Economist*, March 28, 2009, 73–74.

81. Joe Leahy and John Reed, "UK Carmakers Prove Heavy Burden," *Financial Times*, May 22, 2009, 14.

82. Ibid.; and "The New People's Car," *The Economist*.

83. Example informed by Michel Anteby and Nitin Nohria, "Michael Fernandes at Nicholas Piramal," Case 9-408-001 (Boston: Harvard Business School, 2008).

84. Ian Grundy, former head of business development in Europe, Japan, and India for Avecia and then NPIL head of European business development, quoted in ibid., 8.

85. TCL example informed by Tarun Khanna, Felix Oberholzer-Gee, and David Lane, "TCL Multimedia," Case 9-705-502 (Boston: Harvard Business School Publishing, 2006).

86. Terry Yi, president of TCL overseas business unit, quoted in Tarun Khanna, Felix Oberholzer-Gee, and David Lane, "TCL Multimedia," Case 9-705-502 (Boston: Harvard Business School Publishing, 2006), 8.

87. Charls Zhao, president, TCL Thomson Enterprise, quoted in ibid., 1.

88. Li Yuguo, quoted in ibid., 12.

89. Evan Ramstad, "East Meets West in TV Sets: Huge Sino-French Venture Is Still Tuning the Relationship," Wall Street Journal, November 26, 2004, A7.

90. Andrew Edgecliffe-Johnson, Adam Jones, and Justine Lau, "TCL Forced to Close Units in Europe," Financial Times, November 1, 2006; Justine Lau, "Poor Reception for China's Global Push: TCL's Problems Exemplify the Difficulties for Mainland Companies Desperate to Expand Abroad," Financial Times, November 3, 2006.

91. Randy Zhou, analyst, Bank of China International, quoted in Justine Lau, ibid.

92. Saad Al-Barrak, presentation at Harvard Business School.

Chapter 7

1. Ravi Venkatesan, "Ravi Venkatesan, Chairman, Microsoft India," video, product number 9-708-804 (Boston: Harvard Business School Publishing, 2007).

2. Eli Hurvitz, chairman, Teva Pharmaceutical Industries, "Teva Pharmaceutical Industries, Ltd.," video, product number 9-708-806 (Boston: Harvard Business School Publishing, 2007).

3. Alan Rosling, executive director, Tata Sons, interview with authors, April 2007.

4. Daniel Schäfer, "Siemens to Pay €1bn Fines in Effort to Close Bribery Scandal," Financial Times, December 16, 2008, 17.

5. Dionne Searcey, "U.S. Cracks Down on Corporate Bribes," Wall Street Journal, May 26, 2009, A1.

6. Ibid.

7. Saad Al-Barrak, "Zain (MTC) Pre-Class," video, product number 9-709-803 (Boston: Harvard Business Publishing, 2008).

8. Alan Ohnsman and Vipin V. Nair, "Mahindra will Help India Beat China to U.S. Auto Market (Update1)," Bloomberg.com, June 17, 2009, http://www.bloomberg.com/apps/news?pid=20601109&sid=aU7hSULUYEX8. See also Nick Kurczewski, "Mahindra Says Wait and See," New York Times, June 28, 2009, Automobiles, 10.

9. "Tata's Nano Is Headed to U.S.," Detroit Free Press (Freep.com), June 11, 2009, http://www.freep.com/article/20090611/BUSINESS01/906110384/1014/BUSINESS01/Tata+s+Nano+is+headed+to+U.S.

Index

About the Authors

Tarun Khanna is the Jorge Paulo Lemann professor at the Harvard Business School, where he has taught and researched strategy and international business in emerging markets worldwide since 1993. He serves on the boards of several companies and NGOs, and mentors startups in Asia. The World Economic Forum elected him a Young Global Leader (under forty) in 2007, and the Academy of International Business appointed him a Fellow in 2009.

Krishna G. Palepu is the Ross Graham Walker Professor and Senior Associate Dean for International Development at the Harvard Business School, where he currently oversees the school's global activities in Asia, Europe, and Latin America. His research over the last fifteen years has focused on strategy and execution in emerging markets. His recent teaching activities at HBS include chairing the Global CEO program for China and Building Global Enterprises in India. He has worked extensively with top management teams in these areas both as a consultant and as a board member.

Richard J. Bullock worked as a research associate at Harvard Business School on case studies and other teaching materials related to emerging markets. He earned a master's degree in international relations from Yale University, and a bachelor's degree in politics from Princeton University. Prior to graduate school, he worked as a contributor and editor for the Economist Intelligence Unit publication *Business China* and taught English in China under the auspices of the Princeton in Asia program.